Reading the Past

READERS IN CULTURAL CRITICISM

General Editor: *Catherine Belsey*

Posthumanism   *Neil Badmington*
Reading the Past   *Tamsin Spargo*
Reading Images   *Julia Thomas*
Gender   *Anna Tripp*

Readers in Cultural Criticism
Series Standing Order
ISBN 0–333–78660–2 hardcover
ISBN 0–333–75236–8 paperback
(outside North America only)

You can receive future titles in this series as they are published by placing a standing order. Please contact your bookseller or, in case of difficulty, write to us at the address below with your name and address, the title of the series and the ISBN quoted above.

Customer Services Department, Macmillan Distribution Ltd
Houndmills, Basingstoke, Hampshire RG21 6XS, England

Reading the Past

Literature and History

Edited by Tamsin Spargo

palgrave

First published 2000 by
PALGRAVE
Houndmills, Basingstoke, Hampshire RG21 6XS and
175 Fifth Avenue, New York, N. Y. 10010
Companies and representatives throughout the world

PALGRAVE is the new global academic imprint of
St. Martin's Press LLC Scholarly and Reference Division and
Palgrave Publishers Ltd (formerly Macmillan Press Ltd).

ISBN 0–333–77122–2 hardback
ISBN 0–333–77121–4 paperback

This book is printed on paper suitable for recycling and
made from fully managed and sustained forest sources.

A catalogue record for this book is available
from the British Library.

Library of Congress Cataloging-in-Publication Data
Reading the past: Literature and history/edited by Tamsin Spargo
       p. cm.—(Readers in cultural criticism)
   Includes bibliographical references and index.
   ISBN 0–333–77122–2 (cloth) — ISBN 0–333–77121–4 (pbk.)
   1. Literature and history. 2. Literature, Modern—History and
   criticism. 3. Historiography. I. Spargo, Tamsin. II. Series.

PN50 .R38 2000
809' .93358—dc21
                                                        00—040454

10   9   8   7   6   5   4   3   2   1
09 08 07 06 05 04 03 02 01 00

Printed and bound in Great Britain by
Creative Print and Design (Wales), Ebbw Vale

The Ambassadors: Jean de Dinteville and Georges de Selve, by Hans Holbein the younger (1497–1543).
Reproduced courtesy of the National Gallery Company Limited. Research by ISI.

Contents

General Editor's Preface

Culture is the element we inhabit as subjects.

Culture embraces the whole range of practices, customs and representations of a society. In their rituals, stories and images, societies identify what they perceive as good and evil, proper, sexually acceptable, racially other. Culture is the location of values, and the study of cultures shows how values vary from one society to another, or from one historical moment to the next.

But culture does not exist in the abstract. On the contrary, it is in the broadest sense of the term textual, inscribed in the paintings, operas, sculptures, furnishings, fashions, bus tickets and shopping lists which are the currency of both aesthetic and everyday exchange. Societies invest these artefacts with meanings, until in many cases the meanings are so 'obvious' that they pass for nature. Cultural criticism denaturalises and defamiliarises these meanings, isolating them for inspection and analysis.

The subject is what speaks, or, more precisely, what signifies, and subjects learn in culture to reproduce or to challenge the meanings and values inscribed in the signifying practices of the society that shapes them.

If culture is pervasive and constitutive for us, if it resides in the documents, objects and practices that surround us, if it circulates as the meanings and values we learn and reproduce as good citizens, how in these circumstances can we practise cultural *criticism*, where criticism implies a certain distance between the critic and the culture? The answer is that cultures are not homogeneous; they are not even necessarily coherent. There are always other perspectives, so that cultures offer alternative positions for the subjects they also recruit. Moreover, we have a degree of power over the messages we reproduce. A minor modification changes the script, and may alter the meaning; the introduction of a negative constructs a resistance.

The present moment in our own culture is one of intense debate. Sexual alignments, family values, racial politics, the implications of economic differences are all hotly contested. And positions are taken up not only in explicit discussions at political meetings, on television and in the pub. They are often reaffirmed or challenged implicitly in films and advertisements, horoscopes and lonely-hearts columns. Cultural criticism analyses all these forms in order to assess their hold on our consciousness.

There is no interpretative practice without theory, and the more sophisticated the theory, the more precise and perceptive the reading it makes possible. Cultural theory is as well defined now as it has ever been, and as strongly contested as our social values. There could not, in consequence, be a more exciting time to engage in the theory and practice of Cultural Criticism.

Catherine Belsey
Cardiff University

Acknowledgements

I would like to thank Catherine Belsey, Series Editor, and Margaret Bartley and Gabriella Stiles at the publishers, for their help and support. I am also grateful to a number of colleagues, past and present, at Liverpool John Moores University: Timothy Ashplant, Elspeth Graham, Mike Pudlo, Helen Rogers, Berthold Schoene-Harwood and Gerry Smyth.

The editor and publishers wish to thank the following for permission to use copyright material:

Walter Benjamin, for 'Theses on the Philosophy of History' from *Illuminations: Essays and Reflections* by Walter Benjamin, Jonathan Cape. Copyright © 1955 by Suhrkamp Verlag, English translation by Harry Zohn, copyright © 1968, renewed 1996 by Harcourt, Inc, by permission of Random House UK and Harcourt, Inc; Michel de Certeau, for material from *The Writing of History* by Michel de Certeau (1988), pp. 1–14. Copyright © 1988 Columbia University Press, by permission of Columbia University Press; Robert Darnton, for material from *The Great Cat Massacre and Other Episodes in French Cultural History* by Robert Darnton, Allen Lane (1984), pp. 79–101. Copyright © Basic Books, Inc, 1984, by permission of Penguin UK and Basic Books, a member of Perseus Books, LLC; Shoshana Felman, for 'Camus' *The Plague*, or a Monument to Witnessing' from *Testimony: Crises of Witnessing in Literature, Pychoanalysis, and History*, by Shoshana Felman and Dori Laub. Copyright © 1992, by permission of Taylor & Francis/ Routledge Inc; Michel Foucault, for material from *Discipline and Punish: The Birth of the Prison* by Michel Foucault, trs. Alan Sheridan, Allen Lane (1977), pp. 3–23, 30–1, first published as *Surveiller et punir: naissance de la prison* by Editions Gallimard, 1975. Copyright © Alan Sheridan, 1977, by permission of Penguin UK and Georges Borchardt, Inc, on behalf of the author; Stephen Greenblatt, for material from *Renaissance Self-Fashioning from More to Shakespeare* by Stephen Greenblatt (1980), pp. 11–26, by permission of The University of Chicago Press; Keith Jenkins, for 'Why Bother with the Past? Engaging with some issues raised by the "end of history as we have known it"', *Rethinking History*, 1:1 (1997), 56–66, by permission of Taylor & Francis Ltd; Leszek Kolakowski, for 'Emperor

Kennedy Legend: A New Anthropological Debate', *Salmagundi*, 72 (1986), 211–17, also included in *Modernity on Endless Trial* by Leszek Kolakowski, University of Chicago Press (1990), by permission of David Higham Associates on behalf of the author; Carolyn Steedman, for 'The Watercress Seller' from *Past Tenses: Essays on Writing, Autobiography and History* (1992), pp. 193–202, by permission of Rivers Oram Press Ltd; Susan Willis, for material from *Specifying: Black Women Writing the American Experience* by Susan Willis (1987), pp. 83–96, 105–9. Copyright © 1987, by permission of The University of Wisconsin Press.

1

Introduction: Past, Present and Future Pasts

Tamsin Spargo

In the summer of 1999 newspaper and television reporters seemed obsessed with different ways of reading the future. It was hard to avoid stories about the sixteenth-century astrologer Nostradamus's predictions of the end of the world, which happily proved inaccurate, about the possible portents of the solar eclipse, and the meaning of the millennium. Although most interpretations of humanity's impending doom or transformation were presented as laughable or pitiful, the desire to make sense of human existence in time is clearly not restricted to the deluded or fanatical. The approach of the year 2000 saw the publication of countless chronologies and charts of prominent people, the most significant events and achievements of the last two thousand years. Readers, listeners and viewers were asked to vote on the most important figures while supermarket customers were rewarded for spending money with commemorative historical wallcharts, complete with stickers. History was suddenly marketable just as, and perhaps because, some people were saying it was about to end.

While only a few extreme Christian groups argued that the final conflict between good and evil was really nigh, millenarian narratives of time coming to an end for the human race seemed to encourage many people to look back at the past. The cumulative effect of these historical snapshots certainly resembled the montage of scenes of a past life that flashes before the eyes of a dying character in a film. But whose past was being represented in these histories? Why were some people, events, and achievements judged to be historically significant rather than others? What makes the past historical?

Perhaps we should ask first what the past *is* ? The obvious answer is that the past is what happened before the present: it is time that has passed. Thinking in terms of past, present, and future seems natural, inevitable both on a personal level and in broader social, cultural terms. The past is, in a sense, over but in another sense it is only available to us, knowable, as part of the present. The past may be real but it is, by definition, irrecoverable in its pastness.

So, why do we try to read the past? Nostradamus studied the conjunction between astronomical alignments and momentous events in ancient history

1

in order to predict the future within the constraints of his own present. Arguments about the past are often explicitly and, I would argue, always implicitly interventions in debates about the present and the future. When revisionist historians insist that the systematic genocide of Jews in Nazi Germany has been invented or wildly exaggerated they are clearly serving current particular political ends. Those who argue that studying the history of the Holocaust is essential if we are to avoid a repetition are equally clearly motivated by a prospective ethical concern. Learning lessons for the future as well as paying debts to the dead has been the goal of many enquiries into the past. But are these lessons really learned? Knowledge of the history of the Holocaust has not prevented further genocides.

Less obviously politically charged readings of the past may also serve to support particular interpretations of human social existence. Research into similarities between human behaviour through time may underpin arguments about the naturalness or effectiveness of particular social and political formations, while exploration of differences may support the possibility of future change. As the essays in this *Reader* show, the political, ethical and intellectual motivations for reading the past are many and varied, conscious and unconscious. But whatever his or her motivation, anyone who wants to read the past must do precisely that. Nostradamus may have attempted to defy the constraints of temporality by predicting the future, but he could not travel back in time to see what happened in ancient Rome. The information he used as the factual basis of his work came from written accounts of the past. If his predictions were to be correct, then the data provided by his Roman histories would have to be accurate, true. But as a recent controversy has shown, even the most reliable of sources, the most factual, least fictional of texts can be open to question.

The Encarta electronic encyclopaedia, published by Microsoft, was first developed from a print version compiled in the United States in 1993. This first edition was criticised for being too American in its content and tone and the publishers responded by employing compilers in a number of different countries to produce local versions. The impact on the content was dramatic. The telephone, for example, is described in the United Kingdom edition as being invented by 'Scottish-born' Alexander Graham Bell, in the United States edition as the creation of 'American inventor' Alexander Graham Bell, while the Italian edition notes that an Italian, Antonio Meucci, had invented a prototype before Bell.

The publishers were accused of rewriting history for economic profit, offering flattering versions of the past to all concerned and abandoning responsibility to the truth. They replied that the publication of divergent histories was not a distortion of historical truth but a recognition of the relative significance of factual information within different cultures' historical accounts. This could be read as implicitly endorsing the argument that truth is not an absolute value that exists independently but is a context-dependent and so relative or contingent meaning. It suggests that different cultures produce accounts of their pasts that have meaning in and for those cultures. But if one person's true history is someone else's lie, how do we decide between them when the past is out of reach? What sort of claims can we make about a history that is clearly partial? Is the only alternative to Encarta's relativism the sort of history implied by some of the pre-millennial versions, underpinned by a determining religious faith or arrogantly presuming the universality of one culture's, or one social group's, account?

For some people these problems may make the study of the past as dubious an enterprise as predicting the future, but for others they have acted as the spur to developing new ways of reading the traces and texts of different times. While reading the past, or attempting to do so, is an activity that involves many different people, ranging from psychoanalysts, to archaeologists, anthropologists and detectives, this *Reader* is concerned with debates about the past within the practices and disciplines of History and Literature. This will necessarily entail rummaging through some of the baggage of academics working in, and in the terms of, disciplines whose boundaries no longer seem entirely appropriate in the twenty-first century. Nevertheless these disciplines have been a major factor in the production of the very ideas that have challenged their claims to authority and tested the limits of conventional ways of reading the past.

It is impossible in this context to give anything but a reductive summary and the linear narrative form of this short history inevitably imposes a misleading singularity and coherence on the sequence of events and ideas I have selected for inclusion. Readers worried by this can play spot the writer's own priorities and evaluations, or turn immediately to the bibliography for directions to accounts written from alternative perspectives.

The relationship between literary writing and historiography (writing history) has been the subject of recorded debate from Aristotle's *Poetics* to the present day. Aristotle distinguished between history as the study of events that had actually occurred and poetry as the imagining of possible events. As an opposition this seems fairly straightforward, but it was qualified by his assertion that history deals with particular truth, while poetry deals with general or universal truths and is therefore more philosophical. It is only slightly mischievous to suggest that, in granting poetry a higher status linked to its capacity to reveal universal truth, and in insisting on history's more mundane recording role, Aristotle established a tension about the value of the activities that has fuelled disciplinary squabbles ever since. The more serious effect was, of course, to exclude imagination and interpretation from the writing of history and to ally poetry, and its successor literature, to the communication of a universal and timeless human condition. The debates and struggles within the disciplines and by those writing either type of text can be read as attempts to fulfil, confound or overturn Aristotle's opposition.

HISTORY

One history of History tells of its forward march away from the seductions of myth, replete with meaning but short on verifiable truth, towards the sober embrace of its true partner, science. Aristotle's relegation of history to a less elevated position than poetry was challenged in the early modern period when rationalism and empiricism, championed by Francis Bacon, allotted history a more serious epistemological status. Inductive reasoning based on observation by a detached observer was the proper activity of the historian and scientist alike and would contribute to humanity's ever-expanding knowledge of the world. Poetry was pleasing and popular but the imagination was not a proper tool for the serious work of historical enquiry.

The association of history with empirical science was consolidated through the Enlightenment, when the view that human beings could rationally understand and explain more and more of their world was combined with a sense that this would contribute to the progressive improvement of human society. In the nineteenth century the historian's task was famously defined by the German Leopold von Ranke as being to show the past as it really was ('*wie es eigentlich gewesen*'). Written histories were to be unbiased factual records. Ranke is generally regarded as the founder of the modern discipline of History. He established the model that has continued to dominate one traditional approach to the subject, and that has often failed to keep up with radical changes to the scientific methods and epistemologies on which it was modelled.

While Ranke's empiricism is the most famous aspect of his approach to the past, his providentialism may have been just as significant. For Ranke the facts of history are components of God's order waiting to be rationally comprehended. This view resembles that of the key figure in the development of the philosophy of history in the period, Georg Wilhelm Friedrich Hegel. Hegel has been something of a thorn in the side of empiricist historians; he has often been depicted as an interloper, a philosopher who has overcomplicated or misrepresented the business of history.

Hegel viewed the events of human history as part of the unfolding of a general idea, unwittingly fulfilling the demands of Reason, the one true essence. Although many empiricists rejected this overarching explanation and its metaphysical grounding, the idea of a progressive linear history is evident throughout the great narrative histories of the nineteenth century, which 'recorded' and justified the imperial ambitions of the European nation states. Hegel's most famous successor in proposing that history is governed by a particular force was, ironically, Karl Marx, whose political analysis offered a very different interpretation of the events of the past and of the role of the historian.

Marx rejected the illusion of disinterested history and presented his own historical intervention as part of an attempt to change the world. His theory of 'historical materialism' argued that social existence determines consciousness and placed economics and the unequal, conflictual, class relations produced by capitalism at the centre of the historical process. The past is to be examined because it affects, even determines, the possibilities of the present: 'Men make their own history, but they do not make it just as they please; they do not make it under circumstances chosen by themselves, but under circumstances directly encountered, given and transmitted by the past.'[1]

In addition to reading history as struggle, Marx argued that cultural production, including the writing of history, was ideological, promoting the economic interests of the ruling classes by presenting them as natural and universal. Marxism exposed the illusory nature and political interests served by the model of disinterested history but offered an overarching explanatory theory of history that was later seen as too restrictive. Walter Benjamin's 'Theses On the Philosophy of History', included in this volume, explored historical materialism in ways which disrupted any sense of guaranteed progression, while other Marxists, including Antonio Gramsci, Louis Althusser, and Raymond Williams, refined the Marxist theory of the relationship between economics and culture, allotting a more active role to the latter in effecting social change.

Within the discipline of History, Marxism acted as a spur to demands for changes in what and who should be the subjects of historical enquiry. Traditional historiography had broadly concentrated on the lives and actions of the ruling classes and excluded those of the majority of the population. Marxist historians, such as E. P. Thompson, author of *The Making of the English Working Class* (1963), presented alternative histories of the hitherto underrepresented. Women, members of different ethnic groups, gays and lesbians and others similarly criticised the partiality, in both senses, of conventional historiography. Some contributed to the development of a still popular type of history that attempts to recover and represent forgotten or effaced lives and events. Their interventions also explicitly and implicitly challenged the adequacy of any overarching narrative to explain history, whether conservative, liberal or Marxist. By the middle of the twentieth century History had been broken down into multiple, often conflicting, histories.

The way in which historians worked was also changed in the aftermath of what could be read as the last historical event of the imperial age, the 'Great War'. In France in the 1920s the Annales group, including Marc Bloch and

Lucien Febvre, tried to broaden and deepen history. They developed new forms of cultural history that examined different types of human activity, using methods adapted from anthropology and the new discipline of sociology. Their work explored aspects of the social and cultural history of a particular place at a specific time, building up a detailed picture, rather than attempting to outline a progressive narrative. The essay by Robert Darnton in this volume is of more recent date, but is one of the most celebrated examples of this tradition that rapidly replaced the history of kings and queens, wars and discoveries as the main activity of many professional historians.

It is now quite rare to encounter a historian who is not acutely aware both of the contingency and specificity of his or her own social and political position and that this will inform their reading and writing of the past. Although many popular histories and some academic studies are still presented as objective accounts of the past written from a position that is somehow above or outside history, this is an increasingly rare approach. The majority of readings of the past by academic historians are explicitly presented as *interpretations* based on methodical and meticulous analysis of primary sources and factual data. But for some historians and philosophers of history this pluralist approach still underestimates the textual nature of history.

The work of the American historian Hayden White, writing from the 1970s onwards, and that of others including Dominick LaCapra, Frank Ankersmit and Patrick Joyce, is often described as part of a shift or movement called 'the linguistic turn' that explores the textuality of history. The historians who initiated the linguistic turn worked with ideas from literary theory and argued that, far from seeing literature as the fictional opposite of a factual history, historians should acknowledge their intimate relationship as two forms of writing that create, rather than find, meaning.

Although earlier writers had explored the relationship between narrative and history, notably Paul Ricoeur and Roland Barthes, it is the work of Hayden White that has had a particularly dramatic effect on many historians' sense of the role and future of their discipline. White argues that historians do not *find* the meaning of the past by examining the facts, they *invent* or make meanings through their use of language. They do not reconstruct or translate lived stories into prose stories but create meaningful narratives.

White began by analysing the great narrative histories of the nineteenth century. In *Metahistory: The Historical Imagination in Nineteenth Century Europe* (1973) he identified four basic forms of 'emplotment' in historiographical narratives that are associated with specific types of argument and ideological positions. These, provocatively literary, forms were applied to texts by, among others, Michelet, Ranke, Hegel, Marx and Nietzsche. White argued that, as narratives, histories tend to obey the narrative conventions of specific genres. An event can be recounted as tragedy, or, alternatively, as comedy, with a happy ending. Genre, the way the events are presented, determines their political implications. Comic versions of history, for example, are generally conservative because they imply that everything works out well in the end, so there is no need to intervene to change things. White suggested that particular combinations of emplotment, type of argument and ideological implication have a mutual affinity: Romantic, formist, and anarchist; Tragic, mechanistic, and radical; Comic, organicist, and conservative; Satiric, contextualist, and liberal. Although his theoretical grid seems very neat, his analysis of historical narratives shows that most are marked by a dialectical tension. Hegel, for example, employed both Tragic and Comic emplotments on, respectively, microcosmic and macrocosmic levels, both justified by an organicist argument. This, in White's analysis, is why Hegel's work can be read as having both conservative and radical ideological implications.

Even if emplotment was simply a matter of individual choice on the part of the historian, White's insistence on the formal construction rather than transcription of historical meaning demands that we read historiography differently. But, according to White, underpinning the narrative combinations of emplotment, argument and ideological implication are *tropes*, linguistic figures with specific rhetorical functions. Romantic narrative is founded on metaphor, Tragic on metonymy, Comic on synecdoche, and Satiric on irony. White's tropes are not turns of speech in the sense of decorative flourishes but dominant strategies by which known and unknown phenomena are made meaningful within language. The events of the past can only be constituted as objects of study when they are described in language, so all historical enquiry is really analysing textual description that is itself governed by linguistic conventions such as the tropes.

White has expressed his hope that recognising the literary and imaginative components of historiography may help to strengthen it by making apparent what he calls ideological distortions. While this move towards greater self-consciousness might serve simply to reinforce an otherwise conventional approach to writing history, White's arguments about the textual status of the accessible past could be seen as having more radical and unsettling implications. Within the discipline of History, the effects of the linguistic turn have been diverse. Some historians now view their task not as the exploration of traces of the past but as the analysis of different historiographical constructions of the past. They are, in effect, examining the history of History. Others, including Keith Jenkins, have begun to ask new questions about the future directions of History as a discipline and about different ways of pursuing the political and ethical concerns which the subject addresses.

LITERATURE

If reading the past within the discipline of History has taken a sometimes dizzying linguistic turn, what has been going on in literary studies? The neat answer, and a not entirely misleading one, is a return to history. The study of literature in the discipline of English has, as Paul Hamilton has argued, always been pulled in two directions, one formalist and the other historicist.[2] As a new discipline, founded as part of the attempt to forge a social and cultural community in the aftermath of the First World War, English Literature might be read as trying to carve out a niche by differentiating itself from rivals and antecedents, including religious interpretation, both in terms of its object of study and of its method. An ideological imperative to identify the timeless truths that Aristotle believed poetry dealt with made historical difference something of a problem for the founders of the new discipline. The formal properties of literary texts might be a safer object of study.

In the early twentieth century influential schools of criticism associated with F. R. Leavis and with I. A. Richards, among others, emphasised the value of studying literary texts apparently freed from the shackles of historical context. In America, New Criticism explicitly divorced literary texts from their historical moments of production and condemned contextual or historicist approaches as distractions or 'fallacies'. There were critical approaches that made connections between individual works and their historical context. Some critics approached texts as moments in a linear literary history or narrative of great works; others saw the need for contextual reading but located texts against a backdrop constructed from historiographical accounts which were rarely subject to critical scrutiny. As traditional historians tended to approach the sources they read and the histories they wrote as records, so literary critics saw history as background and historical texts, of and on the past, as sources of information.

This assumption was challenged in the 1960s by the Marxist literary critic Raymond Williams, whose redefinition of culture challenged the basis of traditional literary studies and paved the way for a series of radical practices. For Williams culture was the whole way of life of a society, not a collection of great works of art. His broader definition of culture contributed to the impetus for the foundation of the discipline of Cultural Studies, while his insistence that culture is dynamic and changing, reflecting but also acting upon society, transformed radical literary criticism. While Marx saw history as structured by class struggle and culture as an ideological cover-up, Williams read culture as the material of conflict and interplay between residual, dominant and emergent tendencies. Literary texts, as both products and producers of the social, material conditions of existence, played a powerful part in upholding and contesting social orders in this historical dynamic. William's 'cultural materialism' soon became the dominant radical critical practice, but literary-critical approaches to the past were soon subject to a new set of influences.

In the 1970s Hayden White's insistence on historiography as a process of *constructing* a meaningful historical past challenged the idea of direct correspondence between representation and reality and also challenged traditional notions of the historian's role. At around the same time, the ideas of poststructuralist thinkers including Jacques Derrida, Jacques Lacan and Michel Foucault transformed many literary critics' understandings of the relationship between texts and the world and of critical practice. Poststructuralist theory insists that meaning is culturally constructed in the language we use and that it is always unstable, plural and incomplete. Truth is not something that exists independently and can be discovered conclusively but is an effect of politically charged systems of knowledge production. Our own subjectivities are culturally constructed, in language, and are contingent and changing, through time and in relation to our changing circumstances.

In the United States some critics used some aspects of poststructuralist theory to develop a new, apparently apolitical but implicitly conservative, formalism, relegating social and historical conditions to the background again. The return to history in the early 1980s can be read as a reaction to this conservative critical move. Some critics, particularly Marxists, saw this formalist appropriation of poststructuralism as revealing the theories' intrinsic conservatism and quietism. Others, however, including feminists and postcolonial critics, whose concerns had been sidelined or subsumed by Marxism, argued that poststructuralist theories could form the basis for exploring the interimplication of texts and social and historical forces, acknowledging the historicity of texts, the textuality of history and their complex mutual relationships. Critics would not claim to be objective or neutral but a crucial feature of this approach would be the refusal of any overarching narrative of history that explained historical or cultural difference as evidence for its own story about human nature or social relations.

The critics who embarked on the return to history were not interested in doing so in order to discover its truth or to add to the sum of human knowledge in a disinterested fashion. Many were, and are, committed to exploring differences in the way things were in the past, in order to show that the way things are in the present could change. Others are less sure of their positive motivations, but are wary of ahistorical approaches to cultural criticism.

One of the most crucial influences on these critics is the French philosopher and historian Michel Foucault. Foucault's, frequently controversial, work on the past and on history took many forms and cannot be reduced to a single argument or approach. Some of his studies were histories – of madness, punishment, sexuality – but his approach to these topics was very different to that of earlier social and historical enquiries. Foucault's histories involved exploring the production of the very categories of knowledge and types of subjectivity that other histories usually assumed were simply there. The key concept that Foucault deployed was that of discourse.

A discourse is generally understood to be a type of language with specific rules, vocabulary and concepts but in Foucault's terms it is a historically specific material practice that produces knowledge and establishes particular power relations between different subjects who occupy specific positions. Obvious examples include medicine, the law, and psychoanalysis. The implications of the idea of discourse for historical enquiry are shown in the example of Foucault's work in this *Reader*, but there were other repercussions for historians who chose to adopt Foucault's ideas. Traditional History can be seen as a discourse that demands that proper historians work in particular ways to produce specific types of knowledge. Rejecting the terms of the discourse meant risking one's position as a historian or being called, as Foucault was in some critical responses, an anti-historian.

While some historians have endorsed or adopted Foucault's ideas, his influence has, perhaps understandably, been greater in literary studies. Some of Foucault's work approached history as a series of epochs marked by different *epistemes* or governing systems of discursive practices linked to specific types of knowledge production. But rather than offer a narrative of progression from one to another Foucault noted the breaches and ruptures between them. His work suggested the possibility of exploring the ways in which discrete moments organised, categorised, explained and constructed human life in the world not to link them together as part of a linear history but in order to attend to the differences between past and present. For literary critics who were interested in exploring the connections between textual and cultural representation and power relations Foucault's writings suggested new ways of working.

The best known movements influenced by Foucault within literary studies are New Historicism and Cultural Materialism, the former North American, the latter British. A tremendous amount of critical energy in recent years has been expended in elaborating the differences between the two, as well as on defining precisely what they should be viewed as: doctrines, practices, movements, loose groupings. There are significant differences between the two approaches and conflicting interpretations of the implications of those differences. New Historicism is often accused of overemphasising the containment of textual subversion, while Cultural Materialism has been charged with exaggerating the destabilising effects of texts.

In both approaches literary and other types of texts are viewed as being implicated in a complex web of relationships with social and cultural institutions and practices, relationships that are *mutually* determining. The critic's challenge is to explore the representations of the past, without assuming the nature of those relationships in advance in accordance with a determining narrative, while acknowledging his or her own inevitably present-centred position. The techniques include juxtaposing or connecting apparently unrelated types of text, and attending to previously overlooked details, to types of activity or text that might seem trivial, and to the conflicts, tensions and debates evident in any historical moment.

New Historicism and related critical practices have been attacked from right and left for failing to recognise the particularity of literary texts, for turning away from the radical or emancipatory projects of Marxism or socialist criticism, and for fetishising the strange, the wonderful, even difference itself. And while few would deny that new forms of cultural history have reinvigorated as well as challenged the study of past representations and the representation of the past, the pull of traditional disciplinary or discursive practices is still strong. Some apparently innovative readings turn out to be old-fashioned literary criticism served with a dash of history for piquancy: an anecdote about, say, a root vegetable followed by a fairly conventional reading of a canonical play. Meanwhile other explorations of complex representational practices are founded on unacknowledged dependence on old-fashioned narrative history.

Whatever their shortcomings, variations of Cultural Materialism and New Historicism seem to have become the new orthodoxy in many Literature departments and have been instrumental in the development of inter- and multidisciplinary courses in many universities and colleges. Debates about the possibilities and problems of recent forms of historicist cultural criticism inform the essays in this volume by Stephen Greenblatt, Catherine Belsey, and Jürgen Pieters, who are all engaged in theoretical and critical exploration of contemporary uses of the past.

The present of reading the past is, inevitably, almost impossible to describe. Its history has yet to be written. It is tempting to see present ways of reading the past as better than earlier, older approaches: more sophisticated, more subtle, or more self-reflexive. No matter how aware we are of the historical and cultural contingency of our ways of understanding, of knowing, those of us who have been schooled in the Western traditions of reading the past seem repeatedly to treat it as a trial run for the present. But as the essay by Michel de Certeau that closes this *Reader* reminds us, ways of conceptualising the relations between past, present and future are themselves historically and culturally contingent.

History and Literature have, like their forebears religion and myth, offered exciting, useful, moving, and even dangerous, ways of reading the past. Their day may soon be over as other ways of understanding temporal and spatial difference are developed. But for the foreseeable future, constructed of course in the light of the present, the past in some form seems likely to engage the interest of human beings. The past may not have been what history tells us, it may be forever out of reach, but it is not over yet.

2

Emperor Kennedy Legend: A New Anthropological Debate

Leszek Kolakowski

This 6684th annual meeting of the Academy of Science provoked a heated controversy. The main paper presented at the meeting dealt with a little known legend of an Emperor called Kennedy who is said to have ruled two large countries in the remote past BGC (Before the Great Calamity). Dr Rama, the author of the paper, confronted and scrupulously analysed all the sources available. This is not, to be sure, a large collection by comparison with, say, the amount of material we have on another ruler, Alphonse XIII, who is said to have governed another country, called Espagna, some time earlier or later, yet Dr Rama proved that more can be extracted from the existing sources than the scholars previously believed.

As is known, after the Great Calamity which occurred in the years 0–72 (approx.) when about two thirds of the inhabitable land were engulfed by waters and the remaining parts almost destroyed by huge explosions of unknown origin, only eight books from the preceding period were preserved in full. They are:

John Williams, *Creative Gardening*, Omaha, Nebraska (whether Omaha, Nebraska is one or two persons is still a matter of dispute);

Alice Besson, *La vie d'une idiote racontée par elle-même*. Roman (the book seems to have been produced in a country or locality called Gallimard);

Laszlo Varga, *Bridge for Beginners*, translated from Hungarian by Peter Harsch, Llandudno 1966;

Dirk Hoegeveldt, *De arte divinatoria Romanorum*, Lugduni Bat. 1657; *Annuario telefonico di Ferrara*;

Arno Miller, *Neue Tendenzen in amerikanischen Sozialwissenschaften*, Hoser Verlag Erlangen 1979;

Dinah Ellberg, *All my Lovers*.

The eighth book is omitted, as it was written in an entirely unknown script apart from one mysterious word 'Nagoya' printed on the second to the last page; according to the best authorities it was probably a magic incantation designed to frighten off the evil spirits coming from a foreign land. None of the books, for that matter, has been deciphered fully, but some fragments, smaller or larger, do exist now in satisfying translations. It needs mentioning that the numbers in books probably refer to years; since nothing is known, however, about the method according to which time was calculated in the BGC era or when their years began, it is impossible properly to date the events. Moreover, it is not known whether people used to calculate time forward or backwards; it is quite possible, many scholars argue, that they marked years by a number corresponding to the lapse of time still remaining to the Great Calamity, so that, e.g., the year 1657 was actually three hundred years later, and not earlier, than the year 1957.

The Emperor Kennedy Legend is mentioned only in one of the books just listed, which suggested to some scholars that it had not been widely spread or considered important among the savages. However, in almost two dozen books preserved in fragments, as well as in over a hundred and twenty journals that have been recovered so far, thirteen of them almost intact (among them *Chemical Engineering, Trybuna Ludu, Crosswords for Children* – the latter practically unintelligible – *Il Messaggero* and *Vuelta*) the legend appears several times and Dr Rama, after having thoroughly examined the entire material, provided for the first time a coherent interpretation. The main components of the myth, according to his study, are as follows:

1. President (a title of obscure origin, obviously equivalent to 'Emperor') Kennedy ruled simultaneously two big countries called respectively America and USA.

2. He came from a legendary island called Ireland, located in the North; whether this island was identical with another one called Iceland and mentioned in another source, has not yet been definitively established; perhaps just a typographic error made two countries of one.

3. He was rich.

4. He fought the rulers of three other kingdoms called Russia, Soviet Union and Cuba. He, so it seems, defeated them, but then was himself defeated in a battle which took place in the Bay of Pigs. Yet he remained the emperor of both his countries.

5. One of the hostile countries called Berlin (almost certainly another name for Russia) built a huge wall to prevent the Emperor's army from invading it, but the Emperor boldly insulted the enemies from this very wall.

6. He has two brothers; the older was killed before, and the younger after the Emperor's death.

7. The Emperor himself was struck by his enemies and died.

8. His widow Jacqueline subsequently married a 'Millionnaire'.

Dr Rama discovered one more, previously unknown item of information of great importance. In half a page preserved from the journal *Ici Paris* the Emperor is called 'un grand coureur des jupes'. The only plausible translation of this expression is that he often used 'to run in skirts'. Since it is documented that skirts were exclusively female garments, it appears clear that the Emperor was an androgynous figure, embodying both male and female characteristics. Dr Rama corrected as well the mistaken interpretation of the word 'Millionnaire' which until recently was uncritically translated as a 'rich man'. He found a previously neglected comment in a preserved fragment of the 'Miami Star' which says: 'What is a million nowadays? Peanuts.' As the peanut was a very small kind of nut, a 'Millionnaire', far from being a rich man, is a 'poor man', a man who owns very little, just a few peanuts. This fits well in Dr Rama's interpretation.

Dr Rama happens to be a disciple of the famous scholar Mr Levi-Strauss who produces a special kind of pants used both by male and female humans and who therefore argues that everything can be seen as a structure made of a pair of opposites, so that each term of the pair is meaningless without the other; indeed, if you cut off one leg of pants the remaining leg is meaningless. Dr Rama, employing this hermeneutic device, offered the following interpretation of the legend:

Emperor Kennedy's myth was an attempt to reconcile, in mythological imagination, basic irreconcilable contradictions of human life. First, there is the opposition of dreams and reality. In one source America – one of two countries he ruled – is called 'the dream of mankind', whereas another source speaks of the 'harsh reality of USA' which clearly suggests that the 'USA' was considered real. Dream and reality were thus combined in his figure. Secondly, we have the opposition North–South: he came from the North but he ruled the South, as it appears from a remark found in a preserved fragment of a paper which states unambiguously that the 'South is in the grip of Kennedy's magic'. Since in this period South was hot and North was cold, both conditions being unpleasant, albeit for different reasons, the emperor's figure, it appears, was expected to abolish, by magical means, the bad sides of both North and South.

Scholars have worried a lot about how to explain the mythological sense of wars which the Emperor had fought, but here, too, Dr Rama came up with an ingenious interpretation. We remember that the Emperor embodied both male and female characteristics. It seems that he encouraged his subjects to become males (according to the just quoted 'Ici Paris' he made many people 'cocus', which means 'coq', that is roosters. In most mythologies the rooster is a phallic symbol, but the defeat, as mentioned, was inflicted on him by pigs, and pigs, too, were a symbol of masculinity ['those male chauvinist pigs' – we read in a fragment preserved from a brochure 'The Unspeakable Martyrdom of American Women']. Thus, a complicated male–female dialectics emerges from the legend: the male–female figure produces males, is defeated by males, and eventually killed, presumably by a woman or on women's order; this last fact has been established by the confrontation of two sources: in one of a few pages preserved from a booklet 'True facts about the Soviet Union' we read that the 'happiness of Soviet women is beyond description', whereas another source – a page from a journal mysteriously called 'The Times' – speaks of the 'utmost misery of Soviet men'; and so, we see that at least in one of the main hostile countries women were happy and men unhappy, which suggests that this country was a kind of gynaecocracy.

We conclude therefore that the emperor's attempt to overcome the male–female opposition was attacked from both sides – male and female – and ended with the ultimate catastrophe. The legend is to prove that the male–female synthesis is impossible.

The last pair of opposites on which the legend has been built is rich–poor. The emperor was rich but, a source says, he was 'a champion of the poor'. Clearly, he symbolised an attempt to abrogate the linguistic contrast between wealth and poverty. The fact that he was defeated and that his wife became poor (a wife of a 'millionnaire') proves that his effort to bring into harmony those two terms of opposition ended in failure.

The deep, pessimistic meaning of the myth is: the basic contradictions of human life cannot be abolished, any attempt to make them consistent is futile.

Dr Rama's interpretation, though applauded by many scholars, was by no means universally accepted. The strongest attack was launched by Dr Gama, a follower of the famous Dr Sigmund Fraud who was the founder of another (so called analo-psychic) school of hermeneutics. Dr Gama questioned virtually all the points in Dr Rama's interpretation and the entire framework of Mr Levi-Strauss's pants-doctrine. Dr Fraud's theory says that the only thing people want to do all the time is to copulate but, in order to survive, they compel each other to do other things as well, which makes them unhappy; as a result of this unhappiness some write poems; others commit suicide, still others become political leaders, etc. 'I admit', Dr Gama said, 'that Dr Rama found some interesting facts which throw new light on the legend; his fantastic interpretation, however, is utterly untenable; new facts confirm clearly, once again, that only the Fraudian theory is capable of explaining the story. The true meaning is indeed transparent to any unprejudiced mind. The pig, far from being a symbol of masculinity, symbolised an effeminate male, a *castrato*; it is known that people in those times castrated male pigs which they used subsequently as food. The expression "those male chauvinist pigs", far from bearing out Mr Rama's speculation, fits perfectly in the Fraudian doctrine; the expression is an insult, to be sure, but it means castrated males, males unable to produce offspring. The word chauvinist is not yet properly explained but most likely it is cognate to "chauve", meaning bald, hairless, and baldness was another sign of emasculation, whereas hairs stood for male prowess (this can be seen from a sentence in one of the books preserved intact: this hairy beast tried to rape me). The interpretation is thus clear: the emperor was defeated in the land of *castran* ("pigs") and then he had to run in skirts not because he was an androgynous figure, as Dr Rama would have it, but because he was clearly half-male; in other words he was almost certainly castrated. He tried indeed to restore masculinity to other males – presumably castrated as well – but he failed. If in one of the hostile countries women were in fact happy and men unhappy, this was probably because in this mythological land men were castrated. Having gotten rid of the source of their penis envy, the women were happy. What other explanation is more plausible? Consequently, the legend is an expression of the universal human fear of castration and the failure of the emperor symbolises the fact that castration is irreversible. Once again the theory of Dr Fraud was confirmed.'

This was not the end of the meeting, though. Another scholar, Dr Ngama, attacked both previous interpretations. Professor Ngama is a disciple of the great Dr Calamarx; the latter's theory states that there are poor people and rich people and they fight against each other, and in the course of their struggle they invent various mythologies; the mythologies of the rich were to convince everybody that rich should remain rich and the poor must stay poor, whereas the mythologies of the poor stood for the opposite. In the future – Dr Calamarx proved – the poor would slaughter all the rich and everybody would be *very*, very happy ever after. 'It should be obvious to anybody in his sane mind,' Professor Ngama argued, 'that, scientifically speaking, both "theories" produced in this meeting are not only false but reactionary as well. Mr Rama's pseudo-theory amounts to stating that the alleged "structures" he concocted are perennial, in other words that wealthy people will always be wealthy and paupers must remain paupers. As to Mr Gama's pseudo-theory, it states that, instead of fighting against injustice, poor people should only worry about the possible loss of their sexual prowess. Meanwhile, the real meaning of the legend is quite clear. That the emperor himself was rich is irrelevant to the story, as all the emperors in the past have been rich – only in the universal happiness of the future the emperors will be poor. What is relevant is that the emperor was "a champion of the poor", as even my adversaries had to admit. One must therefore conclude that his enemies were champions of the rich, because all the struggles are ultimately reducible to the conflict between rich and poor. All known elements of the myth clearly confirm this interpretation. The emperor was defeated by pigs but pigs, far from being this or that sexual symbol, as the theories of my adversaries purport to "show", were symbolic representations of wealth. Indeed, both speakers preferred to overlook a leaflet signed by the "Absolutely Revolutionary Invincible World Liberation Movement of Toiling Masses" which clearly says: "kill those wealthy pigs!" This noble emperor, champion of the poor, was treacherously murdered by his foes but Mr Rama himself proved that his widow subsequently married a poor man. The message of the legend is: one great warrior for the cause of the poor has been killed but the struggle goes on. The legend obviously belongs to the folklore of poor people and the truth of Dr Calamarx's invincible theory has been once again vindicated.'

Faced with three conflicting theories, the Academy had to find the truth, as usual, by voting. After four ballots which yielded no clear majority, most fellows in the fifth voting finally opted for Dr Gama's explanation and so, the truth of Dr Sigmund Fraud's theory was definitively and scientifically established. Dr Gama was delighted while the two defeated scholars, whose errors had been thus exposed, wept bitterly. To defend a wrong anthropological theory might be punishable by death.

3

The Watercress Seller

Carolyn Steedman

This[1] is about the encounter of one middle-class man with one working-class eight-year-old girl, on the streets of London, sometime in the winter of 1850–1851. By means of this encounter, I want to consider others that have taken place between some adults and some children, over the last two hundred years or so. Not all of them have been the product of real meetings on wintry pavements, as was the one I am going to describe. Some have been fictional, or were meetings made within other kinds of texts, made across time and through the written word, or through a camera lens, or through the glass of social investigation. All of them, I shall argue, have served a particular cultural purpose; and they raise more general questions: about history, about the cultural uses of the past; questions of sexuality, of representation. The problems involved in those meetings were to do with the disjunctures that the participants represented, and that they became aware of in the course of their conversation; but there are also for us, problems of evidence involved in their exchanges. Evidence from children, and about children in the past, throws into relief general problems of historical interpretation. History, as a methodology, is concerned with the reconstruction, interpretation, and use of the past, so it may be the case that it has something to say as well, about that past that occupies all of us, whether we are historians or not – the personal past of each individual childhood.

My interest in these questions came about in two ways. I am a historian who, through the accidents of life, came to spend several years working with children. I taught them, and later I wrote about that teaching. The question I am working on at the moment is historical: the use of the figure of the child, particularly the working-class child, within British socialist theory and the labour movement, at the end of the last century.[2] My experience, of actually working with children, has made me aware of the split that exists between children and 'the child'. Both history and many psychologies tell us, in very different ways, that 'the child' is a construct: that beyond a bit of anatomy and physiology, and perhaps the order of language acquisition, there is not much there that isn't a matter of adult construction, adult projection. There is no 'real', or 'natural' or transcendental child. At the same time, children are *there*, in life as we know it, in social and historical time. They are lived with, worked with; they are there, in networks of social and political relation-ships. And so we will continue to act as if there is a real and natural and transcendental child. We may know enough about the legacies of Words-worthian Romanticism to see what it is we're up with as we search the past for real children. But we will go on doing precisely that: constructing hope, and belief and desire and political futures, using the figure of 'the child'. So there is a tension between what the historian has led me to in the following argument, and what actual relationships with children have led me to. My hope, of course, is that this argument will make a useful connection between the two.

This argument is about an obsession. First of all, it is my obsession, read out of the obsession of a mid-Victorian, middle-class social investigator; and then it is part of a more general cultural obsession. Henry Mayhew, the journalist and social investigator, originally published much of the material that makes up the four volumes of *London Labour and the London Poor* in a series of articles for the *Morning Chronicle* newspaper, that ran from Decem-ber 1849 to February 1850.[3] *London Labour and the London Poor* is usually seen as the first sociological investigation into the life of working-class London. In histories of the development of social investigation, it is typically linked with Charles Booth's mammoth survey of the late 1880s, *Life and Labour of the People of London*. What is particularly valuable for the historian, is that in his much earlier survey, Henry Mayhew recorded his conversations with a very wide range of poor Londoners, and reproduced them in transcript.

During his first period of investigation, sometime in the winter of 1850, he interviewed an eight-year-old seller of watercresses – a street trader – prob-ably somewhere in the Farringdon area, for that was where the child lived, and where she worked. Mayhew interviewed many little girls that winter, and later on, in the 1850s, as he prepared material for the enlarged edition of *London Labour* of 1861. It is important to note here that he interviewed many more female children than male (indeed, he does not seem to have interviewed any boy under the age of eleven). This interest in little girls was certainly to do with his self-confessed concerns about their moral welfare. I think that we should see it as well, as part of a history of sexuality in the nineteenth century. In her discussion that surrounded the age of consent campaigns of the 1880s, Deborah Gorham has drawn our attention to the ways in which the sexual life of girls and women was seen as more significant than that of boys and men, their very being more sexually symbolic.[4] In the same way, as more and more work is done on nineteenth-century construc-tions of feminity, the ideal-type of Victorian woman emerges as a kind of child, sharing frailty of body and innocence of mind with contemporary understandings of girl-children. In these ways, it is not at all surprising that Mayhew was more interested in little girls than he was in little boys.

He spoke that winter then, to many little girls; but the street seller of watercresses was the one who affected him the most. I have tried to deal with his puzzled and complicated approach to this child in both *The Tidy House* and in *Landscape for a Good Woman*. He did not know what to make of her: she puzzled him: she repelled him: he felt attraction towards her. For him she was a child, and not-a-child; and something else besides. He possessed though, an available repertoire of affect with which to write about her: conventional horror and pity, which was the rhetorical mode of the vast majority of nineteenth-century investigators of working-class life. 'There was', he wrote:

> something cruelly pathetic in hearing this infant, so young that her features had scarcely formed themselves, talking of the bitterest struggles of life, with the calm earnestness of one who has endured them all. I did not know how to talk to her. At first, I treated her as a child, speaking on childish subjects; so that I might, by being familiar with her, remove all shyness, and get her to relate her life freely...but the look of amazement that answered me soon put an end to any attempt of fun on my part.

The child confounded him: he could not explain her: the theories of childhood and working-class life he possessed failed him. Indeed, the child went on to talk about play, about games, about family affection, and revealed (more apparently to the historian of the nineteenth century than to Mayhew himself, though it was he who recorded the evidence) a highly organised family life and household economy. 'I always gives mother my money', said the child, explaining that

> she's so very good to me...She's very poor and goes out cleaning rooms sometimes, now she don't work at the fur [trade]. I ain't got no father, he's a father-in-law. No; mother ain't married again – he's a father-in-law. No; I don't mean by that he says kind things to me, for he never hardly speaks. When I gets home after selling cresses, I stops at home. I puts the room to rights; mother doesn't make me do it, I does it myself. I cleans the chairs, though there's only two to clean. I takes a tub and scrubbing brush and flannel, and scrubs the floor – that's what I do three or four times a week...I never had no doll; but I misses little sister – she's only two years old. We don't sleep in the same room; for father and mother sleeps with little sister in one pair, and me and brother and other sister sleeps in the top room. I always goes to bed at seven, 'cos I has to be up so early. ...

What makes this evidence so powerful and so revelatory is, I think, the deep interest that Mayhew experienced, in his own reactions to this little girl, and

to others. Along with the Commissioners of Inquiry into Children's Employment of 1862, and those who worked for the Commission of Inquiry into the
Employment of Children in Agriculture of 1867, both of which offer extens-
ive documentary evidence of upper-middle-class men talking to working-
class children,[5] Mayhew watched and recorded his own reactions to the
smiles that enlivened passive faces, was gratified when a pretty glance or
the rounded cheek of babyhood showed through the dirt. 'She smiled', he
wrote of one pleasingly clean little crossing-sweeper, 'like a baby in its sleep
when thinking of the answer.' These children were true mirrors for these
men, mirrors of their own cultivation of the idea of childhood.

Six years later, in 1856, John Ruskin walked through St Giles on the way
from his house to the British Museum, and took part in that same reaction of
exquisite sadness felt at the contemplation of warped lives, cramped hopes,
opportunity lost. He looked at the children's faces as they played in the
street, and recorded that 'through all of their pale and corrupt misery' they
recalled 'the old Non Angii, and recall it not by their beauty but by their
sweetness of expression, even though signed already with trace and cloud of
coming life'.[6]

This sense of exquisite sadness served these men in some way (exactly how,
I shall suggest in a moment); and as sentiment, it came to form part of an
enduring and romanticised vision of working-class life. Part of what I mean
is to be found for instance, in those passages of *Mary Barton*, where Elizabeth Gaskell describes the cosy littleness of the Barton parlour, simple and
heart-wrenching detail upon domestic detail called up to make us understand
a simplicity and sadness in this form of life.[7] Or to take a more recent
example, another passage which celebrates the same domestic simplicity in
almost the same terms: Richard Hoggart's *Uses of Literacy* of 1957, where a
rag rug comes to symbolise a great and enduring simplicity of working-class
life.[8] I would suggest that it was a need that propelled this sentimentality, the
same need that propelled the watching of poor London children in the 1850s.
This need is part of a romance, a longing, that in Mayhew's and Ruskin's
prose, is for something gone, and lost beyond all retrieval. I hope to be able
to make this particular point clearer in a moment.

In quite fundamental ways, Henry Mayhew could not *see* the Little Watercress Girl. He was, for instance, quite uncertain about her status on a
developmental map. His inability to see her as an eight-year-old, in the
way that we might see her, has been given theoretical foundation by Steven
Marcus, in his discussion of Sigmund Freud's similar difficulties in this
regard, when he contemplated the adolescent Dora.[9] Deborah Gorham, in
discussing Victorian child-prostitution (or rather, the moral panic that
surrounded the idea of child prostitution in the 1880s) reminds us that
working-class women, girls, and girl-children, were human beings of lesser
social worth than themselves, in the eyes of the middle- and upper-class men

who bought their sexual services (or – perhaps – dreamed of such sexual contact: it is clear that child prostitution really did not exist in the mid-Victorian Metropolis).[10] There was that dream or purpose at work too, in Mayhew's encounter with the Little Watercress Girl, a chimera of a belief that there existed a far more common purpose for stopping girls and young women in the street than investigation into their trade and economic circumstances. That was not Henry Mayhew's purpose, but that purpose hovers there, throughout the whole interview. He himself expressed concern about the sexual danger that little girls ran, stopping strange men in the streets to try to sell them bootlaces and matches.

Mayhew could not see this child; but I have spent ten years wanting to. In writing *The Tidy House*, I discovered that one of the things I was up to was equating one of the writers of the story, one of these modern children, a child called Carla, with The Little Watercress Girl. ...That equation, of the modern child with the Victorian child, got me a long way; it was a device that allowed me to explore a history of working-class childhood. But after writing the book, and to deflect my attention from seeing what it was that I had wanted and needed from Carla and from that other, long-dead eight-year-old, I set out instead on the path of trying to discover what it was that Mayhew might have seen and understood as he stood there talking to that child, winter-time, Farringdon, 1850. ...

I started looking for Mayhew's looking with Gustave Doré's image of the 1870s, of children playing in a rookery, and assumed that something of his representation of street life would have dictated Mayhew's vision, as much as it did my historical one.[11] I then moved to (roughly) contemporaneous photographs, at first, ones taken by John Thomson of 1876, that display the same sense of an alien culture displaying its rituals to the observer, and to his other images of working-class childhood, notably his 'Beggar Child' of 1876.[12] Why do the details of that particular photograph mean so much to me? Why do I dwell on the necklace as much as on the sores on the dancing girl's face? I want to read these photographs: to be allowed in – quite as much as did this horde of male photographers who wandered the highways and by-ways of poor London in the 1860s, 1870s and 1880s, snapping poor children. (Or more often, taking them to a studio and snapping them there.) I felt closer to Mayhew's vision with John Allison Spence's 'Slum Child' of 1851, seeing how powerful would seem the smile of childhood to the middle-class observer, were it to surface through the grime recorded here; and seeing how the impassive stare of Robert Crawshaw's 'Two Beggar Girls' might have disturbed Mayhew very much indeed.[13]

In this pursuit of Mayhew's perception, I found my little watercress girl, in John Allison Spence's 'Rag Picker's Daughter' of 1849. Still, in my imagination, when that child of Mayhew's does not wear Carla's face of 1976, she is here. I wanted her like this of course, wanted her not to be looking at the camera, not to be fixed by Mayhew's inquiry; but herself, looking elsewhere.

There were two things that I was not aware of, or was unwilling to admit, as I collected slides of these photographs. The first repression has become clearer, as historical scholarship has got to work on the photographic image. I am thinking here of work on the unstable nature of the pornographic image in the mid/late nineteenth century – a series of questions that have been particularly scrutinised through the photographs that Arthur Munby took of Hannah Cullwick, where certain poses he placed her in, which are irreducibly pornographic to the modern eye, were obviously not intended to be so by him. (Others were, and we can read them as such.) Certainly, and for a very long time, I passed over the pages in my major source book for these photographs, which show little girls in explicitly erotic poses. I divided the portraits of street life in Ovenden and Melville's *Victorian Children* from these. I was, I think, evading the connection of images, a connection which lies irreducibly in the figure of the little girl herself (all the photographs in a book called *Victorian Children* are of little girls). Perhaps, in this way, I was ignoring an important source of Mayhew's vision (and indeed, of my own). When I discovered, rather late in the day, that my source book for these searches and imaginings was indeed, a modern text book of kiddy porn, my suspicions about the febrility of my search were confirmed;[14] and so was my understanding of the irreducible fact that the lost object cannot be found.

For even at the time of my pursuit of someone else's vision, I did know that the Little Watercress Girl was indeed Henry Mayhew's child, a figure wrought out of his perception and his transcription of her words. She is not to be found looking away from his gaze, as the rag-picker's daughter looks away. This is particularly hard for me. All disciplines possess their romance, and of course, there is a romance of historical practice. Beyond all the hard and practical work in the archives, the patient compilation of an argument from fragmentary sources, there is a wish, or a desire: *that it might be found*; that the past may be delivered up whole. My own romance is still that I may find this child, that there is enough evidence in her narrative, enough detail of her life and the life of her household, to trace her, perhaps through census material, or through an as-yet-unfound survey of street-trading in Clerkenwell, dated 1849–1851.

This romance, this particular romance, is my own desire for this child, read in the light of Mayhew's desire for her (which was indeed, different from mine; and the same, in many ways). In one way, I have found her, for I now see her as the shade of *Landscape for a Good Woman*, the means by which I allowed myself to recall my own childhood, and write another account of working-class childhood. She was important because of a series of particular meanings that are attached to watercress, to coldness – being cold – to confrontations with male authority, to my father, to being eight years old; and to a fairy-tale, Andersen's 'The Snow Queen', which is itself about a great many of these things.[15] More generally than all of this: the Little Watercress Girl is what I want: the past, which is lost and which I cannot have; my own childhood. She is my fantasy child; and in a different way, she was Mayhew's fantasy child too.

You will see then, I hope, that historical inquiry into childhood must lead us to these real theoretical and practical difficulties. From my perspective, it is clear that we need to do several things. We need to make plainer to ourselves the arena of romanticism and post-romanticism within which we describe and theorise childhood. This will involve recognising how little distinction we actually make between real children and our fantasies of children. Then perhaps, seeing the usefulness of this confusion (the usefulness of recognising the confusion) we may be able to use it for intellectual purposes. We need to understand the place of our own childhood in our scholarly as much as our psychic life, and to see that the historical framework within which we work can make paedophiles of us all, at some moment or another: that as we watch, talk to, teach and write about children, we desire them, want something from them, which is our own lost childhood.

Childhood is a particular problem for the historian: we are up to something when we work on the history of childhood that we are not up to when we work on other categories of people in the past. The problem is to do with the place that childhood occupies in Western culture: the way in which our dealings with children are seen as an objective measure of our civilisation and our humanity. It is for this reason that the kind of history that records a steady march to an enlightened present, lingers persistently in the history of childhood. It is for instance, the history that we all learn at school: that once there were poor little climbing boys, and that then kind people rescued them by putting them in school: and that things are better now.[16] Both the romantic movement and psycho-analysis have taught us that in cultural terms, and over the last two hundred years, childhood is that which lies eternally within us, and the thing we can never have: which is our own particular piece of lost time. I would argue, with Dominick LaCapra in *History and Criticism*, that the historian has a massive transferential relationship to the past.[17] I would say that this transference becomes particularly acute and particularly interesting when children are the subjects of historical research, because of the place that children occupy in human imagination and human culture. The history of childhood, and its historiography, are important, because they will tell us something particular about what we are up to in 'doing history'.

I can't go beyond this. What I have done is tell you about my own transferential relationship to the past – and I hope, something about

Henry Mayhew and an eight-year-old girl. What we can talk about, and what I hope you will be interested in discussing, is class and gender in the study of childhood, and the way in which, over the last two hundred years of cultural life, the little girl has become 'the child'.

4

Workers Revolt: The Great Cat Massacre of the Rue Saint-Séverin

Robert Darnton

The funniest thing that ever happened in the printing shop of Jacques Vincent, according to a worker who witnessed it, was a riotous massacre of cats. The worker, Nicolas Contat, told the story in an account of his apprenticeship in the shop, rue Saint-Séverin, Paris, during the late 1730s.[1] Life as an apprentice was hard, he explained. There were two of them: Jerome, the somewhat fictionalised version of Contat himself, and Léveillé. They slept in a filthy, freezing room, rose before dawn, ran errands all day while dodging insults from the journeymen and abuse from the master, and received nothing but slops to eat. They found the food especially galling. Instead of dining at the master's table, they had to eat scraps from his plate in the kitchen. Worse still, the cook secretly sold the leftovers and gave the boys cat food – old, rotten bits of meat that they could not stomach and so passed on to the cats, who refused it.

This last injustice brought Contat to the theme of cats. They occupied a special place in his narrative and in the household of the rue Saint-Séverin. The master's wife adored them, especially *la grise* (the grey), her favourite. A passion for cats seemed to have swept through the printing trade, at least at the level of the masters, or *bourgeois* as the workers called them. One bourgeois kept twenty-five cats. He had their portraits painted and fed them on roast fowl. Meanwhile, the apprentices were trying to cope with a profusion of alley cats who also thrived in the printing district and made the boys' lives miserable. The cats howled all night on the roof over the apprentices' dingy bedroom, making it impossible to get a full night's sleep. As Jerome and Léveillé had to stagger out of bed at four or five in the morning to open the gate for the earliest arrivals among the journeymen, they began the day in a state of exhaustion while the bourgeois slept late. The master did not even work with the men, just as he did not eat with them. He let the foreman run the shop and rarely appeared in it, except to vent his violent temper, usually at the expense of the apprentices.

One night the boys resolved to right this inequitable state of affairs. Léveillé, who had an extraordinary talent for mimickry, crawled along the roof until he reached a section near the master's bedroom, and then he took to howling and meowing so horribly that the bourgeois and his wife did not sleep a wink. After several nights of this treatment, they decided they were being bewitched. But instead of calling the curé – the master was exceptionally devout and the mistress exceptionally attached to her confessor – they commanded the apprentices to get rid of the cats. The mistress gave the order, enjoining the boys above all to avoid frightening her *grise*.

Gleefully Jerome and Léveillé set to work, aided by the journeymen. Armed with broom handless, bars of the press, and other tools of their trade, they went after every cat they could find, beginning with *la grise*. Léveillé smashed its spine with an iron bar and Jerome finished it off. Then they stashed it in a gutter while the journeymen drove the other cats across the rooftops, bludgeoning every one within reach and trapping those who tried to escape in strategically placed sacks. They dumped sackloads of half-dead cats in the courtyard. Then the entire workshop gathered round and staged a mock trial, complete with guards, a confessor, and a public executioner. After pronouncing the animals guilty and administering last rites, they strung them up on an improvised gallows. Roused by gales of laughter, the mistress arrived. She let out a shriek as soon as she saw a bloody cat dangling from a noose. Then she realised it might be *la grise*. Certainly not, the men assured her: they had too much respect for the house to do such a thing. At this point the master appeared. He flew into a rage at the general stoppage of work, though his wife tried to explain that they were threatened by a more serious kind of insubordination. Then master and mistress withdrew, leaving the men delirious with 'joy', 'disorder', and 'laughter'.[2]

The laughter did not end there. Léveillé re-enacted the entire scene in mime at least twenty times during subsequent days when the printers wanted to knock off for some hilarity. Burlesque re-enactments of incidents in the life of the shop, known as *copies* in printers' slang, provided a major form of entertainment for the men. The idea was to humiliate someone in the shop by satirising his peculiarities. A successful *copie* would make the butt of the joke fume with rage – *prendre la chèvre* (take the goat) in the shop slang – while his mates razzed him with 'rough music'. They would run their composing sticks across the tops of the type cases, beat their mallets against the chases, pound on cupboards, and bleat like goats. The bleating (*bais* in the slang) stood for the humiliation heaped on the victims, as in English when someone 'gets your goat'. Contat emphasised that Léveillé produced the funniest *copies* anyone had ever known and elicited the greatest choruses of rough music. The whole episode, cat massacre compounded by *copies*, stood out as the most hilarious experience in Jerome's entire career.

Yet it strikes the modern reader as unfunny, if not downright repulsive. Where is the humour in a group of grown men bleating like goats and banging with their tools while an adolescent re-enacts the ritual slaughter of a defenceless animal? Our own inability to get the joke is an indication of the distance that separates us from the workers of pre-industrial Europe. The perception of that distance may serve as the starting point of an investigation, for anthropologists have found that the best points of entry in an attempt to penetrate an alien culture can be those where it seems to be most opaque. When you realise that you are not getting something – a joke, a proverb, a ceremony – that is particularly meaningful to the natives, you can see where to grasp a foreign system of meaning in order to unravel it. By getting the joke of the great cat massacre, it may be possible to 'get' a basic ingredient of artisanal culture under the Old Regime.

It should be explained at the outset that we cannot observe the killing of the cats at firsthand. We can study it only through Contat's narrative, written about twenty years after the event. There can be no doubt about the authenticity of Contat's quasi-fictional autobiography, as Giles Barber has demonstrated in his masterful edition of the text. It belongs to the line of autobiographical writing by printers that stretches from Thomas Platter to Thomas Gent, Benjamin Franklin, Nicolas Restif de la Bretonne, and Charles Manby Smith. Because printers, or at least compositors, had to be reasonably literate in order to do their work, they were among the few artisans who could give their own accounts of life in the working classes two, three, and four centuries ago. With all its misspellings and grammatical flaws, Contat's is perhaps the richest of these accounts. But it cannot be regarded as a mirror-image of what actually happened. It should be read as Contat's version of a happening, as his attempt to tell a story. Like all story telling, it sets the action in a frame of reference; it assumes a certain repertory of associations and responses on the part of its audience; and it provides meaningful shape to the raw stuff of experience. But since we are attempting to get at its meaning in the first place, we should not be put off by its fabricated character. On the contrary, by treating the narrative as fiction or meaningful fabrication we can use it to develop an ethnological *explication de texte*.

The first explanation that probably would occur to most readers of Contat's story is that the cat massacre served as an oblique attack on the master and his wife. Contat set the event in the context of remarks about the disparity between the lot of workers and the bourgeois – a matter of the basic elements in life: work, food, and sleep. The injustice seemed especially flagrant in the case of the apprentices, who were treated like animals while the animals were promoted over their heads to the position the boys should have occupied, the place at the master's table. Although the apprentices seem most abused, the text makes it clear that the killing of the cats expressed a hatred for the bourgeois that had spread among all the workers: 'The masters love cats; consequently [the workers] hate them.' After masterminding the massacre, Léveillé became the hero of the shop, because 'all the workers are in league against the masters. It is enough to speak badly of them [the masters] to be esteemed by the whole assembly of typographers.'[3]

Historians have tended to treat the era of artisanal manufacturing as an idyllic period before the onset of industrialisation. Some even portray the workshop as a kind of extended family in which master and journeymen laboured at the same tasks, ate at the same table, and sometimes slept under the same roof.[4] Had anything happened to poison the atmosphere of the printing shops in Paris by 1740?

During the second half of the seventeenth century, the large printing houses, backed by the government, eliminated most of the smaller shops, and an oligarchy of masters seized control of the industry.[5] At the same time, the situation of the journeymen deteriorated. Although estimates vary and statistics cannot be trusted, it seems that their number remained stable: approximately 335 in 1666, 339 in 1701, and 340 in 1721. Meanwhile the number of masters declined by more than half, from eighty-three to thirty-six, the limit fixed by an edict of 1686. That meant fewer shops with larger work forces, as one can see from statistics on the density of presses: in 1644 Paris had seventy-five printing shops with a total of 180 presses; in 1701 it had fifty-one shops with 195 presses. This trend made it virtually impossible for journeymen to rise into the ranks of the masters. About the only way for a worker to get ahead in the craft was to marry a master's widow, for masterships had become hereditary privileges, passed on from husband to wife and from father to son.

The journeymen also felt threatened from below because the masters tended increasingly to hire *alloués*, or underqualified printers, who had not undergone the apprenticeship that made a journeyman eligible, in principle, to advance to a mastership. The *alloués* were merely a source of cheap labour, excluded from the upper ranks of the trade and fixed, in their inferior status, by an edict of 1723. Their degradation stood out in their name: they were *à louer* (for hire), not *compagnons* (journeymen) of the master. They personified the tendency of labour to become a commodity instead of a partnership. Thus Contat served his apprenticeship and wrote his memoirs when times were hard for journeymen printers, when the men in the shop in the rue Saint-Séverin stood in danger of being cut off from the top of the trade and swamped from the bottom.

How this general tendency became manifest in an actual workshop may be seen from the papers of the Société typographique de Neuchâtel (STN). To be sure, the STN was Swiss, and it did not begin business until seven years after Contat wrote his memoirs (1762). But printing practices were essentially the same way everywhere in the eighteenth century. The STN's archives conform in dozens of details to Contat's account of his experience. (They even mention the same shop foreman, Colas, who supervised Jerome for a while at the Imprimerie Royale and took charge of the STN's shop for a brief stint in 1779.) And they provide the only surviving record of the way masters hired, managed, and fired printers in the early modern era.

The STN's wage book shows that workers usually stayed in the shop for only a few months.[6] They left because they quarrelled with the master, they got in fights, they wanted to pursue their fortune in shops further down the road, or they ran out of work. Compositors were hired by the job, *labeur* or *ouvrage* in printer's slang. When they finished a job, they frequently were fired, and a few pressmen had to be fired as well in order to maintain the balance between the two halves of the shop, the *casse* or composing sector and the *presse* or pressroom (two compositors usually set enough type to occupy a team of two pressmen). When the foreman took on new jobs, he hired new hands. The hiring and firing went on at such a fierce pace that the work force was rarely the same from one week to the next. Jerome's fellow workers in the rue Saint-Séverin seem to have been equally volatile. They, too, were hired for specific *labeurs*, and they sometimes walked off the job after quarrels with the bourgeois – a practice common enough to have its own entry in the glossary of their slang which Contat appended to his narrative: *emporter son Saint Jean* (to carry off your set of tools or quit). A man was known as an *ancien* if he remained in the shop for only a year. Other slang terms suggest the atmosphere in which the work took place: *une chèvre capitale* (a fit of rage), *se donner la gratte* (to get in a fight), *prendre la barbe* (to get drunk), *faire la déroute* (to go pub crawling), *promener sa chape* (to knock off work), *faire des loups* (to pile up debts).[7]

The violence, drunkenness, and absenteeism show up in the statistics of income and output one can compile from the STN's wage book. Printers worked in erratic spurts – twice as much in one week as in another, the weeks varying from four to six days and the days beginning anywhere from four in the morning until nearly noon. In order to keep the irregularity within bounds, the masters sought out men with two supreme traits: assiduousness and sobriety. If they also happened to be skilled, so much the better. A recruiting agent in Geneva recommended a compositor who was willing to set out for Neuchâtel in typical terms: 'He is a good worker, capable of doing any job he gets, not at all a drunkard and assiduous at his labour.'[8]

The STN relied on recruiters because it did not have an adequate labour pool in Neuchâtel and the streams of printers on the typographical *tours de France* sometimes ran dry. The recruiters and employers exchanged letters that reveal a common set of assumptions about eighteenth-century artisans: they were lazy, flighty, dissolute, and unreliable. They could not be trusted, so the recruiter should not loan them money for travel expenses and the employer could keep their belongings as a kind of security deposit in case they skipped off after collecting their pay. It followed that they could be discarded without compunction, whether or not they had worked diligently, had families to support, or fell sick. The STN ordered them in 'assortments' just as it ordered paper and type. It complained that a recruiter in Lyon 'sent us a couple in such a bad state that we were obliged to ship them off'[9] and lectured him about failing to inspect the goods: 'Two of those whom you have sent to us have arrived all right, but so sick that they could infect all the rest; so we haven't been able to hire them. No one in town wanted to give them lodging. They have therefore left again and took the route for Besançon, in order to turn themselves in at the *hôpital*.'[10] A bookseller in Lyon advised them to fire most of their men during a slack period in their printing in order to flood the labour supply in eastern France and 'give us more power over a wild and undisciplinable race, which we cannot control'.[11] Journeymen and masters may have lived together as members of a happy family at some time somewhere in Europe, but not in the printing houses of eighteenth-century France and Switzerland.

Contat himself believed that such a state had once existed. He began his description of Jerome's apprenticeship by invoking a golden age when printing was first invented and printers lived as free and equal members of a 'republic', governed by its own laws and traditions in a spirit of fraternal 'union and friendship'.[12] He claimed that the republic still survived in the form of the *chapelle* or workers' association in each shop. But the government had broken up general associations; the ranks had been thinned by *alloués*; the journeymen had been excluded from masterships; and the masters had withdrawn into a separate world of *haute cuisine* and *grasses matinées*. The master in the rue Saint-Séverin ate different food, kept different hours, and talked a different language. His wife and daughters dallied with worldly abbés. They kept pets. Clearly, the bourgeois belonged to a different subculture – one which meant above all that he did not work. In introducing his account of the cat massacre, Contat made explicit the contrast between the worlds of worker and master that ran throughout the narrative: 'Workers, apprentices, everyone works. Only the masters and mistresses enjoy the sweetness of sleep. That makes Jerome and Léveillé resentful. They resolve not to be the only wretched ones. They want their master and mistress as associates (*associés*).'[13] That is, the boys wanted to restore a mythical past when masters and men worked in friendly association. They also may have had in mind the more recent extinction of the smaller printing shops. So they killed the cats.

But why cats? And why was the killing so funny? Those questions take us beyond the consideration of early modern labour relations and into the obscure subject of popular ceremonies and symbolism.

Folklorists have made historians familiar with the ceremonial cycles that marked off the calendar year for early modern man.[14] The most important of these was the cycle of carnival and Lent, a period of revelry followed by a period of abstinence. During carnival the common people suspended the normal rules of behaviour and ceremoniously reversed the social order or turned it upside down in riotous procession. Carnival was a time for cutting up by youth groups, particularly apprentices, who organised themselves in 'abbeys' ruled by a mock abbot or king and who staged charivaris or burlesque processions with rough music in order to humiliate cuckolds, husbands who had been beaten by their wives, brides who had married below their age group, or someone else who personified the infringement of traditional norms. Carnival was high season for hilarity, sexuality, and youth run riot – a time when young people tested social boundaries by limited outbursts of deviance, before being reassimilated in the world of order, submission, and Lentine seriousness. It came to an end on Shrove Tuesday or Mardi Gras, when a straw mannequin, King Carnival or Caramantran, was given a ritual trial and execution. Cats played an important part in some charivaris. In Burgundy, the crowd incorporated cat torture into its rough music. While mocking a cuckold or some other victim, the youths passed around a cat, tearing its fur to make it howl. *Faire le chat*, they called it. The Germans called charivaris *Katzenmusik*, a term that may have been derived from the howls of tortured cats.[15]

Cats also figured in the cycle of Saint John the Baptist, which took place on June 24, at the time of the summer solstice. Crowds made bonfires, jumped over them, danced around them, and threw into them objects with magical power, hoping to avoid disaster and obtain good fortune during the rest of the year. A favourite object was cats – cats tied up in bags, cats suspended from ropes, or cats burned at the stake. Parisians liked to incinerate cats by the sackful, while the Courimauds (*cour à miaud* or cat chasers) of Saint Chamond preferred to chase a flaming cat through the streets. In parts of Burgundy and Lorraine they danced around a kind of burning May pole with a cat tied to it. In the Metz region they burned a dozen cats at a time in a basket on top of a bonfire. The ceremony took place with great pomp in Metz itself, until it was abolished in 1765. The town dignitaries arrived in procession at the Place du Grand-Saulcy, lit the pyre, and a ring of riflemen from the garrison fired off volleys while the cats disappeared screaming in the flames. Although the practice varied from place to place, the ingredients were everywhere the same: a *feu de joie* (bonfire), cats, and an aura of hilarious witch-hunting.[16]

In addition to these general ceremonies, which involved entire communities, artisans celebrated ceremonies peculiar to their craft. Printers processed and feasted in honour of their patron, Saint John the Evangelist, both on his saint's day, December 27, and on the anniversary of his martyrdom,

May 6, the festival of Saint Jean Porte Latine. By the eighteenth century, the masters had excluded the journeymen from the confraternity devoted to the saint, but the journeymen continued to hold ceremonies in their chapels.[17] On Saint Martin's day, November 11, they held a mock trial followed by a feast. Contat explained that the chapel was a tiny 'republic', which governed itself according to its own code of conduct. When a worker violated the code, the foreman, who was the head of the chapel and not part of the management, entered a fine in a register: leaving a candle lit, five sous; brawling, three livres; insulting the good name of the chapel, three livres; and so on. On Saint Martin's, the foreman read out the fines and collected them. The workers sometimes appealed their cases before a burlesque tribunal composed of the chapel's 'ancients', but in the end they had to pay up amidst more bleating, banging of tools, and riotous laughter. The fines went for food and drink in the chapel's favourite tavern, where the hell-raising continued until late in the night.[18]

Taxation and commensality characterised all the other ceremonies of the chapel. Special dues and feasts marked a man's entry into the shop (*bienvenue*), his exit (*conduite*), and even his marriage (*droit de chevet*). Above all, they punctuated a youth's progress from apprentice to journeyman. Contat described four of these rites, the most important being the first, called the taking of the apron, and the last, Jerome's initiation as a full-fledged *compagnon*.

The taking of the apron (*la prise de tablier*) occurred soon after Jerome joined the shop. He had to pay six livres (about three days' wages for an ordinary journeyman) into a kitty, which the journeymen supplemented by small payments of their own (*faire la reconnaissance*). Then the chapel repaired to its favourite tavern, Le Panier Fleury in the rue de la Huchette. Emissaries were dispatched to procure provisions and returned loaded down with bread and meat, having lectured the shopkeepers of the neighbourhood on which cuts were worthy of typographers and which could be left for cobblers. Silent and glass in hand, the journeymen gathered around Jerome in a special room on the second floor of the tavern. The subforeman approached, carrying the apron and followed by two 'ancients', one from each of the 'estates' of the shop, the *casse* and the *presse*. He handed the apron, newly made from close-woven linen, to the foreman, who took Jerome by the hand and led him to the centre of the room, the subforeman and 'ancients' falling in behind. The foreman made a short speech, placed the apron over Jerome's head and tied the strings behind him, as everyone drank to the health of the initiate. Jerome was then given a seat with the chapel dignitaries at the head of the table. The rest rushed for the best places they could find and fell on the food. They gobbled and guzzled and called out for more. After several Gargantuan rounds, they settled down to shop talk – and Contat lets us listen in:

'Isn't it true,' says one of them, 'that printers know how to shovel it in? I am sure that if someone presented us with a roast mutton, as big as you like, we would leave nothing but the bones behind. . . .' They don't talk about theology nor philosophy and still less of politics. Each speaks of his job: one will talk to you about the *casse*, another the *presse*, this one of the tympan, another of the ink ball leathers. They all speak at the same time, whether they can be heard or not.

At last, early in the morning after hours of swilling and shouting, the workers separated – sotted but ceremonial to the end: 'Bonsoir, Monsieur notre prote [foreman]'; 'Bonsoir, Messieurs les compositeurs'; 'Bonsoir, Messieurs les imprimeurs'; 'Bonsoir Jerome'. The text explains that Jerome will be called by his first name until he is received as a journeyman.[19]

That moment came four years later, after two intermediary ceremonies (the *admission à l'ouvrage* and the *admission à la banque*) and a vast amount of hazing. Not only did the men torment Jerome, mocking his ignorance, sending him on wild goose chases, making him the butt of practical jokes, and overwhelming him with nasty chores; they also refused to teach him anything. They did not want another journeyman in their over-flooded labour pool, so Jerome had to pick up the tricks of the trade by himself. The work, the food, the lodging, the lack of sleep, it was enough to drive a boy mad, or at least out of the shop. In fact, however, it was standard treatment and should not be taken too seriously. Contat recounted the catalogue of Jerome's troubles in a light-hearted manner, which suggested a stock comic genre, the *misère des apprentis*.[20] The *misères* provided farcial accounts, in doggerel verse or broadsides, of a stage in life that was familiar and funny to everyone in the artisanate. It was a transitional stage, which marked the passage from childhood to adulthood. A young man had to sweat his way through it so that he would have paid his dues – the printers demanded actual payments, called *bienvenues* or *quatre heures*, in addition to razzing the apprentices – when he reached full membership in a vocational group. Until he arrived at that point, he lived in a fluid or liminal state, trying out adult conventions by subjecting them to some hell-raising of his own. His elders tolerated his pranks, called *copies* and *joberies* in the printing trade, because they saw them as wild oats, which needed to be sown before he could settle down. Once settled, he would have internalised the conventions of his craft and acquired a new identity, which was often symbolised by a change in his name.[21]

Jerome became a journeyman by passing through the final rite, *compagnonnage*. It took the same form as the other ceremonies, a celebration over food and drink after the candidate paid an initiation fee and the journeymen chipped in with *reconnaissance*. But this time Contat gave a summary of the foreman's speech:[22]

The newcomer is indoctrinated. He is told never to betray his colleagues and to maintain the wage rate. If a worker doesn't accept a price [for a job] and leaves the shop, no one in the house should do the job for a smaller price. Those are the laws among the workers. Faithfulness and probity are recommended to him. Any worker who betrays the others, when something forbidden, called *marron* [chestnut], is being printed, must be expelled ignominiously from the shop. The workers blacklist him by circular letters sent around all the shops of Paris and the provinces.... Aside from that, anything is permitted: excessive drinking is considered a good quality, gallantry and debauchery as youthful feats, indebtedness as a sign of wit, irreligion as sincerity. It's a free and republican territory in which everything is permitted. Live as you like but be an *honnête homme*, no hypocrisy.

Hypocrisy turned out in the rest of the narrative to be the main characteristic of the bourgeois, a superstitious religious bigot. He occupied a separate world of pharasaical bourgeois morality. The workers defined their 'republic' against that world and against other journeymen's groups as well – the cobblers, who ate inferior cuts of meat, and the masons or carpenters who were always good for a brawl when the printers, divided into 'estates' (the *casse* and the *presse*) toured country taverns on Sundays. In entering an 'estate', Jerome assimilated an ethos. He identified himself with a craft; and as a full-fledged journeyman compositor, he received a new name. Having gone through a rite of passage in the full, anthropological sense of the term, he became a *Monsieur*.[23]

So much for ceremonies. What about cats? It should be said at the outset that there is an indefinable *je ne sais quoi* about cats, a mysterious something that has fascinated mankind since the time of the ancient Egyptians. One can sense a quasi-human intelligence behind a cat's eyes. One can mistake a cat's howl at night for a human scream, torn from some deep, visceral part of man's animal nature. Cats appealed to poets like Baudelaire and painters like Manet, who wanted to express the humanity in animals along with the animality of men – and especially of women.[24]

This ambiguous ontological position, a straddling of conceptual categories, gives certain animals – pigs, dogs, and cassowaries as well as cats – in certain cultures an occult power associated with the taboo. That is why Jews do not eat pigs, according to Mary Douglas, and why Englishmen can insult one another by saying 'son-of-a-bitch' rather than 'son-of-a-cow', according to Edmund Leach.[25] Certain animals are good for swearing, just as they are 'good for thinking' in Lévi-Strauss's famous formula. I would add that others – cats in particular – are good for staging ceremonies. They have ritual value. You cannot make a charivari with a cow. You do it with cats: you decide to *faire le chat*, to make *Katzenmusik*.

The torture of animals, especially cats, was a popular amusement through-out early modern Europe. You have only to look at Hogarth's *Stages of Cruelty* to see its importance, and once you start looking you see people torturing animals everywhere. Cat killings provided a common theme in literature, from *Don Quixote* in early seventeenth-century Spain to *Germinal* in late nineteenth-century France.[26] Far from being a sadistic fantasy on the part of a few half-crazed authors, the literary versions of cruelty to animals expressed a deep current of popular culture, as Mikhail Bakhtin has shown in his study of Rabelais.[27] All sorts of ethnographic reports confirm that view. On the *dimanche des brandons* in Semur, for example, children used to attach cats to poles and roast them over bonfires. In the *jeu du chat* at the Fete-Dieu in Aix-en-Provence, they threw cats high in the air and smashed them on the ground. They used expressions like 'patient as a cat whose claws are being pulled out' or 'patient as a cat whose paws are being grilled'. The English were just as cruel. During the Reformation in London, a Protestant crowd shaved a cat to look like a priest, dressed it in mock vestments, and hanged it on the gallows at Cheapside.[28] It would be possible to string out many other examples, but the point should be clear: there was nothing unusual about the ritual killing of cats. On the contrary, when Jerome and his fellow workers tried and hanged all the cats they could find in the rue Saint-Séverin, they drew on a common element in their culture. But what significance did that culture attribute to cats?

To get a grip on that question, one must rummage through collections of folktales, superstitions, proverbs, and popular medicine. The material is rich, varied, and vast but extremely hard to handle. Although much of it goes back to the Middle Ages, little can be dated. It was gathered for the most part by folklorists in the late nineteenth and early twentieth centuries, when sturdy strains of folklore still resisted the influence of the printed word. But the collections do not make it possible to claim that this or that practice existed in the printing houses of mid-eighteenth-century Paris. One can only assert that printers lived and breathed in an atmosphere of traditional customs and beliefs which permeated everything. It was not everywhere the same – France remained a patchwork of *pays* rather than a unified nation until late in the nineteenth century – but everywhere some common motifs could be found. The commonest were attached to cats. Early modern Frenchmen probably made more symbolic use of cats than of any other animal, and they used them in distinct ways, which can be grouped together for the purposes of discussion, despite the regional peculiarities.

First and foremost, cats suggested witchcraft. To cross one at night in virtually any corner of France was to risk running into the devil or one of his agents or a witch abroad on an evil errand. White cats could be as satanic as the black, in the daytime as well as at night. In a typical encounter, a peasant woman of Bigorre met a pretty white house cat who had strayed in the fields.

She carried it back to the village in her apron, and just as they came to the house of a woman suspected of witchcraft, the cat jumped out, saying 'Merci, Jeanne'.[29] Witches transformed themselves into cats in order to cast spells on their victims. Sometimes, especially on Mardi Gras, they gathered for hideous sabbaths at night. They howled, fought, and copulated horribly under the direction of the devil himself in the form of a huge tomcat. To protect yourself from sorcery by cats there was one, classic remedy: maim it. Cut its tail, clip its ears, smash one of its legs, tear or burn its fur, and you would break its malevolent power. A maimed cat could not attend a sabbath or wander abroad to cast spells. Peasants frequently cudgelled cats who crossed their paths at night and discovered the next day that bruises had appeared on women believed to be witches – or so it was said in the lore of their village. Villagers also told stories of farmers who found strange cats in barns and broke their limbs to save the cattle. Invariably a broken limb would appear on a suspicious woman the following morning.

Cats possessed occult power independently of their association with witchcraft and deviltry. They could prevent the bread from rising if they entered bakeries in Anjou. They could spoil the catch if they crossed the path of fishermen in Brittany. If buried alive in Béarn, they could clear a field of weeds. They figured as staple ingredients in all kinds of folk medicine aside from witches' brews. To recover from a bad fall, you sucked the blood out of a freshly amputated tail of a tomcat. To cure yourself from pneumonia, you drank blood from a cat's ear in red wine. To get over colic, you mixed your wine with cat excrement. You could even make yourself invisible, at least in Brittany, by eating the brain of a newly killed cat, provided it was still hot.

There was a specific field for the exercise of cat power: the household and particularly the person of the master or mistress of the house. Folktales like 'Puss 'n Boots' emphasised the identification of master and cat, and so did superstitions such as the practice of tying a black ribbon around the neck of a cat whose mistress had died. To kill a cat was to bring misfortune upon its owner or its house. If a cat left a house or stopped jumping on the sickbed of its master or mistress, the person was likely to die. But a cat lying on the bed of a dying man might be the devil, waiting to carry his soul off to hell. According to a sixteenth-century tale, a girl from Quintin sold her soul to the devil in exchange for some pretty clothes. When she died, the pallbearers could not lift her coffin; they opened the lid, and a black cat jumped out. Cats could harm a house. They often smothered babies. They understood gossip and would repeat it out of doors. But their power could be contained or turned to your advantage if you followed the right procedures, such as greasing their paws with butter or maiming them when they first arrived. To protect a new house, Frenchmen enclosed live cats within its walls – a very old rite, judging from cat skeletons that have been exhumed from the walls of medieval buildings.

Finally, the power of cats was concentrated on the most intimate aspect of domestic life: sex. *Le chat, la chatte, le minet* mean the same thing in French slang as 'pussy' does in English, and they have served as obscenities for centuries.[30] French folklore attaches special importance to the cat as a sexual metaphor or metonym. As far back as the fifteenth century, the petting of cats was recommended for success in courting women. Proverbial wisdom identified women with cats: 'He who takes good care of cats will have a pretty wife.' If a man loved cats, he would love women; and vice versa: 'As he loves his cat, he loves his wife', went another proverb. If he did not care for his wife, you could say of him, 'He has other cats to whip'. A woman who wanted to get a man should avoid treading on a cat's tail. She might postpone marriage for a year – or for seven years in Quimper and for as many years as the cat meowed in parts of the Loire Valley. Cats connoted fertility and female sexuality everywhere. Girls were commonly said to be 'in love like a cat'; and if they became pregnant, they had 'let the cat go to the cheese'. Eating cats could bring on pregnancy in itself. Girls who consumed them in stews gave birth to kittens in several folktales. Cats could even make diseased apple trees bear fruit, if buried in the correct manner in upper Brittany.

It was an easy jump from the sexuality of women to the cuckolding of men. Caterwauling could come from a satanic orgy, but it might just as well be toms howling defiance at each other when their mates were in heat. They did not call as cats, however. They issued challenges in their masters' names, along with sexual taunts about their mistresses: 'Reno! Francois!' 'Où allez-vous? – Voir la femme à vous. – Voir la femme à moi! Rouah!' (Where are you going? – To see your wife. – To see my wife! Ha!). Then the toms would fly at each other like the cats of Kilkenny, and their sabbath would end in a massacre. The dialogue differed according to the imaginations of the listeners and the onomatopoetic power of their dialect, but it usually emphasised predatory sexuality.[31] 'At night all cats are grey', went the proverb, and the gloss in an eighteenth-century proverb collection made the sexual hint explicit: 'That is to say that all women are beautiful enough at night.'[32] Enough for what? Seduction, rape, and murder echoed in the air when the cats howled at night in early modern France. Cat calls summoned up *Katzenmusik*, for charivaris often took the form of howling under a cuckold's window on the eve of Mardi Gras, the favourite time for cat sabbaths.

Witchcraft, orgy, cuckoldry, charivari, and massacre, the men of the Old Regime could hear a great deal in the wail of a cat. What the men of the rue Saint-Séverin actually heard is impossible to say. One can only assert that cats bore enormous symbolic weight in the folklore of France and that the lore was rich, ancient, and widespread enough to have penetrated the printing shop. In order to determine whether the printers actually drew on the ceremonial and symbolic themes available to them, it is necessary to take another look at Contat's text.

The text made the theme of sorcery explicit from the beginning. Jerome and Léveillé could not sleep because 'some bedevilled cats make a sabbath all night long'.[33] After Léveillé added his cat calls to the general caterwauling, 'the whole neighbourhood is alarmed. It is decided that the cats must be agents of someone casting a spell.' The master and mistress considered summoning the curé to exorcise the place. In deciding instead to commission the cat hunt, they fell back on the classic remedy for witchcraft: maiming. The bourgeois – a superstitious, priest-ridden fool – took the whole business seriously. To the apprentices it was a joke. Léveillé in particular functioned as a joker, a mock 'sorcerer' staging a fake 'sabbath', according to the terms chosen by Contat. Not only did the apprentices exploit their master's super-stition in order to run riot at his expense, but they also turned their rioting against their mistress. By bludgeoning her familiar, *la grise*, they in effect accused her of being the witch. The double joke would not be lost on anyone who could read the traditional language of gesture.

The theme of charivari provided an additional dimension to the fun. Although it never says so explicitly, the text indicates that the mistress was having an affair with her priest, a 'lascivious youth', who had memorised obscene passages from the classics of pornography – Aretino and *L'Acade-mie des dames* – and quoted them to her, while her husband droned on about his favourite subjects, money and religion. During a lavish dinner with the family, the priest defended the thesis 'that it is a feat of wit to cuckold one's husband and that cuckolding is not a vice'. Later, he and the wife spent the night together in a country house. They fit perfectly into the typical triangle of printing shops: a doddering old master, a middle-aged mistress, and her youthful lover.[34] The intrigue cast the master in the role of a stock comic figure: the cuckold. So the revelry of the workers took the form of a charivari. The apprentices managed it, operating within the liminal area where novitiates traditionally mocked their superiors, and the journeymen responded to their antics in the traditional way, with rough music. A riotous, festival atmosphere runs through the whole episode, which Contat described as a *fête:* 'Léveillé and his comrade Jerome preside over the *fête*', he wrote, as if they were kings of a carnival and the cat bashing corresponded to the torturing of cats on Mardi Gras or the *fête* of Saint John the Baptist.

As in many Mardi Gras, the carnival ended in a mock trial and execution. The burlesque legalism came naturally to the printers because they staged their own mock trials every year at the *fête* of Saint Martin, when the chapel squared accounts with its boss and succeeded spectacularly in getting his goat. The chapel could not condemn him explicitly without moving into open insubordination and risking dismissal. (All the sources, including the papers of the STN, indicate that masters often fired workers for insolence and misbehaviour. Indeed, Léveillé was later fired for a prank that attacked the bourgeois more openly.) So the workers tried the bourgeois in absentia, using a symbol that would let their meaning show through without being explicit enough to justify retaliation. They tried and hanged the cats. It would be going too far to hang *la grise* under the master's nose after being ordered to spare it; but they made the favourite pet of the house their first victim, and in doing so they knew they were attacking the house itself, in accordance with the traditions of cat lore. When the mistress accused them of killing *la grise*, they replied with mock deference that 'nobody would be capable of such an outrage and that they have too much respect for that house'. By executing the cats with such elaborate ceremony, they condemned the house and declared the bourgeois guilty – guilty of overworking and underfeeding his apprentices, guilty of living in luxury while his journeymen did all the work, guilty of withdrawing from the shop and swamping it with *alloués* instead of labouring and eating with the men, as masters were said to have done a generation or two earlier, or in the primitive 'republic' that existed at the beginning of the printing industry. The guilt extended from the boss to the house to the whole system. Perhaps in trying, confessing, and hanging a collection of half-dead cats, the workers meant to ridicule the entire legal and social order.

They certainly felt debased and had accumulated enough resentment to explode in an orgy of killing. A half-century later, the artisans of Paris would run riot in a similar manner, combining indiscriminate slaughter with improvised popular tribunals.[35] It would be absurd to view the cat massacre as a dress rehearsal for the September Massacres of the French Revolution, but the earlier outburst of violence did suggest a popular rebellion, though it remained restricted to the level of symbolism.

Cats as symbols conjured up sex as well as violence, a combination perfectly suited for an attack on the mistress. The narrative identified her with *la grise*, her *chatte favorite*. In killing it, the boys struck at her: 'It was a matter of consequence, a murder, which had to be hidden.' The mistress reacted as if she had been assaulted: 'They ravished from her a cat without an equal, a cat that she loved to madness.' The text described her as lascivious and 'impassioned for cats' as if she were a she-cat in heat during a wild cat's sabbath of howling, killing, and rape. An explicit reference to rape would violate the proprieties that were generally observed in eighteenth-century writing. Indeed, the symbolism would work only if it remained veiled – ambivalent enough to dupe the master and sharp enough to hit the mistress in the quick. But Contat used strong language. As soon as the mistress saw the cat execution she let out a scream. Then the scream was smothered in the realisation that she had lost her *grise*. The workers assured her with feigned sincerity of their respect and the master arrived. ' "Ah! the scoundrels," he says. "Instead of working they are killing cats." Madame to Monsieur: "These wicked men can't kill the masters; they have killed my cat." . . . It seems to her that all the blood of the workers would not be sufficient to redeem the insult.'

It was metonymic insult, the eighteenth-century equivalent of the modern schoolboy's taunt: 'Ah, your mother's girdle!' But it was stronger, and more obscene. By assaulting her pet, the workers ravished the mistress symbol-ically. At the same time, they delivered the supreme insult to their master. His wife was his most precious possession, just as her *chatte* was hers. In killing the cat, the men violated the most intimate treasure of the bourgeois household and escaped unharmed. That was the beauty of it. The symbolism disguised the insult well enough for them to get away with it. While the bourgeois fumed over the loss of work, his wife, less obtuse, virtually told him that the workers had attacked her sexually and would like to murder him. Then both left the scene in humiliation and defeat. 'Monsieur and Madame retire, leaving the workers in liberty. The printers, who love dis-order, are in a state of great joy. Here is an ample subject for their laughter, a beautiful *copie*, which will keep them amused for a long time.'

This was Rabelaisian laughter. The text insists upon its importance: 'The printers know how to laugh, it is their sole occupation.' Mikhail Bakhtin has shown how the laughter of Rabelais expressed a strain of popular culture in which the riotously funny could turn to riot, a carnival culture of sexuality and sedition in which the revolutionary element might be contained within symbols and metaphors or might explode in a general uprising, as in 1789. The question remains, however, what precisely was so funny about the cat massacre? There is no better way to ruin a joke than to analyse it or to overload it with social comment. But this joke cries out for commentary – not because one can use it to prove that artisans hated their bosses (a truism that may apply to all periods of labour history, although it has not been appreciated adequately by eighteenth-century historians), but because it can help one to see how workers made their experience meaningful by playing with themes of their culture.

The only version of the cat massacre available to us was put into writing, long after the fact, by Nicolas Contat. He selected details, ordered events, and framed the story in such a way as to bring out what was meaningful for him. But he derived his notions of meaning from his culture just as naturally as he drew in air from the atmosphere around him. And he wrote down what he had helped to enact with his mates. The subjective character of the writing does not vitiate its collective frame of reference, even though the written account must be thin compared with the action it describes. The workers' mode of expression was a kind of popular theatre. It involved pantomime, rough music, and a dramatic 'theatre of violence' improvised in the work place, in the street, and on the rooftops. It included a play within a play, because Léveillé re-enacted the whole farce several times as *copies* in the

shop. In fact, the original massacre involved the burlesquing of other ceremonies, such as trials and charivaris. So Contat wrote about a burlesque of a
burlesque, and in reading it one should make allowances for the refraction of
cultural forms across genres and over time.

Those allowances made, it seems clear that the workers found the massacre funny because it gave them a way to turn the tables on the bourgeois.
By goading him with cat calls, they provoked him to authorise the massacre
of cats, then they used the massacre to put him symbolically on trial for
unjust management of the shop. They also used it as a witch hunt, which
provided an excuse to kill his wife's familiar and to insinuate that she herself
was the witch. Finally, they transformed it into a charivari, which served as a
means to insult her sexually while mocking him as a cuckold. The bourgeois
made an excellent butt of the joke. Not only did he become the victim of a
procedure he himself had set in motion, he did not understand how badly he
had been had. The men had subjected his wife to symbolic aggression of the
most intimate kind, but he did not get it. He was too thick-headed, a classic
cuckold. The printers ridiculed him in splendid Boccaccian style and got off
scot-free.

The joke worked so well because the workers played so skilfully with a
repertory of ceremonies and symbols. Cats suited their purposes perfectly.
By smashing the spine of *la grise* they called the master's wife a witch and a
slut, while at the same time making the master into a cuckold and a fool. It
was metonymic insult, delivered by actions, not words, and it struck home
because cats occupied a soft spot in the bourgeois way of life. Keeping pets
was as alien to the workers as torturing animals was to the bourgeois.
Trapped between incompatible sensitivities, the cats had the worst of both
worlds.

The workers also punned with ceremonies. They made a roundup of cats
into a witch hunt, a festival, a charivari, a mock trial, and a dirty joke. Then
they redid the whole thing in pantomime. Whenever they got tired of working, they transformed the shop into a theatre and produced *copies* – their
kind of copy, not the authors'. Shop theatre and ritual punning suited the
traditions of their craft. Although printers made books, they did not use
written words to convey their meaning. They used gestures, drawing on the
culture of their craft to inscribe statements in the air.

Insubstantial as it may seem today, this joking was a risky business in the
eighteenth century. The risk was part of the joke, as in many forms of
humour, which toy with violence and tease repressed passions. The workers
pushed their symbolic horseplay to the brink of reification, the point at
which the killing of cats would turn into an open rebellion. They played on
ambiguities, using symbols that would hide their full meaning while letting
enough of it show through to make a fool of the bourgeois without giving
him a pretext to fire them. They tweaked his nose and prevented him from

protesting against it. To pull off such a feat required great dexterity. It showed that workers could manipulate symbols in their idiom as effectively as poets did in print.

The boundaries within which this jesting had to be contained suggest the limits to working-class militancy under the Old Regime. The printers identified with their craft rather than their class. Although they organised in chapels, staged strikes, and sometimes forced up wages, they remained subordinate to the bourgeois. The master hired and fired men as casually as he ordered paper, and he turned them out into the road when he sniffed insubordination. So until the onset of proletarianisation in the late nineteenth century, they generally kept their protests on a symbolic level. A *copie*, like a carnival, helped to let off steam; but it also produced laughter, a vital ingredient in early artisanal culture and one that has been lost in labour history. By seeing the way a joke worked in the horseplay of a printing shop two centuries ago, we may be able to recapture that missing element – laughter, sheer laughter, the thigh-slapping, rib-cracking Rabelaisian kind, rather than the Voltairian smirk with which we are familiar.

5

Eruptions of Funk: Historicising Toni Morrison

Susan Willis

'I begin to feel those little bits of color floating up into me – deep in me. That streak of green from the june-bug light, the purple from the berries trickling along my thighs. Mama's lemonade yellow runs sweet in me. Then I feel like I'm laughing between my legs, and the laughing gets all mixed up with the colors, and I'm afraid I'll come, and afraid I won't. But I know I will. And I do. And it be rainbow all inside.' (*TBE*, pp. 103–4)

This is the way Polly Breedlove in *The Bluest Eye* remembers the experience of orgasm – *remembers* it, because in the grim and shabby reality of her present, orgasm (which we might take as a metaphor for any deeply pleasurable experience) is no longer possible.[1] Living in a storefront, her husband fluctuating between brutality and apathy, her son estranged, her daughter just plain scared, Polly has no language to describe the memory of a past pleasure, except one drawn from her distant childhood.

The power of this passage is not just related to the fact that it evokes the most intense female experience possible. Much of the impact is produced by the way it describes. Morrison defamiliarises the portrayal of sensual experience. Adjectives become substantives, giving taste to colour and making it possible for colours to trickle and flow and, finally, to be internalised like the semen of an orgasmic epiphany.

As often happens in Morrison's writing, sexuality converges with history and functions as a register for the experience of change, i.e., historical transition. Polly's remembrance of childhood sensuality coincides with her girlhood in the rural South. Both are metaphorically condensed and juxtaposed with the alienation she experiences as a black emigrant and social lumpen in a Northern industrial city. The author's metaphoric language produces an estrangement of alienation. Although her metaphors are less bold in their form and content, they still achieve an effect very similar to that of the negritude poets. Indeed, the image of an internal rainbow evokes the poetics of surrealism, but in a language less disjunctive because prose reveals the historical and artistic process through which the image is produced.[2]

44

When Polly Breedlove reminisces, her present collides with her past and spans her family's migration from the hills of Alabama to a small Kentucky town and her own subsequent journey as the wife of one of the many black men who, in the late thirties and early forties, sought factory jobs in the industrial North. The rural homeland is the source of the raw material of experience and praxis, which in the border-state small town is abstracted to colours, tastes, and tactile sensations. Ohio is, then, the site where images are produced out of the discontinuity between past and present.

Neither Morrison's use of metaphor, nor her general drive to return to origins is rooted in a nostalgia for the past. Rather, the metaphoric rendition of past experience represents a process for coming to grips with historical transition. Migration to the North signifies more than a confrontation with (and contamination by) the white world. It implies a transition in social class. Throughout Morrison's writing, the white world is equated with the bourgeois class – its ideology and life-style. This is true of *Song of Solomon* in which Macon Dead's attitudes toward rents and property make him more 'white' than 'black'. This is true of *Tar Baby* in which notions of bourgeois morality and attitudes concerning the proper education and role of women have created a contemporary 'tar baby', a black woman in cultural limbo. And it is made dramatically clear in *The Bluest Eye*, whose epigrammatic introduction and subsequent chapter headings are drawn from a white, middle-class 'Dick-and-Jane' reader. In giving voice to the experience of growing up black in a society dominated by white, middle-class ideology, Morrison is writing against the privatised world of suburban house and nuclear family, whose social and psychological fragmentation does not need her authorial intervention, but is aptly portrayed in the language of the reader: 'Here is the family. Mother, Father, Dick, and Jane live in the green-and-white house. They are very happy' (*TBE*, p. 7).

The problem at the centre of Morrison's writing is how to maintain an Afro-American cultural heritage once the relationship to the black rural South has been stretched thin over distance and generations. Although a number of black Americans will criticise her problematising of Afro-American culture, seeing in it a symptom of Morrison's own relationship to white bourgeois society as a successful writer and editor, there are a number of social and historical factors that argue in support of her position. These include the dramatic social changes produced by recent wide-scale migration of industry to the South, which has transformed much of the rural population into wage labourers; the development, particularly in the Northern cities, of a black bourgeoisie; and the coming into being, under late capitalism, of a full-blown consumer society capable of homogenising society by recouping cultural difference. The temporal focus of each of Morrison's novels pinpoints strategic moments in black American history during which social and cultural forms underwent disruption and transformation.

Both *The Bluest Eye* and *Sula* focus on the forties, a period of heavy black migration to the cities, when, particularly in the Midwest, black 'neighbour-hoods' came into being as annexes of towns that had never before had a sizeable black population. *Sula* expands the period of the forties by looking back to the First World War, when blacks as a social group were first incorporated into a modern capitalist system as soldiers, and it looks ahead to the sixties, when cultural identity seems to flatten out, and, as Helene Sabat observes, all young people tend to look like the 'Deweys', the book's nameless and indistinguishable orphans. *Song of Solomon* focuses on the sixties, when neighbourhoods are perceived from the outside and called ghettos, a time of urban black political activism and general countercultural awareness. And *Tar Baby*, Morrison's most recent book, is best charac-terised as a novel of the eighties, in which the route back to cultural origins is very long and tenuous, making many individuals cultural exiles.

With this as an outline of modern black history in the United States, Morrison develops the social and psychological aspects that characterise the lived experience of historical transition. For the black emigrant to the North, the first of these is alienation. As Morrison defines it, alienation is not simply the result of an individual's separation from his or her cultural centre, although this is a contributory factor that reinforces the alienation produced by the transition to wage labour. For the black man incorporated into the wartime labour pool (as for many white Appalachians),[3] selling one's labour for the creation of surplus value was only half of alienation, whose brutal second half was the grim reality of unemployment once war production was no longer necessary. The situation for the black woman was somewhat different. Usually employed as a maid and therefore only marginally incor-porated as a wage labourer, her alienation was the result of striving to achieve the white bourgeois social model (in which she worked but did not live), which is itself produced by the system of wage labour under capitalism. As housemaid in a prosperous lakeshore home, Polly Breedlove lives a form of schizophrenia, in which her marginality is constantly confronted with a world of Hollywood movies, white sheets, and tender blond children. When at work or at the movies, she separates herself from her own kinky hair and decayed tooth. The tragedy of a woman's alienation is its effect on her role as mother. Her emotions split, Polly showers tenderness and love on her employer's child, and rains violence and disdain on her own.

Morrison's aim in writing is very often to disrupt alienation with what she calls eruptions of 'funk' (*TBE*, p. 68). Dismayed by the tremendous influence of bourgeois society on young black women newly arrived from deep South cities like 'Meridian, Mobile, Aiken and Baton Rouge', Morrison describes the women's loss of spontaneity and sensuality. They learn 'how to behave. The careful development of thrift, patience, high morals, and good manners. In short, how to get rid of the funkiness. The dreadful funkiness of passion, the funkiness of nature, the funkiness of the wide range of human emotions' (*TBE*, p. 68).

For Polly Breedlove, alienation is the inability to experience pleasure ever again – orgasm or otherwise – whereas for the 'sugar-brown Mobile girls' (*TBE*, p. 68), whose husbands are more successful and therefore better assimilated into bourgeois society, alienation is the purposeful denial of pleasure. Once again Morrison translates the loss of history and culture into sexual terms and demonstrates the connection between bourgeois society and repression:

He must enter her surreptitiously, lifting the hem of her nightgown only to her navel. He must rest his weight on his elbows when they make love, ostensibly to avoid hurting her breasts but actually to keep her from having to touch or feel too much of him.

While he moves inside her, she will wonder why they didn't put the necessary but private parts of the body in some more convenient place – like the armpit, for example, or the palm of the hand. Someplace one could get to easily, and quickly, without undressing. She stiffens when she feels one of her paper curlers coming undone from the activity of love; imprints in her mind which one it is that is coming loose so she can quickly secure it once he is through. She hopes he will not sweat – the damp may get into her hair; and that she will remain dry between her legs – she hates the glucking sound they make when she is moist. When she senses some spasm about to grip him, she will make rapid movements with her hips, press her fingernails into his back, suck in her breath, and pretend she is having an orgasm. (*TBE*, p. 69)

At a sexual level, alienation is the denial of the body, produced when sensuality is redefined as indecent. Sounds and tactile sensations that might otherwise have precipitated or highlighted pleasure provoke annoyance or disdain. Repression manifests itself in the fastidious attention given to tomorrow's Caucasian-inspired coiffure and the decathexis of erogenous stimulation. Although repression inhibits sexual pleasure, it does not liberate a woman from sexuality. In faking an orgasm, the woman negates her pleasure for the sake of her husband's satisfaction, thus defining herself as a tool of his sexual gratification.

To break through repressed female sexuality, Morrison contrasts images of stifled womanhood with girlhood sensuality. In *The Bluest Eye*, the author's childhood alter ego, Claudia, is fascinated by all bodily functions and the physical residues of living in the world. She rebels at being washed, finding her scrubbed body obscene due to its 'dreadful and humiliating absence of dirt' (*TBE*, p. 21). Even vomit is interesting for its colour and consistency as it 'swaddles down the pillow onto the sheet' (*TBE*, p. 13). In wondering how anything can be 'so neat and nasty at the same time' (*TBE*, p. 13), Claudia shows a resistance toward the overdetermination of sensual experience, which, as Morrison sees it, is the first step toward repression. Openness to a full range of sensual experience may be equated with poly-morphous sexuality, typified by the refusal of many young children to be thought of as either a boy or a girl. As my own four-year-old daughter sees it, 'Little girls grow up to be big boys', and because there is no firm distinction between the sexes, her teddy bear is 'both a boy and a girl'. The refusal to categorise sensual experience – and likewise sex – captures the essence of unrepressed childhood, which Morrison evokes as a mode of existence prior to the individual's assimilation into bourgeois society.

The ultimate horror of bourgeois society against which Morrison writes and the end result of both alienation and repression is reification.[4] None of Morrison's black characters actually accedes to the upper reaches of bour-geois reification, but there are some who come close. They are saved only because they remain marginal to the bourgeois class and are imperfectly assimilated to bourgeois values. In *Song of Solomon*, Hagar offers a good example. Rejected by her lover, she falls into a state of near-catatonia, oblivious to all around her. However, chancing to look in a mirror, she is horrified by her appearance and marvels that anyone could love a woman with her looks. Thus roused from her withdrawal, Hagar embarks on a daylong shopping spree, driven by the desire to be the delightful image promised by her brand-name purchases:

> She bought a Playtex garter belt, I. Miller No Color hose, Fruit of the Loom panties, and two nylon slips – one white, one pink – one pair of Joyce Fancy Free and one of Con Brio ('Thank heaven for little Joyce heels'). . . .
> The cosmetics department enfolded her in perfume, and she read hun-grily the labels and the promise. Myrurgia for primeval woman who creates for him a world of tender privacy where the only occupant is you, mixed with Nina Ricci's L'Air du Temps. Yardley's Flair with Tuv-aché's Nectaroma and D'Orsay's Intoxication. (*SOS*, pp. 314–15)

Hagar's shopping spree culminates in a drenching downpour. Her shopping bags soaked, everything – her 'Sunny Glow' and 'fawn-trimmed-in-sea-foam shortie nightgown' – her wished-for identity and future – falls into the wet and muddy street. Returning home, Hagar collapses with fever and dies after days of delirium.

Hagar's hysteria and death mark the limits of her assimilation into bourgeois culture. Neither through withdrawal nor through commodity consumption can Hagar transform herself into an object. Her marginality, by reason of race and lumpen background, is the basis for her inalienable human dimension. As Morrison might have put it, she is simply too black, too passionate, too human ever to become reified.

Reification, although never attained by any of Morrison's characters – not even those drawn from the white world[5] – is, instead, embodied in a number of figural images from *The Bluest Eye*. These are the celluloid images of Shirley Temple or her 'cute' face on a blue-and-white china cup, and the candy-wrapper images of Mary Jane. Most of all, reification is evident in the plastic smile and moronic blue eyes of a white Christmas baby doll. When Claudia destroys these – dismembering the doll and poking its eyes out – her rebellion is not just aimed at the idea of beauty incarnated in a white model. She is also striking out against the horrifying dehumanisation that acceptance of the model implies – both for the black who wears it as a mask and for the white who creates commodified images of the self.

For Morrison, everything is historical; even objects are embedded in history and are the bearers of the past. For those characters closest to the white bourgeois world, objects contain the residues of repressed and unrealised desires. For Ruth Foster in *Song of Solomon*, the daughter of the town's first black doctor and wife of the slumlord Macon Dead, a watermark on a table is the stubborn and ever-present reminder of her husband's remorseless rejection. The bowl of flowers around which their hatred crystallised is no longer present; only its sign remains, an opaque residue indelibly written into the table. If, for the bourgeois world, experience is capable of being abstracted to the level of sign, this is not the case for the world of the marginal characters. To cite another example from *Song of Solomon*, Pilate, Ruth Foster's sister-in-law and in every way her antithesis, enjoys a special relationship to all levels of natural experience – including a specific shade of blue sky. Now, colour does not function as a sign in the way that the watermark on the table does. Although it bears a concrete relationship to a real object (the blue ribbons on Pilate's mother's hat), it is not an abstract relationship in the way that the watermark stands for the bowl of flowers. For Ruth Foster, the watermark is an 'anchor' to the mental and sexual anguish imprisoned in the sign. In contrast, when Pilate points to a patch of sky and remarks that it is the same colour as her mother's bonnet ribbons, she enables her nephew Milkman (Ruth Foster's overly sheltered son) to experience a unique moment of sensual perception. The experience is liberational because Pilate is not referring to a specific bonnet – or even to a specific mother; rather, the colour blue triggers the whole range of emotions associated with maternal love, which Pilate offers to anyone who will share the experience of colour with her.

In contrast to the liberational aspect of *Song of Solomon*, Morrison's most recent novel, *Tar Baby*, registers a deep sense of pessimism. Here, cultural exiles – both white and black – come together on a Caribbean island where they live out their lives in a neatly compartmentalised bourgeois fashion: the candy magnate Valerian Street[6] in his stereophonic-equipped greenhouse; his wife, cloistered in her bedroom; and the servants, Odine and Sydney, ensconced in their comfortable quarters. Daily life precludes 'eruptions of funk', a lesson poignantly taught when Margaret Lenore discovers the bedraggled wild man, Son, in her closet. Although Son's appearance suggests Rastafarianism and outlawry, any shock value stirred by his discovery is cancelled when he, too, proves to be just another exile. Except for one brief incident, when Odine kills a chicken and in plucking it recalls a moment from her distant past when she worked for a poultry butcher, there are no smells, tastes, or tactile experiences to summon up the past. Rather, there is a surfeit of foods whose only quality is the calories they contain.

In contrast with Morrison's earlier novels, the past in *Tar Baby* is never brought to metaphoric juxtaposition with the present. Rather, it is held separate and bracketed by dream. When Valerian Street, sipping a brandy in his greenhouse, lapses into daydream, his recollection of the past, which in essence contrasts entrepreneurial capitalism to modern corporate capitalism, does not intrude on his present retirement. The past is past, and the significant historical transition evoked is perceived as inaccessible and natural.

The past is made more remote when it informs a night-time dream. This is the case for Sydney, who every night dreams of his boyhood in Baltimore. 'It was a tiny dream he had each night that he would never recollect from morning to morning. So he never knew what it was exactly that refreshed him.'[7] For the black man hanging to the coat-tails of the white upper bourgeoisie, who thinks of himself as a 'Philadelphia Negro' (*TB*, p. 61), the back streets of Baltimore are a social debit. His desire for assimilation to white bourgeois culture and the many years spent in service to the bourgeois class negate his ever experiencing the deep sensual and emotional pleasure that Pilate has whenever she beholds a blue sky or bites into a vine-ripened tomato.

With every dreamer dreaming a separate dream, there are no bridges to the past and no possibility of sharing an individual experience as part of a group's social history. Although a reminiscence like Pilate's recognition of the colour blue can be communicated, a dream, as Son finds out, cannot be pressed into another dreamer's head. Son's dream of 'yellow houses with white doors' and 'fat black ladies in white dresses minding the pie table in the church' (*TB*, p. 119) is an image of wish fulfilment, rooted in private nostalgia. It bears no resemblance to his real past as we later come to understand it out of what the novel shows us of Eloe, Florida, where tough black women with little time for pie tables have built their own rough-hewn, unpainted homes.

For the 'tar baby', Jadine, fashioned out of the rich white man's indulgence and the notions of culture most appealing to bourgeois America (European education and Paris 'haute couture'), the past is irretrievable and no longer perceived as desirable. As the individual whose cultural exile is the most profound, Jadine is haunted by waking visions, born out of guilt and fear. In her most terrifying vision, a mob of black women – some familiar, some only known by their names – crowds into her room. Revealing, then waving, their breasts at her, they condemn Jadine for having abandoned the traditional maternal role of black women.

Whereas Jadine lives her separation from the past and rejection of traditional cultural roles with tormented uncertainty and frenzied activity, Milkman, in Morrison's previous novel, experiences his alienation from black culture as a hollow daily monotony. Jadine, whose desire to find self and be free leads to jet hops between Paris, the Caribbean, and New York, has not had the benefit of a powerful cultural mentor like Pilate, who awakens Milkman's desire to know his past. In contrast, all of Jadine's possible cultural heroes are bracketed by her rupture with the past and her class position. Jadine rejects family – her Aunt Odine, for her homey ways and maternal nature – and culture – the black islanders, so remote from Jadine's trajectory into the future that she never even bothers to learn their names.

Milkman, on the other hand, has been born and raised in the ghetto, albeit in the biggest house. He has never been to college, but he has had the benefit of teachers – both the street-wise Guitar and the folk-wise Pilate. If Milkman's present is a meaningless void of bourgeois alienation, the possibility of a past opens out to him like a great adventure. A quest for gold initiates Milkman's journey into the past – and into the self – but gold is not the novel's real object. Imagining that gold will free him from his father's domination and his family's emotional blackmail, Milkman comes to realise that only by knowing the past can he hope to have a future.

There is a sense of urgency in Morrison's writing, produced by the realisation that a great deal is at stake. The novels may focus on individual characters like Milkman and Jadine, but the salvation of individuals is not the point. Rather, these individuals, struggling to reclaim or redefine themselves, are portrayed as epiphenomenal to community and culture, and it is the strength and continuity of the black cultural heritage as a whole that is at stake and being tested.

As Morrison sees it, the most serious threat to black culture is the obliterating influence of social change. The opening line from *Sula* might well have been the novel's conclusion, so complete is the destruction it records: 'In that place, where they tore the night shade and blackberry patches from their roots to make room for the Medallion City Golf Course, there was once a neighborhood.'[8] This is the community Morrison is writing to reclaim. Its history, terminated and dramatically obliterated, is condensed into a single sentence whose content spans from rural South to urban redevelopment. Here, as throughout Morrison's writing, natural imagery refers to the past, the rural South, the reservoir of culture that has been uprooted – like the blackberry bushes – to make way for modernisation. In contrast, the future is perceived of as an amorphous, institutionalised power embodied in the notion of 'Medallion City', which suggests neither nature nor a people. Joining the past to the future is the neighbourhood, which occupies a very different temporal moment (which history has shown to be transitional), and defines a very different social mode, as distinct from its rural origins as it is from the amorphous urban future.

It is impossible to read Morrison's four novels without coming to see the neighbourhood as a concept crucial to her understanding of history. The neighbourhood defines a Northern social mode rather than a Southern one, for it describes the relationship of an economic satellite, contiguous to a larger metropolis rather than separate subsistence economies like the Southern rural towns of Shalimar and Eloe. It is a Midwestern phenomenon rather than a Northeastern big-city category, because it defines the birth of principally first-generation, Northern, working-class black communities. It is a mode of the forties rather than the sixties or the eighties, and it evokes the many locally specific black populations in the North before these became assimilated to a larger, more generalised, and less regionally specific sense of black culture that we today refer to as the 'black community'.

The fact that Milkman embarks on a quest for his past is itself symptomatic of the difference between the forties neighbourhood and the sixties community. In contrast with Milkman, the black youth of the forties had no need to uncover and decipher the past simply because enough of it was still present, born on successive waves of Southern black immigrants. For Milkman the past is a riddle, a reality locked in the verses of a children's song (the 'song of Solomon') whose meaning is no longer explicit because time has separated the words from their historical content. Childhood and the way children perceive the world are again a figure for a mode of existence prior to the advent of capitalism and bourgeois society. And in *Song of Solomon*, it coincides with the function of song in all marginal cultures as the unwritten text of history and culture.

Milkman's quest is a journey through geographic space in which the juxtaposition of the city and the countryside represents the relationship of the present to the past. In tracing his roots from the Detroit ghetto, where he was familiar with Pilate's version of the Solomon song; to Danville, Pennsylvania, where his father grew up; and then to Shalimar, Virginia, where his grandfather was born and children still sing of Solomon, Milkman deciphers the twin texts of history: song and genealogy. In so doing, he reconstructs a dialectic of historical transition, in which individual genealogy evokes the history of black migration and the chain of economic expropriation from hinterland to village, and village to metropolis. The end point of Milkman's journey is the starting point of his race's history in this country: slavery. The confrontation with the reality of slavery, coming at the end of Milkman's penetration into historical process, is liberational because slavery is not portrayed as the origin of history and culture. Instead, the novel opens out to Africa, the source, and takes flight on the wings of Milkman's great-grandfather, the original Solomon. With the myth of the 'flying Africans' (*SOS*, p. 332) Morrison transforms the moment of coming to grips with slavery as an allegory of liberation.

The fact that geographic space functions for history is symptomatic of a time when a people's past no longer forms a continuity with the present. It is one of the features that differentiates literary modernism from realism, in which people's lives are portrayed as integral to the flow of history. Because the past is perceived as problematical and historical transition is represented by the relationship among countryside, village, and city, *Song of Solomon* is very similar to the great modernist novels of the Latin American 'Boom' (the literary movement born with the Cuban Revolution and brought to an end with the assassination of Allende). In Morrison's *Song of Solomon*, as in the Peruvian Mario Vargas Llosa's *La Casa Verde*, the synchronic relationship defined in geographic space stands for a diachronic relationship. The most interesting feature about these modernist texts is that, in reading them, the reader, like Milkman, restores diachrony to the text and, in so doing, realises the historical dialectic that the text presents as inaccessible.
[...]

At one level, Morrison writes to awaken her reader's sensitivity, to shake up and disrupt the sensual numbing that accompanies social and psychological alienation. This is the function of her 'eruptions of funk', which include metaphors drawn from past moments of sensual fulfilment as well as the use of lack, deformity, and self-mutilation as figures for liberation. At a deeper level, and as a consequence of these features, Morrison's writing often allows an alternative social world to come into being. When this happens, 'otherness' no longer functions as an extension of domination (as it does when blackness is beheld from the point of view of racist bourgeois society, or when the crippled, blind, and deformed are compared to the terrorising totality of a whole and therefore 'perfect' body). Rather, the space created by otherness permits a reversal of domination and transforms what was once perceived from without as 'other' into the explosive image of a utopian mode. Morrison's most radical 'eruption of funk' is the vision of an alternative social world. It comes into view when Macon Dead peers into Pilate's window; when the child Nel, the product of her mother's stifled bourgeois morality, scratches at Sula's screen door; and when the intimidated and fearful Pecola visits her upstairs neighbours, the three prostitutes.

It is not gratuitous that in all these cases the definition of social utopia is based on a three-woman household. This does not imply a lesbian orientation, because in all cases the women are decidedly heterosexual. Rather, these are societies that do not permit heterosexuality as it articulates male domination to be the determining principle for the living and working relationships of the group, as it is in capitalist society.

Morrison's three-woman utopian households contrast dramatically with an earlier literary version that occurs, paradoxically again, in Faulkner's *Absalom! Absalom!* During the grinding culmination of the Civil War, the men all gone – siphoned off by the army – the economy reduced to bare subsistence, the novel brings together three women: Judith, Sutpen's daughter and heir; Clytie, Sutpen's black non-heir; and the young spinstress, Miss Rosa, Sutpen's non-betrothed. Taking refuge in the shell of a once-prosperous manor house, they eke out their survival on a day-to-day basis:

> So we waited for him. We led the busy eventless lives of three nuns in a barren and poverty-stricken convent: the walls we had were safe, impervious enough, even if it did not matter to the walls whether we ate or not. And amicably, not as two white women and a negress, not as three negroes or three whites, not even as three women, but merely as three creatures who still possessed the need to eat but took no pleasure in it, the need to sleep but from it no joy in weariness or regeneration, and in whom sex was some forgotten atrophy like the rudimentary gills we call the tonsils or the still-opposable thumbs for old climbing.[9]

In considering the cataclysm of the Civil War and its destruction of traditional Southern society, Faulkner is led to imagine the basis for a potentially radical new form of social organisation, based on subsistence rather than accumulation and women rather than men. However, the incipient possibility of social utopia dies stillborn, because the male principle and the system of patrimony have not been transformed or refuted, but merely displaced. Sutpen, even in his absence, is still the centre of the household. Race, too, is not confronted or transcended. Rather, it, like sex, is simply dismissed. And with it go all vestiges of humanity.

The tremendous differences between Faulkner and Morrison, which include historical period, race, and sex, lie at the heart of their dramatically opposed images: the one dystopian; the other utopian. Rather than dwell on the social and historical factors that shape their fiction, I will emphasise the ways in which historical differences are manifested in the texts. Faulkner's dehumanised monads and the routinised lives they lead contrast sharply with Morrison's portrayal of Pilate's household, in which individual differences between the three women function to test the social dynamic within the group, and between it and society at large. Faulkner's retrenched espousal of the male-dominated social model and his tenacious refusal to imagine anything else condition his bleak vision of society. On the other hand, Morrison's projection of a social utopia arises from its confrontation with and reversal of the male-dominated bourgeois social model. Rather than systematically levelling social problems, Morrison foregrounds them. The utopian aspect of her vision is produced by the totality of its opposition to society at large – not by its individual members. This makes her portrayal very different from classical literary utopias, whose individuals are presented as perfect and harmonious models. None of Morrison's individual characters in any of her three utopias is perfect. Rather than supplying answers to social problems, they give rise to questions about social relationships and society as a whole. Thus, Pilate demonstrates the insufficiency of the agrarian social mode to provide for its members once they are transplanted to urban consumer society. Her strength and resourcefulness cannot be passed on to her daughter and granddaughter because each is more distant from the rural society in which Pilate worked and grew up. Their experience of insufficiency leads to hollow consumption (Reba's of sex and Hagar's of commodities) and demonstrates the way consumer society penetrates and impoverishes human relationships.

When in *Tar Baby* 'funk' erupts as myth, its potential for estranging fetishised relationships is minimised because of its distance from the urban and suburban settings that condition the lives of more and more Americans, both black and white. Son's quest for the mythic community of blind maroon horsemen that ends *Tar Baby* may represent a dramatic departure from his previous endeavours, but it does not bring disruption into the heart of social practice, as occurs when the image of Pilate's household bursts upon Macon Dead's alienated and numbed sensibilities. Although *Song of Solomon* also has a mythic dimension, myth is not the novel's only form of 'funk'. Then, too, myth is integral to Milkman's concrete past, as he discovers by following his family's route back to slavery, whereas for Son, it represents a very distant cultural source not directly linked to his present.

'Funk' is really nothing more than the intrusion of the past into the present. It is most oppositional when it juxtaposes a not-so-distant social mode to those evolved under bourgeois society. Morrison's method might be thought of as a North American variant of the magical realism that we have come to associate with Gabriel García Márquez. If in his *One Hundred Years of Solitude* pleasurable delight is synonymous with barbed political criticism, this is because the text's metaphoric incidents and characters are created out of the juxtaposition of First and Third World realities. Just as domination and dependency create separation and inequality between North and South America, so too do Márquez's metaphors represent the unresolved contradiction between two possible readings: the one mythic and pleasurable, the other historical and critical. The same holds true for Morrison, only the terms of her geographic and historical equation are bound up and framed by the history of the United States. North/South, black/white, these are the ingredients of Morrison's magical realism whose tension-fraught and unresolved juxtapositions articulate the continuation of domination in our society and the persistence of racism, and at the same time provoke Morrison's creative and critical imagination.

6

The Body of the Condemned

Michel Foucault

On 2 March 1757 Damiens the regicide was condemned 'to make the *amende honorable* before the main door of the Church of Paris', where he was to be 'taken and conveyed in a cart, wearing nothing but a shirt, holding a torch of burning wax weighing two pounds'; then, 'in the said cart, to the Place de Grève, where, on a scaffold that will be erected there, the flesh will be torn from his breasts, arms, thighs and calves with red-hot pincers, his right hand, holding the knife with which he committed the said parricide, burnt with sulphur, and, on those places where the flesh will be torn away, poured molten lead, boiling oil, burning resin, wax and sulphur melted together and then his body drawn and quartered by four horses and his limbs and body consumed by fire, reduced to ashes and his ashes thrown to the winds' (*Pièces originales...*, pp. 372–4).

'Finally, he was quartered,' recounts the *Gazette d'Amsterdam* of 1 April 1757. 'This last operation was very long, because the horses used were not accustomed to drawing; consequently, instead of four, six were needed; and when that did not suffice, they were forced, in order to cut off the wretch's thighs, to sever the sinews and hack at the joints...

'It is said that, though he was always a great swearer, no blasphemy escaped his lips; but the excessive pain made him utter horrible cries, and he often repeated: "My God, have pity on me! Jesus, help me!" The spectators were all edified by the solicitude of the parish priest of St Paul's who despite his great age did not spare himself in offering consolation to the patient.'

Bouton, an officer of the watch, left us his account: 'The sulphur was lit, but the flame was so poor that only the top skin of the hand was burnt, and that only slightly. Then the executioner, his sleeves rolled up, took the steel pincers, which had been especially made for the occasion, and which were about a foot and a half long, and pulled first at the calf of the right leg, then at the thigh, and from there at the two fleshy parts of the right arm; then at the breasts. Though a strong, sturdy fellow, this executioner found it so difficult to tear away the pieces of flesh that he set about the same spot two or three times, twisting the pincers as he did so, and what he took away formed at each part a wound about the size of a six-pound crown piece.

'After these tearings with the pincers, Damiens, who cried out profusely, though without swearing, raised his head and looked at himself; the same executioner dipped an iron spoon in the pot containing the boiling potion, which he poured liberally over each wound. Then the ropes that were to be harnessed to the horses were attached with cords to the patient's body; the horses were then harnessed and placed alongside the arms and legs, one at each limb.

'Monsieur Le Breton, the clerk of the court, went up to the patient several times and asked him if he had anything to say. He said he had not; at each torment, he cried out, as the damned in hell are supposed to cry out, "Pardon, my God! Pardon, Lord." Despite all this pain, he raised his head from time to time and looked at himself boldly. The cords had been tied so tightly by the men who pulled the ends that they caused him indescribable pain. Monsieur le Breton went up to him again and asked him if he had anything to say; he said no. Several confessors went up to him and spoke to him at length; he willingly kissed the crucifix that was held out to him; he opened his lips and repeated: "Pardon, Lord."

'The horses tugged hard, each pulling straight on a limb, each horse held by an executioner. After a quarter of an hour, the same ceremony was repeated and finally, after several attempts, the direction of the horses had to be changed, thus: those at the arms were made to pull towards the head, those at the thighs towards the arms, which broke the arms at the joints. This was repeated several times without success. He raised his head and looked at himself. Two more horses had to be added to those harnessed to the thighs, which made six horses in all. Without success.

'Finally, the executioner, Samson, said to Monsieur Le Breton that there was no way or hope of succeeding, and told him to ask their Lordships if they wished him to have the prisoner cut into pieces. Monsieur Le Breton, who had come down from the town, ordered that renewed efforts be made, and this was done; but the horses gave up and one of those harnessed to the thighs fell to the ground. The confessors returned and spoke to him again. He said to them (I heard him): "Kiss me, gentlemen." The parish priest of St Paul's did not dare to, so Monsieur de Marsilly slipped under the rope holding the left arm and kissed him on the forehead. The executioners gathered round and Damiens told them not to swear, to carry out their task and that he did not think ill of them; he begged them to pray to God for him, and asked the parish priest of St Paul's to pray for him at the first mass.

'After two or three attempts, the executioner Samson and he who had used the pincers each drew out a knife from his pocket and cut the body at the thighs instead of severing the legs at the joints; the four horses gave a tug and carried off the two thighs after them, namely, that of the right side first, the other following; then the same was done to the arms, the shoulders, the arm-pits and the four limbs; the flesh had to be cut almost to the bone, the horses pulling hard carried off the right arm first and the other afterwards.

'When the four limbs had been pulled away, the confessors came to speak to him; but his executioner told them that he was dead, though the truth was that I saw the man move, his lower jaw moving from side to side as if he were talking. One of the executioners even said shortly afterwards that when they had lifted the trunk to throw it on the stake, he was still alive. The four limbs were untied from the ropes and thrown on the stake set up in the enclosure in line with the scaffold, then the trunk and the rest were covered with logs and faggots, and fire was put to the straw mixed with this wood.

'...In accordance with the decree, the whole was reduced to ashes. The last piece to be found in the embers was still burning at half-past ten in the evening. The pieces of flesh and the trunk had taken about four hours to burn. The officers of whom I was one, as also was my son, and a detachment of archers remained in the square until nearly eleven o'clock.

'There were those who made something of the fact that a dog had lain the day before on the grass where the fire had been, had been chased away several times, and had always returned. But it is not difficult to understand that an animal found this place warmer than elsewhere' (quoted in Zevaes, pp. 201–14).

Eighty years later, Léon Faucher drew up his rules 'for the House of young prisoners in Paris':

'Art. 17. The prisoners' day will begin at six in the morning in winter and at five in summer. They will work for nine hours a day throughout the year. Two hours a day will be devoted to instruction. Work and the day will end at nine o'clock in winter and at eight in summer.

Art. 18. *Rising*. At the first drum-roll, the prisoners must rise and dress in silence, as the supervisor opens the cell doors. At the second drum-roll, they must be dressed and make their beds. At the third, they must line up and proceed to the chapel for morning prayer. There is a five-minute interval between each drum-roll.

Art. 19. The prayers are conducted by the chaplain and followed by a moral or religious reading. This exercise must not last more than half an hour.

Art. 20. *Work*. At a quarter to six in the summer, a quarter to seven in winter, the prisoners go down into the courtyard where they must wash their hands and faces, and receive their first ration of bread. Immediately afterwards, they form into work-teams and go off to work, which must begin at six in summer and seven in winter.

Art. 21. *Meal*. At ten o'clock the prisoners leave their work and go to the refectory; they wash their hands in their courtyards and assemble in divisions. After the dinner, there is recreation until twenty minutes to eleven.

Art. 22. *School.* At twenty minutes to eleven, at the drum-roll, the prisoners form into ranks, and proceed in divisions to the school. The class lasts two hours and consists alternately of reading, writing, drawing and arithmetic.

Art. 23. At twenty minutes to one, the prisoners leave the school, in divisions, and return to their courtyards for recreation. At five minutes to one, at the drum-roll, they form into work-teams.

Art. 24. At one o'clock they must be back in the workshops: they work until four o'clock.

Art. 25. At four o'clock the prisoners leave their workshops and go into the courtyards where they wash their hands and form into divisions for the refectory.

Art. 26. Supper and the recreation that follows it last until five o'clock: the prisoners then return to the workshops.

Art. 27. At seven o'clock in the summer, at eight in winter, work stops; bread is distributed for the last time in the workshops. For a quarter of an hour one of the prisoners or supervisors reads a passage from some instructive or uplifting work. This is followed by evening prayer.

Art. 28. At half-past seven in summer, half-past eight in winter, the prisoners must be back in their cells after the washing of hands and the inspection of clothes in the courtyard; at the first drum-roll, they must undress, and at the second get into bed. The cell doors are closed and the supervisors go the rounds in the corridors, to ensure order and silence' (Faucher, pp. 274–82).

We have, then, a public execution and a time-table. They do not punish the same crimes or the same type of delinquent. But they each define a certain penal style. Less than a century separates them. It was a time when, in Europe and in the United States, the entire economy of punishment was redistributed. It was a time of great 'scandals' for traditional justice, a time of innumerable projects for reform. It saw a new theory of law and crime, a new moral or political justification of the right to punish; old laws were abolished, old customs died out. 'Modern' codes were planned or drawn up: Russia, 1769; Prussia, 1780; Pennsylvania and Tuscany, 1786; Austria, 1788; France, 1791, Year IV, 1808 and 1810. It was a new age for penal justice.

Among so many changes, I shall consider one: the disappearance of torture as a public spectacle. Today we are rather inclined to ignore it; perhaps, in its time, it gave rise to too much inflated rhetoric; perhaps it has been attributed too readily and too emphatically to a process of 'humanisation', thus dispensing with the need for further analysis. And, in any case, how important is such a change, when compared with the great institutional transformations, the formulation of explicit, general codes and unified rules of procedure; with the almost universal adoption of the jury system, the

definition of the essentially corrective character of the penalty and the
tendency, which has become increasingly marked since the nineteenth century, to adapt punishment to the individual offender? Punishment of a less
immediately physical kind, a certain discretion in the art of inflicting pain, a
combination of more subtle, more subdued sufferings, deprived of their
visible display, should not all this be treated as a special case, an incidental
effect of deeper changes? And yet the fact remains that a few decades saw the
disappearance of the tortured, dismembered, amputated body, symbolically
branded on face or shoulder, exposed alive or dead to public view. The body
as the major target of penal repression disappeared.

By the end of the eighteenth and the beginning of the nineteenth century,
the gloomy festival of punishment was dying out, though here and there it
flickered momentarily into life. In this transformation, two processes were at
work. They did not have quite the same chronology or the same *raison d'être*.
The first was the disappearance of punishment as a spectacle. The ceremonial
of punishment tended to decline; it survived only as a new legal or administrative practice. The *amende honorable* was first abolished in France in
1791, then again in 1830 after a brief revival; the pillory was abolished in
France in 1789 and in England in 1837. The use of prisoners in public works,
cleaning city streets or repairing the highways, was practised in Austria,
Switzerland and certain of the United States, such as Pennsylvania. These
convicts, distinguished by their 'infamous dress' and shaven heads, 'were
brought before the public. The sport of the idle and the vicious, they often
become incensed, and naturally took violent revenge upon the aggressors. To
prevent them from returning injuries which might be inflicted on them, they
were encumbered with iron collars and chains to which bomb-shells were
attached, to be dragged along while they performed their degrading service,
under the eyes of keepers armed with swords, blunderbusses and other
weapons of destruction' (Roberts Vaux, *Notices*, 21, quoted in Teeters,
1937, p. 24). This practice was abolished practically everywhere at the end
of the eighteenth or the beginning of the nineteenth century. The public
exhibition of prisoners was maintained in France in 1831, despite violent
criticism – 'a disgusting scene', said Réal; it was finally abolished in April
1848. While the chain-gang, which had dragged convicts across the whole of
France, as far as Brest and Toulon, was replaced in 1837 by inconspicuous
black-painted cell-carts, punishment had gradually ceased to be a spectacle.
And whatever theatrical elements it still retained were now downgraded, as if
the functions of the penal ceremony were gradually ceasing to be understood, as if this rite that 'concluded the crime' was suspected of being in some
undesirable way linked with it. It was as if the punishment was thought to
equal, if not to exceed, in savagery the crime itself, to accustom the spectators to a ferocity from which one wished to divert them, to show them the
frequency of crime, to make the executioner resemble a criminal, judges

murderers, to reverse roles at the last moment, to make the tortured criminal an object of pity or admiration. As early as 1764, Beccaria remarked: 'The murder that is depicted as a horrible crime is repeated in cold blood, remorselessly' (Beccaria, p. 101). The public execution is now seen as a hearth in which violence bursts again into flame.

Punishment, then, will tend to become the most hidden part of the penal process. This has several consequences: it leaves the domain of more or less everyday perception and enters that of abstract consciousness; its effectiveness is seen as resulting from its inevitability, not from its visible intensity; it is the certainty of being punished and not the horrifying spectacle of public punishment that must discourage crime; the exemplary mechanics of punishment changes its mechanisms. As a result, justice no longer takes public responsibility for the violence that is bound up with its practice. If it too strikes, if it too kills, it is not as a glorification of its strength, but as an element of itself that it is obliged to tolerate, that it finds difficult to account for. The apportioning of blame is redistributed: in punishment-as-spectacle a confused horror spread from the scaffold; it enveloped both executioner and condemned; and, although it was always ready to invert the shame inflicted on the victim into pity or glory, it often turned the legal violence of the executioner into shame. Now the scandal and the light are to be distributed differently; it is the conviction itself that marks the offender with the unequivocally negative sign: the publicity has shifted to the trial, and to the sentence; the execution itself is like an additional shame that justice is ashamed to impose on the condemned man; so it keeps its distance from the act, tending always to entrust it to others, under the seal of secrecy. It is ugly to be punishable, but there is no glory in punishing. Hence that double system of protection that justice has set up between itself and the punishment it imposes. Those who carry out the penalty tend to become an autonomous sector; justice is relieved of responsibility for it by a bureaucratic concealment of the penalty itself. It is typical that in France the administration of the prisons should for so long have been the responsibility of the Ministry of the Interior, while responsibility for the *bagnes*, for penal servitude in the convict ships and penal settlements, lay with the Ministry of the Navy or the Ministry of the Colonies. And beyond this distribution of roles operates a theoretical disavowal: do not imagine that the sentences that we judges pass are activated by a desire to punish; they are intended to correct, reclaim, 'cure'; a technique of improvement represses, in the penalty, the strict expiation of evil-doing, and relieves the magistrates of the demeaning task of punishing. In modern justice and on the part of those who dispense it there is a shame in punishing, which does not always preclude zeal. This sense of shame is constantly growing: the psychologists and the minor civil servants of moral orthopaedics proliferate on the wound it leaves.

The disappearance of public executions marks therefore the decline of the spectacle; but it also marks a slackening of the hold on the body. In 1787, in an address to the Society for Promoting Political Enquiries, Benjamin Rush remarked: 'I can only hope that the time is not far away when gallows, pillory, scaffold, flogging and wheel will, in the history of punishment, be regarded as the marks of the barbarity of centuries and of countries and as proofs of the feeble influence of reason and religion over the human mind' (Teeters, 1935, p. 30). Indeed, sixty years later, Van Meenen, opening the second penitentiary congress, in Brussels, recalled the time of his childhood as of a past age: 'I have seen the ground strewn with wheels, gibbets, gallows, pillories; I have seen hideously stretched skeletons on wheels' (*Annales de la Charité*, pp. 529–30). Branding had been abolished in England (1834) and in France (1832); in 1820, England no longer dared to apply the full punishment reserved for traitors (Thistlewood was not quartered). Only flogging still remained in a number of penal systems (Russia, England, Prussia). But, generally speaking, punitive practices had become more reticent. One no longer touched the body, or at least as little as possible, and then only to reach something other than the body itself. It might be objected that imprisonment, confinement, forced labour, penal servitude, prohibition from entering certain areas, deportation – which have occupied so important a place in modern penal systems – are 'physical' penalties: unlike fines, for example, they directly affect the body. But the punishment–body relation is not the same as it was in the torture during public executions. The body now serves as an instrument or intermediary: if one intervenes upon it to imprison it, or to make it work, it is in order to deprive the individual of a liberty that is regarded both as a right and as property. The body, according to this penality, is caught up in a system of constraints and privations, obligations and prohibitions. Physical pain, the pain of the body itself, is no longer the constituent element of the penalty. From being an art of unbearable sensations punishment has become an economy of suspended rights. If it is still necessary for the law to reach and manipulate the body of the convict, it will be at a distance, in the proper way, according to strict rules, and with a much 'higher' aim. As a result of this new restraint, a whole army of technicians took over from the executioner, the immediate anatomist of pain: warders, doctors, chaplains, psychiatrists, psychologists, educationalists; by their very presence near the prisoner, they sing the praises that the law needs: they reassure it that the body and pain are not the ultimate objects of its punitive action. Today a doctor must watch over those condemned to death, right up to the last moment – thus juxtaposing himself as the agent of welfare, as the alleviator of pain, with the official whose task it is to end life. This is worth thinking about. When the moment of execution approaches, the patients are injected with tranquillisers. A utopia of judicial reticence: take away life, but prevent the patient from feeling it; deprive the prisoner of all rights, but do not inflict pain; impose penalties free of all pain. Recourse to psycho-pharmacology and to various physiological 'disconnectors', even if it is temporary, is a logical consequence of this 'non-corporal' penality.

The modern rituals of execution attest to this double process: the disappearance of the spectacle and the elimination of pain. The same movement has affected the various European legal systems, each at its own rate: the same death for all – the execution no longer bears the specific mark of the crime or the social status of the criminal; a death that lasts only a moment – no torture must be added to it in advance, no further actions performed upon the corpse; an execution that affects life rather than the body. There are no longer any of those long processes in which death was both retarded by calculated interruptions and multiplied by a series of successive attacks. There are no longer any of those combinations of tortures that were organised for the killing of regicides, or of the kind advocated, at the beginning of the eighteenth century, by the anonymous author of *Hanging not Punishment Enough* (1701), by which the condemned man would be broken on the wheel, then flogged until he fainted, then hung up with chains, then finally left to die slowly of hunger. There are no longer any of those executions in which the condemned man was dragged along on a hurdle (to prevent his head smashing against the cobble-stones), in which his belly was opened up, his entrails quickly ripped out, so that he had time to see them, with his own eyes, being thrown on the fire; in which he was finally decapitated and his body quartered.[1] The reduction of these 'thousand deaths' to strict capital punishment defines a whole new morality concerning the act of punishing.

As early as 1760, a hanging machine had been tried out in England (for the execution of Lord Ferrer). It made use of a support, which opened under the feet of the condemned man, thus avoiding slow deaths and the altercations that occurred between victim and executioner. It was improved and finally adopted in 1783, the same year in which the traditional procession from Newgate to Tyburn was abolished, and in which the opportunity offered by the rebuilding of the prison, after the Gordon Riots, was used to set up the scaffolds in Newgate itself (see Hibbert, pp. 85–6). The celebrated article 3 of the French Code of 1791 – 'Every man condemned to death will have his head cut off' – bears this triple signification: an equal death for all ('Crimes of the same kind will be punished by the same kind of punishment, whatever the rank and state of the guilty man may be', in the words of the motion proposed by Guillotin and passed on 1 December 1789); one death per condemned man, obtained by a single blow, without recourse to those 'long and consequently cruel' methods of execution, such as the gallows, denounced by Le Peletier; lastly, punishment for the condemned man alone, since decapitation, the capital punishment of the nobility, was the least shaming for the criminal's family (Le Peletier, p. 720). The guillotine, first used in March 1792, was the perfect vehicle for these principles. Death was reduced to a visible, but instantaneous event. Contact between the law, or those who carry it out, and the body of the criminal, is reduced to a split second. There is no physical confrontation; the executioner need be no more than a meticulous watchmaker. 'Experience and reason demonstrate that the method used in the past to cut off the head of a criminal exposed him to a torture more frightful than the loss of life alone, which is the express intention of the law; the execution should therefore be carried out in a single moment and with a single blow; examples show how difficult it is to achieve this. For the method to work perfectly, it must necessarily depend on invariable mechanical means whose force and effect may also be determined ... It is an easy enough matter to have such an unfailing machine built; decapitation will be performed in a moment according to the intention of the new law. If this apparatus seems necessary, it will cause no sensation and will be scarcely noticed' (Saint-Edme, p. 161). The guillotine takes life almost without touching the body, just as prison deprives of liberty or a fine reduces wealth. It is intended to apply the law not so much to a real body capable of feeling pain as to a juridical subject, the possessor, among other rights, of the right to exist. It had to have the abstraction of the law itself.

No doubt something of the old public execution was, for a time, superimposed in France on the sobriety of the new method. Parricides – and the regicides who were regarded as such – were led to the scaffold wearing a black veil; there, until 1832, one of their hands was cut off. Thereafter, nothing remained but the ornamental crêpe. Thus it was in the case of Fieschi, the would-be assassin of Louis-Philippe, in November 1836: 'He will be taken to the place of execution wearing a shirt, barefoot, his head covered with a black veil; he will be exhibited upon a scaffold while an usher reads the sentence to the people, and he will be immediately executed.' We should remember Damiens – and note that the last addition to penal death was a mourning veil. The condemned man was no longer to be seen. Only the reading of the sentence on the scaffold announced the crime – and that crime must be faceless. (The more monstrous a criminal was, the more he must be deprived of light: he must not see, or be seen. This was a common enough notion at the time. For the parricide one should 'construct an iron cage or dig an impenetrable dungeon that would serve him as an eternal retreat' – De Molène, pp. 275–7). The last vestige of the great public execution was its annulment: a drapery to hide a body. Benoît, triply infamous (his mother's murderer, a homosexual, an assassin), was the first of the parricides not to have a hand cut off: 'As the sentence was being read, he stood on the scaffold supported by the executioners. It was a horrible sight; wrapped in a large white shroud, his face covered with black crêpe, the parricide escaped the gaze of the silent crowd, and beneath these mysterious and gloomy clothes, life was manifested only by frightful cries, which soon expired under the knife' (*Gazette des tribunaux*, 30 August 1832).

At the beginning of the nineteenth century, then, the great spectacle of physical punishment disappeared; the tortured body was avoided; the theatrical representation of pain was excluded from punishment. The age of sobriety in punishment had begun. By 1830–48, public executions, preceded by torture, had almost entirely disappeared. Of course, this generalisation requires some qualification. To begin with, the changes did not come about at once or as part of a single process. There were delays. Paradoxically, England was one of the countries most loath to see the disappearance of the public execution: perhaps because of the role of model that the institution of the jury, public hearings and respect of habeas corpus had given to her criminal law; above all, no doubt, because she did not wish to diminish the rigour of her penal laws during the great social disturbances of the years 1780–1820. For a long time Romilly, Mackintosh and Fowell Buxton failed in their attempts to attenuate the multiplicity and severity of the penalties laid down by English law – that 'horrible butchery', as Rossi described it. Its severity (in fact, the juries regarded the penalties laid down as excessive and were consequently more lenient in their application) had even increased: in 1760, Blackstone had listed 160 capital crimes in English legislation, while by 1819 there were 223. One should also take into account the advances and retreats that the process as a whole underwent between 1760 and 1840; the rapidity of reform in certain countries such as Austria, Russia, the United States, France under the Constituent Assembly, then the retreat at the time of the counter-revolutions in Europe and the great social fear of the years 1820–48; more or less temporary changes introduced by emergency courts or laws; the gap between the laws and the real practice of the courts (which was by no means a faithful reflection of the state of legislation). All these factors account for the irregularity of the transformation that occurred at the turn of the century.

It should be added that, although most of the changes had been achieved by 1840, although the mechanisms of punishment had by then assumed their new way of functioning, the process was far from complete. The reduction in the use of torture was a tendency that was rooted in the great transformation of the years 1760–1840, but it did not end there; it can be said that the practice of the public execution haunted our penal system for a long time and still haunts it today. In France, the guillotine, that machine for the production of rapid and discreet deaths, represented a new ethic of legal death. But the Revolution had immediately endowed it with a great theatrical ritual. For years it provided a spectacle. It had to be removed to the Barrière Saint-Jacques; the open cart was replaced by a closed carriage; the condemned man was hustled from the vehicle straight to the scaffold; hasty executions were organised at unexpected times. In the end, the guillotine had to be placed inside prison walls and made inaccessible to the public (after the execution of Weidmann in 1939), by blocking the streets leading to the prison in which the scaffold was hidden, and in which the execution would take place in secret (the execution of Buffet and Bontemps at the Santé in 1972). Witnesses who described the scene could even be prosecuted, thereby ensuring that the execution should cease to be a spectacle and remain a strange secret between the law and those it condemns. One has only to point out so many precautions to realise that capital punishment remains fundamentally, even today, a spectacle that must actually be forbidden.

Similarly, the hold on the body did not entirely disappear in the mid-nineteenth century. Punishment had no doubt ceased to be centred on torture as a technique of pain; it assumed as its principal object loss of wealth or rights. But a punishment like forced labour or even imprisonment – mere loss of liberty – has never functioned without a certain additional element of punishment that certainly concerns the body itself: rationing of food, sexual deprivation, corporal punishment, solitary confinement. Are these the unintentional, but inevitable, consequence of imprisonment? In fact, in its most explicit practices, imprisonment has always involved a certain degree of physical pain. The criticism that was often levelled at the penitentiary system in the early nineteenth century (imprisonment is not a sufficient punishment: prisoners are less hungry, less cold, less deprived in general than many poor people or even workers) suggests a postulate that was never explicitly denied: it is just that a condemned man should suffer physically more than other men. It is difficult to dissociate punishment from additional physical pain. What would a non-corporal punishment be?

There remains, therefore, a trace of 'torture' in the modern mechanisms of criminal justice – a trace that has not been entirely overcome, but which is enveloped, increasingly, by the non-corporal nature of the penal system.

The reduction in penal severity in the last 200 years is a phenomenon with which legal historians are well acquainted. But, for a long time, it has been regarded in an overall way as a quantitative phenomenon: less cruelty, less pain, more kindness, more respect, more 'humanity'. In fact, these changes are accompanied by a displacement in the very object of the punitive operation. Is there a diminution of intensity? Perhaps. There is certainly a change of objective.

If the penality in its most severe forms no longer addresses itself to the body, on what does it lay hold? The answer of the theoreticians – those who, about 1760, opened up a new period that is not yet at an end – is simple, almost obvious. It seems to be contained in the question itself: since it is no longer the body, it must be the soul. The expiation that once rained down upon the body must be replaced by a punishment that acts in depth on the heart, the thoughts, the will, the inclinations. Mably formulated the principle once and for all: 'Punishment, if I may so put it, should strike the soul rather than the body' (Mably, p. 326).

It was an important moment. The old partners of the spectacle of punishment, the body and the blood, gave way. A new character came on the scene, masked. It was the end of a certain kind of tragedy; comedy began, with shadow play, faceless voices, impalpable entities. The apparatus of punitive justice must now bite into this bodiless reality.

Is this any more than a mere theoretical assertion, contradicted by penal practice? Such a conclusion would be over-hasty. It is true that, today, to punish is not simply a matter of converting a soul; but Mably's principle has not remained a pious wish. Its effects can be felt throughout modern penality.

To begin with, there is a substitution of objects. By this I do not mean that one has suddenly set about punishing other crimes. No doubt the definition of offences, the hierarchy of their seriousness, the margins of indulgence, what was tolerated in fact and what was legally permitted – all this has considerably changed over the last 200 years; many crimes have ceased to be so because they were bound up with a certain exercise of religious authority or a particular type of economic activity; blasphemy has lost its status as a crime; smuggling and domestic larceny some of their seriousness. But these displacements are perhaps not the most important fact: the division between the permitted and the forbidden has preserved a certain constancy from one century to another. On the other hand, 'crime', the object with which penal practice is concerned, has profoundly altered: the quality, the nature, in a sense the substance of which the punishable element is made, rather than its formal definition. Under cover of the relative stability of the law, a mass of subtle and rapid changes has occurred. Certainly the 'crimes' and 'offences' on which judgement is passed are juridical objects defined by the code, but judgement is also passed on the passions, instincts, anomalies, infirmities, maladjustments, effects of environment or heredity; acts of aggression are punished, so also, through them, is aggressivity; rape, but at the same time perversions; murders, but also drives and desires. But, it will be objected, judgement is not actually being passed on them; if they are referred to at all it is to explain the actions in question, and to determine to what extent the subject's will was involved in the crime. This is no answer. For it *is* these shadows lurking behind the case itself that are judged and punished. They are judged indirectly as 'attenuating circumstances' that introduce into the verdict not only 'circumstantial' evidence, but something quite different, which is not juridically codifiable: the knowledge of the criminal, one's estimation of him, what is known about the relations between him, his past and his crime, and what might be expected of him in the future. They are also judged by the interplay of all those notions that have circulated between medicine and jurisprudence since the nineteenth century (the 'monsters' of Georget's times, Chaumié's 'psychical anomalies', the 'perverts' and 'maladjusted' of our own experts) and which, behind the pretext of explaining an action, are ways of defining an individual. They are punished by means of a punishment that has the function of making the offender 'not only desirous, but also capable, of living within the law and of providing for his own needs'; they are punished by the internal economy of a penalty which, while intended to punish the crime, may be altered (shortened or, in certain cases, extended) according to changes in the prisoner's behaviour; and they are punished by the 'security measures' that accompany the penalty (prohibition of entering certain areas, probation, obligatory medical treatment), and which are intended not to punish the offence, but to supervise the individual, to neutralise his dangerous state of mind, to alter his criminal tendencies, and to continue even when this change has been achieved. The criminal's soul is not referred to in the trial merely to explain his crime and as a factor in the juridical apportioning of responsibility; if it is brought before the court, with such pomp and circumstance, such concern to understand and such 'scientific' application, it is because it too, as well as the crime itself, is to be judged and to share in the punishment. Throughout the penal ritual, from the preliminary investigation to the sentence and the final effects of the penalty, a domain has been penetrated by objects that not only duplicate, but also dissociate the juridically defined and coded objects. Psychiatric expertise, but also in a more general way criminal anthropology and the repetitive discourse of criminology, find one of their precise functions here: by solemnly inscribing offences in the field of objects susceptible of scientific knowledge, they provide the mechanisms of legal punishment with a justifiable hold not only on offences, but on individuals; not only on what they do, but also on what they are, will be, may be. The additional factor of the offender's soul, which the legal system has laid hold of, is only apparently explanatory and limitative, and is in fact expansionist. During the 150 or 200 years that Europe has been setting up its new penal systems, the judges have gradually, by means of a process that goes back very far indeed, taken to judging something other than crimes, namely, the 'soul' of the criminal.

And, by that very fact, they have begun to do something other than pass judgement. Or, to be more precise, within the very judicial modality of judgement, other types of assessment have slipped in, profoundly altering its rules of elaboration. Ever since the Middle Ages slowly and painfully built up the great procedure of investigation, to judge was to establish the truth of a crime, it was to determine its author and to apply a legal punishment. Knowledge of the offence, knowledge of the offender, knowledge of the law: these three conditions made it possible to ground a judgement in truth. But now a quite different question of truth is inscribed in the course of the penal judgement. The question is no longer simply: 'Has the act been established and is it punishable?' But also: 'What *is* this act, what *is* this act of violence or this murder? To what level or to what field of reality does it belong? Is it a phantasy, a psychotic reaction, a delusional episode, a perverse action?' It is no longer simply: 'Who committed it?' But: 'How can we assign the causal process that produced it? Where did it originate in the author himself? Instinct, unconscious, environment, heredity?' It is no longer simply: 'What law punishes this offence?' But: 'What would be the most appropriate measures to take? How do we see the future development of the offender? What would be the best way of rehabilitating him?' A whole set of assessing, diagnostic, prognostic, normative judgements concerning the criminal have become lodged in the framework of penal judgement. Another truth has penetrated the truth that was required by the legal machinery; a truth which, entangled with the first, has turned the assertion of guilt into a strange scientifico-juridical complex. A significant fact is the way in which the question of madness has evolved in penal practice. According to the 1810 code, madness was dealt with only in terms of article 64. Now this article states that there is neither crime nor offence if the offender was of unsound mind at the time of the act. The possibility of ascertaining madness was, therefore, a quite separate matter from the definition of an act as a crime; the gravity of the act was not altered by the fact that its author was insane, nor the punishment reduced as a consequence; the crime itself disappeared. It was impossible, therefore, to declare that someone was both guilty and mad; once the diagnosis of madness had been accepted, it could not be included in the judgement; it interrupted the procedure and loosened the hold of the law on the author of the act. Not only the examination of the criminal suspected of insanity, but the very effects of this examination had to be external and anterior to the sentence. But, very soon, the courts of the nineteenth century began to misunderstand the meaning of article 64. Despite several decisions of the supreme court of appeal confirming that insanity could not result either in a light penalty, or even in an acquittal, but required that the case be dismissed, the ordinary courts continued to bring the question of insanity to bear on their verdicts. They accepted that one could be both guilty and mad; less guilty the madder one was; guilty certainly, but someone to be put away and treated rather than punished; not only a guilty man, but also dangerous, since quite obviously sick, etc. From the point of view of the penal code, the result was a mass of juridical absurdities. But this was the starting point of an evolution that jurisprudence and legislation itself was to precipitate in the course of the next 150 years: already the reform of 1832, introducing attenuating circumstances, made it possible to modify the sentence according to the supposed degrees of an illness or the forms of a semi-insanity. And the practice of calling on psychiatric expertise, which is widespread in the assize courts and sometimes extended to courts of summary jurisdiction, means that the sentence, even if it is always formulated in terms of legal punishment, implies, more or less obscurely, judgements of normality, attributions of causality, assessments of possible changes, anticipations as to the offender's future. It would be wrong to say that all these operations give substance to a judgement from the outside; they are directly integrated in the process of forming the sentence. Instead of insanity eliminating the crime according to the original meaning of article 64, every crime and even every offence now carries within it, as a legitimate suspicion, but also as a right that may be claimed, the hypothesis of insanity, in any case of anomaly. And the sentence that condemns or acquits is not simply a judgement of guilt, a legal decision that lays down punishment; it bears within it an assessment of normality and a technical prescription for a possible normalisation. Today the judge – magistrate or juror – certainly does more than 'judge'.

And he is not alone in judging. Throughout the penal procedure and the implementation of the sentence there swarms a whole series of subsidiary authorities. Small-scale legal systems and parallel judges have multiplied around the principal judgement: psychiatric or psychological experts, magistrates concerned with the implementation of sentences, educationalists, members of the prison service, all fragment the legal power to punish; it might be objected that none of them really shares the right to judge; that some, after sentence is passed, have no other right than to implement the punishment laid down by the court and, above all, that others – the experts – intervene before the sentence not to pass judgement, but to assist the judges in their decision. But as soon as the penalties and the security measures defined by the court are not absolutely determined, from the moment they may be modified along the way, from the moment one leaves to others than the judges of the offence the task of deciding whether the condemned man 'deserves' to be placed in semi-liberty or conditional liberty, whether they may bring his penal tutelage to an end, one is handing over to them mechanisms of legal punishment to be used at their discretion: subsidiary judges they may be, but they are judges all the same. The whole machinery that has been developing for years around the implementation of sentences, and their adjustment to individuals, creates a proliferation of the authorities of judicial decision-making and extends its powers of decision well beyond the sentence. The psychiatric experts, for their part, may well refrain from judging. Let us examine the three questions to which, since the 1958 ruling, they have to address themselves: Does the convicted person represent a danger to society? Is he susceptible to penal punishment? Is he curable or readjustable? These questions have nothing to do with article 64, nor with the possible insanity of the convicted person at the moment of the act. They do not concern 'responsibility'. They concern nothing but the administration of the penalty, its necessity, its usefulness, its possible effectiveness; they make it possible to show, in an almost transparent vocabulary, whether the mental hospital would be a more suitable place of confinement than the prison, whether this confinement should be short or long, whether medical treatment or security measures are called for. What, then, is the role of the psychiatrist in penal matters? He is not an expert in responsibility, but an adviser on punishment; it is up to him to say whether the subject is 'dangerous', in what way one should be protected from him, how one should intervene to alter him, whether it would be better to try to force him into submission or to treat him. At the very beginning of its history, psychiatric expertise was called upon to formulate 'true' propositions as to the part that the liberty of the offender had played in the act he had committed; it is now called upon to suggest a prescription for what might be called his 'medico-judicial treatment'.

To sum up, ever since the new penal system – that defined by the great codes of the eighteenth and nineteenth centuries – has been in operation, a general process has led judges to judge something other than crimes; they have been led in their sentences to do something other than judge; and the power of judging has been transferred, in part, to other authorities than the judges of the offence. The whole penal operation has taken on extra-juridical elements and personnel. It will be said that there is nothing extraordinary in this, that it is part of the destiny of the law to absorb little by little elements that are alien to it. But what is odd about modern criminal justice is that, although it has taken on so many extra-juridical elements, it has done so not in order to be able to define them juridically and gradually to integrate them into the actual power to punish: on the contrary, it has done so in order to make them function within the penal operation as non-juridical elements; in order to stop this operation being simply a legal punishment; in order to exculpate the judge from being purely and simply he who punishes. 'Of course, we pass sentence, but this sentence is not in direct relation to the crime. It is quite clear that for us it functions as a way of treating a criminal. We punish, but this is a way of saying that we wish to obtain a cure.' Today, criminal justice functions and justifies itself only by this perpetual reference to something other than itself, by this unceasing reinscription in non-juridical systems. Its fate is to be redefined by knowledge.

Beneath the increasing leniency of punishment, then, one may map a displacement of its point of application; and through this displacement, a whole field of recent objects, a whole new system of truth and a mass of roles hitherto unknown in the exercise of criminal justice. A corpus of knowledge, techniques, 'scientific' discourses is formed and becomes entangled with the practice of the power to punish.

This book [*Discipline and Punish*] is intended as a correlative history of the modern soul and of a new power to judge; a genealogy of the present scientificolegal complex from which the power to punish derives its bases, justifications and rules, from which it extends its effects and by which it masks its exorbitant singularity.

But from what point can such a history of the modern soul on trial be written? If one confined oneself to the evolution of legislation or of penal procedures, one would run the risk of allowing a change in the collective sensibility, an increase in humanisation or the development of the human sciences to emerge as a massive, external, inert and primary fact. By studying only the general social forms, as Durkheim did, one runs the risk of positing as the principle of greater leniency in punishment processes of individualisation that are rather one of the effects of the new tactics of power, among which are to be included the new penal mechanisms. This study obeys four general rules:

1. Do not concentrate the study of the punitive mechanisms on their 'repressive' effects alone, on their 'punishment' aspects alone, but situate them in a whole series of their possible positive effects, even if these seem marginal at first sight. As a consequence, regard punishment as a complex social function.

2. Analyse punitive methods not simply as consequences of legislation or as indicators of social structures, but as techniques possessing their own specificity in the more general field of other ways of exercising power. Regard punishment as a political tactic.

3. Instead of treating the history of penal law and the history of the human sciences as two separate series whose overlapping appears to have had on one or the other, or perhaps on both, a disturbing or useful effect, according to one's point of view, see whether there is not some common matrix or whether they do not both derive from a single process of 'epistemologico-juridical' formation; in short, make the technology of power the very principle both of the humanisation of the penal system and of the knowledge of man.

[...]

That punishment in general and the prison in particular belong to a political technology of the body is a lesson that I have learnt not so much from history as from the present. In recent years, prison revolts have occurred throughout the world. There was certainly something paradoxical about their aims, their slogans and the way they took place. They were revolts against an entire state of physical misery that is over a century old: against cold, suffocation and overcrowding, against decrepit walls, hunger, physical maltreatment. But they were also revolts against model prisons, tranquillisers, isolation, the medical or educational services. Were they revolts whose aims were merely material? Or contradictory revolts: against the obsolete, but also against comfort; against the warders, but also against the psychiatrists? In fact, all these movements – and the innumerable discourses that the prison has given rise to since the early nineteenth century – have been about the body and material things. What has sustained these discourses, these memories and invectives are indeed those minute material details. One may, if one is so disposed, see them as no more than blind demands or suspect the existence behind them of alien strategies. In fact, they were revolts, at the level of the body, against the very body of the prison.

What was at issue was not whether the prison environment was too harsh or too aseptic, too primitive or too efficient, but its very materiality as an instrument and vector of power; it is this whole technology of power over the body that the technology of the 'soul' – that of the educationalists, psychologists and psychiatrists – fails either to conceal or to compensate, for the simple reason that it is one of its tools. I would like to write the history of this prison, with all the political investments of the body that it gathers together in its closed architecture. Why? Simply because I am interested in the past? No, if one means by that writing a history of the past in terms of the present. Yes, if one means writing the history of the present.[2]

7

At the Table of the Great: More's Self-Fashioning and Self-Cancellation

Stephen Greenblatt

'A PART OF HIS OWN'

A dinner party at Cardinal Wolsey's. Years later, in the Tower, More recalled the occasion and refashioned it in *A Dialogue of Comfort Against Tribulation* as a 'merry tale', one of those sly jokes that interlace his most serious work. The story reaches back to a past that, in the gathering darkness of 1534, might well have seemed to More almost mythical, back before the collapse of his career, the collapse of his whole world. Perhaps as important, it reaches back to a time before More had decided to embark upon his career. He pictures himself as an ambitious, clever young man, eager to make a good impression, but at the same time an outsider: in his fictionalised version, he is a Hungarian visitor to Germany. The vainglorious prelate – transparently Wolsey – had that day made an oration so splendid in his own estimation that he sat as if on thorns until he could hear it commended by his guests. After casting about in vain for a discreet way of introducing the subject, the cardinal finally asked bluntly what the company thought of his oration. Eating and conversation came to an abrupt halt: 'Every man was fallen in so deep a study for the finding of some exquisite praise.'[1] Then one by one in order, each guest brought forth his flattering speech. When the young More had played his part, he felt confident that he had acquitted himself well, the more so in that he was to be followed by an ignorant priest. But the priest – a 'wily fox' – far surpassed him in the craft of flattery, and both in turn were bested by the last to speak, a 'good ancient honorable flatterer' who, when he saw that he could not exceed the elaborate compliments already produced, spoke not a word, 'but as he that were ravished unto heavenward with the wonder of the wisdom and eloquence that my Lord's grace had uttered in that oration, he fet [i.e., fetched] a long sigh with an "oh" from the bottom of his breast, and held up both hands, and lifted up his head, and cast up his eyes into the welkin, and wept' (pp. 215–16).

74

How much of More is in this little story! The jibes at the ignorant priest who 'could speak no Latin at all' and at the rich, worldly cardinal are the last sparks of that humanist indignation at clerical abuses that he once shared with Erasmus and that had somehow survived fifteen years of bitter anti-Protestant polemics. The setting recalls the rich significance for More of the dinner party, emblem of human society both in its foolish vanity and in its precious moments of communion. Above all, the acute observation of social comedy links the story to More's lifelong fascination with the games people play. The particular game in this case is the satisfaction of self-love, played by fools who rejoice to think 'how they be continually praised all about as though all the world did nothing else day nor night, but ever sit and sing *sanctus sanctus sanctus* upon them' (p. 212). The rich and powerful have the means to realise this fantasy: in their 'pleasant frenzy' they hire flatterers who do nothing but sing their praises.

This is the distillation of More's long career in the dangerous, glittering world of Renaissance politics, the essence of his observation of king and cardinal: bloated vanity, ravenous appetite, folly. The spectacle at once repelled and fascinated him; he could never bring himself simply to renounce the world in holy indignation. On the contrary, he made himself into a consummately successful performer: from modest beginnings in the early 1490s as a young page in the household of Lord Chancellor Morton, four decades of law, diplomacy, parliamentary politics, and court-ship brought More in 1529, as Wolsey's successor, to the Lord Chancellor-ship, the highest office in the realm. Then, as if to confirm all of his darkest reflections on power and privilege, his own position quickly deteriorated beneath the pressure of the king's divorce. In May 1532, attempting to save himself, More resigned the chancellorship on the pretext of ill health, but he was too important and too visible to be granted a silent, unmo-lested retirement. Refusal to subscribe to the Oath of Supremacy – that is, to acknowledge that the king was Supreme Head of the Church in England – brought him in 1534 to the Tower and, on 6 July 1535, to the scaffold.

This chapter will describe the complex interplay in More's life and writings of self-fashioning and self-cancellation, the crafting of a public role and the profound desire to escape from the identity so crafted, and I propose that we keep in our minds the image of More sitting at the table of the great in a peculiar mood of ambition, ironic amusement, curiosity, and revulsion. It is as if he were watching the enactment of a fiction, and he is equally struck by the unreality of the whole performance and by its immense power to impose itself upon the world. This is, in fact, one of the central perceptions of the *Dialogue of Comfort*, repeated again and again in an endless variety of guises. No sooner is one fantasy laid to rest than another pops up to be grappled with in turn and defeated, until the whole world, the great body of man's longings, anxieties, and goals, shimmers like a mirage, compelling, tenacious, and utterly unreal.

But why should men submit to fantasies that will not nourish or sustain them? In part, More's answer is *power*, whose quintessential sign is the ability to impose one's fictions upon the world: the more outrageous the fiction, the more impressive the manifestation of power. The vain cardinal may be in the grip of madness, but he can compel others to enter the madness and reinforce it. So too, a generation earlier, Richard III cast his ruthless seizure of the throne in the guise of an elaborate process of offer, refusal, renewed offer, and reluctant acceptance. The point is not that anyone is deceived by the charade, but that everyone is forced either to participate in it or to watch it silently. In a brilliant passage of his *History of Richard III*, More imagines the talk among the common people who have just witnessed the sinister farce. They marvel at the whole performance, since no one could be expected to be taken in by it, but then, as one of them observes, 'men must sometime for the manner sake not be aknowen what they know'.[2] After all, a bishop goes through a similar charade at his consecration, though everyone knows he has paid for his office. And likewise, at a play, everyone may know that the man playing sultan is, in fact, a cobbler, but if anyone is foolish enough to 'call him by his own name while he standeth in his majesty, one of his tormentors might hap to break his head'.

> And so they said that these matters be king's games, as it were stage plays, and for the more part played upon scaffolds. In which poor men be but the lookers-on. And they that wise be will meddle no farther. For they that sometime step up and play with them, when they cannot play their parts, they disorder the play and do themselves no good. (p. 81)

To try to break through the fiction is dangerous – one can have one's head broken. To try to take a part of one's own, 'to step up and play with them', is equally dangerous. On the one hand, the great have the means to enforce their elaborate, theatrical ceremonies of pride; on the other, those ceremonies are usually performed, ominously, on scaffolds.

But if wealth and force are the props on which such ceremonies are based, why should the great bother with the masquerade at all? More's observation that few, if any, among the performers or the audience are taken in by the elaborate pretence obviates a purely political explanation such as Machiavelli, describing similar rituals, provides. For Machiavelli, the prince engages in deceptions for one very clear reason: to survive. The successful prince must be 'a great feigner and dissembler; and men are so simple and so ready to obey present necessities, that one who deceives will always find those who allow themselves to be deceived'.[3] The observation hovers characteristically between cynicism and revolt, cold counsel and satire, but at least there is only one layer of deception: strip off that layer and you reach the naked realities of appetite and fear. The initiated observer can always see beneath the surface and understand how appearances are manipulated by the cunning prince.

In More, appearances have a more problematical relationship to reality. His is a world in which everyone is profoundly committed to upholding conventions in which no one believes; somehow belief has ceased to be necessary. The conventions serve no evident human purpose, not even deceit, yet king and bishop cannot live without them. Strip off the layer of theatrical delusion and you reach nothing at all. That is why Machiavelli's world seems so much more accessible than More's to the inquiring intellect: 'My intention being to write something of use to those who understand, it appears to me more proper to go to the real truth of the matter than to its imagination; and many have imagined republics and principalities which have never been seen or known to exist in reality; for how we live is so far removed from how we ought to live, that he who abandons what is done for what ought to be done, will rather learn to bring about his own ruin than his preservation' (p. 56). There are spiralling ironies in this famous passage from *The Prince*, but the vertigo is arrested by a passionate commitment to life in this world and by a hard, steady confidence that it is possible to penetrate 'to the real truth of the matter'.

More, of course, could claim with even greater confidence to know the 'real truth', but his was a truth of an entirely different order, capable of *cancelling*, but not *clarifying*, human politics. In neither of his great political works, the *History of Richard III* and *Utopia*, does he invoke this ultimate religious truth as a decisive explanation: in the former, he writes a historical narrative in imitation of classical models; in the latter, he illuminates contemporary politics with the light not of his faith but of his imagination, inventing one of those republics 'which have never been seen or known to exist in reality'. His work then has neither the cold clarity of cynicism nor the confident purposefulness of providential history showing God unfold his great plan through the agency of second causes. For Machiavelli and the providential historian alike, the political world is transparent; for More, it is opaque. And his great faith, his sense of the absolute truth, seems only to have increased that opacity, by rendering political life essentially *absurd*.

More did, to be sure, spend much of his career acting as if Parliament, the Privy Council, the law courts, and the royal court were anything but absurd, as if his own considerable gift for compromise, subtle manoeuvre, and partial reform might well contribute to a rational amelioration of social life and a comfortable position for himself and his family. The tragic drama of his end may obscure for us his remarkable ability to survive and flourish for decades in perilous political waters. After all, the survival rate for those closest to Henry VIII roughly resembles the actuarial record of the First Politburo.

More could scarcely have succeeded for as long as he did had his response to power consisted merely of remarking its absurdity. He was evidently a canny judge of human motives, possessed a firm grasp of the complex network of material interests that underlay the intricate formalities of Tudor government, and knew well how to make his own place within these formalities. The actual texture of his long public life is thick with the ceremonies of power. And yet when he tries to explain why the great bother with these ceremonies, why they stage elaborate theatrical rituals, he concludes ultimately not in a sense of rational calculation but in a sense of the absurd: because they are mad, possessed by 'fond fantasies', incapable of distinguishing between truth and fiction. It is not only Machiavellian calculation but humanist reform that finds its limits in this madness: political life cannot be resolved into underlying forces, cannot be treated as a code that the initiated understand and manipulate, because it is fundamentally insane, its practitioners in the grip of 'frenzies'. And it is not only political life, in the narrow sense, that is so judged, but the great body of man's social relations.

To understand More, we must take this haunting perception of universal madness very seriously, not, in other words, simply as a rhetorical device or conventional turn of phrase, but as a central and enduring response to existence. It is a response he shared, like so much else, with Erasmus, whose *Praise of Folly* is its supreme and definitive expression. But *The Praise of Folly* is a dangerous tool for exploiting More's response to life, in part because of the fundamental differences between Erasmus and More (the former a dissatisfied monk, impatient with confinement; the latter a dissatisfied layman, impatient with liberty), in part because of the success and familiarity of Erasmus's great work. Only when we pass from the confidence, flexibility, and charm of the literary masterpiece to the nervous instability over which it triumphed can we feel how disturbing as a lived experience is the sense of the absurd, how it marked for More a profound alienation from his society, from the greater part of his acquaintance, from himself. It is as if, in the midst of intensely valued attachments to family and friends, he carried within himself the perspective of the London Charterhouse in which he had lived, without vow, for four years, a perspective from which not only the ceremonies of the great but most of his own involvements seemed to him manifestations of limitless folly. 'I assure thee, on my faith,' he told his daughter in his cell in the Tower, 'if it had not been for my wife and you that be my children, whom I accompt the chief part of my charge, I would not have failed long ere this to have closed myself in as strait a room – and straiter too.'[4]

Admiration for More should not be permitted to efface the disturbing estrangement of this summary utterance at the end of his life. To be sure, More is responding in a characteristically brilliant and one might say witty way to the horrible conditions in which he found himself: he consoles his grieving daughter by transforming the suffering inflicted upon him into a gift, in effect making his destiny his choice. (And indeed that destiny was in a very real sense his choice, though not a choice he actively sought to make.) But there is more than comfort against tribulation here; in his words to Margaret, More gives voice to a lifelong current of contempt for a world reduced in his mind to madness, a rejection not only of all the pride, cruelty, and ambition of men, but of much that he himself seemed to cherish, a desire to escape into the fastness of a cell. In part, this attitude should no doubt be traced less to qualities peculiar to More than to the style of late medieval culture with its intense shiver of revulsion against the world it nonetheless embraced.[5] But our knowledge of More's participation in a larger cultural mood should not diminish our sensitivity to its actual effect in his life and writings.

To grasp the precise character of what I have called More's estrangement, we might compare it with the mood evoked by Holbein's famous work *The Ambassadors*, painted in London two years before More's execution. Jean de Dinteville, seigneur de Polisy and Francis I's ambassador to the English court, and his friend Georges de Selve, shortly to be bishop of Lavaur, stand at either side of a two-shelved table. They are young, successful men, whose impressively wide-ranging interests and accomplishments are elegantly recorded by the objects scattered with careful casualness on the table: celestial and terrestrial globes, sundials, quadrants and other instruments of astronomy and geometry, a lute, a case of flutes, a German book of arithmetic, kept open by a square, and an open German hymn book, on whose pages may be seen part of Luther's translation of the 'Veni Creator Spiritus' and his 'Shortened Version of the Ten Commandments'. The hymn book suggests more, of course, than the interest in music that is elsewhere indicated; its presence in the portrait of two important Catholic statesmen may signal the French king's attempt, by cynically advancing the Lutheran cause in England, to further tension between Henry VIII and the emperor Charles V, or, alternatively, it may mark that moment in European history in which it still seemed possible to cultivated men of good will that the Catholic Church and the Reformers could meet on common ground and resolve their differences. If More had once harboured such a hope, the moment for him was long past.[6]

Dinteville and Selve are depicted in the context of the highest hopes and achievements of their age. The objects on the table between them, set off splendidly by the rich Turkish cloth and the exquisite mosaic pavement, represent a mastery of the Quadrivium, that portion of the Seven Liberal Arts comprising Music, Arithmetic, Geometry, and Astronomy, while a mastery of the Trivium – Grammar, Logic, and Rhetoric – is implied by the very profession of the two figures.[7] They are thus in possession of the instruments – both literal and symbolic – by which men bring the world into

focus, represent it in proper perspective. Indeed, in addition to their significance as emblems of the Liberal Arts, the objects on the table virtually
constitute a series of textbook illustrations for a manual on the art of
perspective.[8] The Renaissance invested this art with far more than technical
significance; for Neoplatonism in particular, the power to map, mirror, or
represent the world bore witness to the spark of the divine in man. As Ficino
writes, 'Since man has observed the order of the heavens, when they move,
whither they proceed and with what measures, and what they produce, who
could deny that man possesses as it were almost the same genius as the
Author of the heavens? And who could deny that man could somehow also
make the heavens, could he only obtain the instruments and the heavenly
material, since even now he makes them, though of a different material, but
still with a very similar order.'[9]

The terrestrial and celestial spheres, the sword and the book, the state and
the church, Protestantism and Catholicism, the mind as measurer of all
things and the mind as unifying force, the arts and the sciences, the power
of images and the power of words – all are conjoined then in Holbein's
painting and integrated in a design as intricate as the pavement. And yet
slashing across the pavement, intruding upon these complex harmonies and
disrupting them, is the extraordinary anamorphic representation of the
death's-head. Viewed frontally, the skull is an unreadable blur in the centre
foreground of the painting; only from the proper position at the side of the
painting is it suddenly revealed.[10]

The death's-head is most obviously a bravura display of Holbein's virtuosity, elsewhere manifested in his rendering of the complex network of surfaces on the geometrical instruments,[11] but it also bears a more integral
relation to the composition as a whole. In a major study of the painting
and its subjects, Mary F. S. Hervey observed that Dinteville's cap is adorned
by a small brooch on which is engraved a silver skull, and concluded that the
ambassador must have adopted the death's-head as his personal badge or
devise.[12] This theory is plausible, but it should not be made to suggest too
ornamental a function for elements that, in one's experience of the painting,
are far more disquieting. The skull as *devise* is at once a gesture of self-
adornment and a gesture of self-cancellation. Death may be reduced on
Dinteville's cap to a fashionable piece of jewellery, an enhancement of the
self, but this reduction seems as much mocked as confirmed by the large alien
presence that has intruded into this supremely civilised world of human
achievement.[13] The anamorphic death's-head draws to itself another discordant element in the painting: the broken string of the lute, an emblematic play
upon the very idea of discord.[14] Together these suggest a subtle but powerful
countercurrent to the forces of harmony, reconciliation, and confident intellectual achievement embodied elsewhere in the picture's objects and figures.
None of these antitypes is immediately visible – the ornamental skull and

broken string reveal themselves only to the closest scrutiny, only, that is, if one abandons the large, encompassing view of the painting and approaches the canvas with such myopic closeness that the whole gives way to a mass of individual details. To see the large death's-head requires a still more radical abandonment of what we take to be 'normal' vision; we must throw the entire painting out of perspective in order to bring into perspective what our usual mode of perception cannot comprehend.

Death's presence in Holbein's painting is at once more elusive and more disturbing than the conventional representations of death in late medieval art. In the familiar *transi* tombs, for example, the putrescent, worm-eaten corpse on the bottom level may be said to mock the figure above, dressed in robes of high office.[15] But the mockery affirms the viewer's understanding of the relation between life and death, indeed simplifies that understanding. In this sense, the *transi* tombs, for all their horrible imagery, are expressions of a certain kind of confidence: the confidence of a clear perception of things, a willingness to contemplate the inevitable future of the flesh without mystification or concealment. We can see the body both in its dignity and in its disgrace. In *The Ambassadors*, such clear, steady sight is impossible; death is affirmed not in its power to destroy the flesh, or as is familiar from late medieval literature, in its power to horrify and cause unbearable pain, but in its uncanny inaccessibility and absence. What is unseen or perceived as only a blur is far more disquieting than what may be faced boldly and directly, particularly when the limitations of vision are grasped as *structural*, the consequence more of the nature of perception than of the timidity of the perceiver.

The anamorphic skull casts a shadow on the elegant floor – the shadow of the shadow of death, Hervey neatly calls it – and thus demonstrates its substantiality, but the shadow falls in a different direction from those cast by the ambassadors or the objects on the table.[16] Its presence is thus at once affirmed and denied; if it can become visible to us, when we take up the appropriate position at the angle of the painting, it is manifestly not accessible to the figures in the painting (in the sense that the books and instruments *are* assumed to be accessible). To be sure, Dinteville has his silver death's-head brooch, but we feel far more the incommensurability between this ornament and the skull on the floor than their accord. And this incommensurability is confirmed by the fact that we must distort and, in essence, efface the figures in order to see the skull. That this effacement is moving – that it is felt as a kind of death – is a function of Holbein's mastery of those representational techniques that pay tribute to the world, that glorify the surfaces and textures of things, that celebrate man's relatedness to the objects of his making. For there is nothing in the painting that is not the product of human fashioning – no flower, no lapdog, no distant landscape glimpsed through an open window. The heavens and the earth are

present only as the objects of measurement and representation, the objects of
the globemaker's art. It is only when one takes leave of this world – quite
literally takes leave by walking away from the front of the canvas – that one
can see the single alien object, the skull. The skull expresses the death that the
viewer has, in effect, himself brought about by changing his perspective, by
withdrawing his gaze from the figures of the painting. For that gaze is, the
skull implies, reality-conferring; without it, the objects so lovingly represented in their seeming substantiality vanish. To move a few feet away
from the frontal contemplation of the painting is to efface everything within
it, to bring death into the world.

I have spoken of the skull as alien and inhuman, but to do so is itself an
ironic distortion, for it is the one object in the painting that is at once human
and completely *natural* in the sense of being untouched by artifice. There are,
to be sure, the faces and hands of Dinteville and Selve, and yet so strong is
the sense of *pose* as Holbein depicts them that they seem, of all the objects in
the painting, the most artificially crafted. They possess a calculated impene-
trability that suggests, in the hands, the carefully fashioned casualness counselled by Castiglione and, in the faces, the masking counselled by
Machiavelli.[17] The skull then is virtually unique in its inaccessibility to the
power of human shaping affirmed everywhere else in the painting; it is the
sole occupant of a category that nonetheless counterpoises all of the other
objects.

Yet paradoxically this skull, emblem of that which resists and outlasts
artifice, is treated aesthetically with the most spectacular display of the
painter's ingenuity and skill, just as paradoxically the death's-head, emblem
of the negation of human achievement, is worn by Dinteville as a fashionable
ornament, a badge of status akin to the Order of Saint Michael he wears
around his neck. The effect of these paradoxes is to resist any clear location
of reality in the painting, to question the very concept of locatable reality
upon which we conventionally rely in our mappings of the world, to subordinate the sign systems we so confidently use to a larger doubt. Holbein
fuses a radical questioning of the status of the world with a radical questioning of the status of art. For the painting insists, passionately and profoundly, on the representational power of art, its central role in man's
apprehension and control of reality, even as it insists, with uncanny persuas-
iveness, on the fictional character of that entire so-called reality and the art
that pretends to represent it. In the context of our normal relationship to a
painting – indeed in the context of the physical stance we conventionally
assume before any object we have chosen to perceive – the marginal position
is an eccentric flight of fancy, virtually a non-place, just as the skull exists in a
non-place in relation to all the other objects Holbein depicts. But to enter
this non-place is to alter everything in the painting and to render impossible
a simple return to normal vision. Of course, we do return and reassume that

perspective that seems to 'give' us the world, but we do so in a state of estrangement. In the same artistic moment, the moment of passage from the centre of the painting to the periphery, life is effaced by death, representation by artifice. The non-place that is the place of the skull has reached out and touched phenomenal reality, infecting it with its own alienation. Jean de Dinteville and Georges de Selve, so present to us in their almost hallucinatory substantiality, are revealed to be pigments on stretched canvas, an illusionist's trick. They who seem to be present before us exist nowhere, exist then in utopia.

For I justify this long discussion of *The Ambassadors* on the ground that it plunges us, with the sensuous immediacy and simultaneity that only a painting can achieve, into the full complexity of More's estrangement and the richness of his art. The world of Dinteville and Selve was More's world; with the image before us of the table laden with books and instruments, we may recall Roper's account of the period during which More was, in Elton's phrase, Henry VIII's 'pet humanist'. 'When he had done his own devotions', Roper writes, the king would send for More 'into his traverse, and there sometime in matters of astronomy, geometry, divinity, and such other faculties, and sometimes of his worldly affairs, to sit and confer with him. And other while would he in the night have him up into his leads, there for to consider with him the diversities, courses, motions, and operations of the stars and planets.'[18] The conclusion of the anecdote in Roper is wonderfully revealing: finding himself increasingly trapped by these flattering royal attentions, More 'began thereupon somewhat to dissemble his nature', in other words, to become a bore, until his company was no longer so much in demand. If this seems to lead us away from Holbein's ambassadors, presumably vying for the king's attention, it is only because More had in supreme measure those skills of rhetoric and learning that a Dinteville would have assiduously cultivated.

It is not, however, the French humanists whom More most resembles but the genius who painted them (and indeed we may speculate that the magnificent achievement of Holbein's portraits of More and his family owes something to the special bond of understanding that we are trying to sketch here). If More's interests embraced astronomy, music, rhetoric, geometry, geography, and arithmetic, he was also profoundly capable of withdrawing from these interests, altering his perspective in such a way as to unsettle any underlying assumptions upon which all these methods of ordering and measuring the world were based. More important still, this engagement and detachment do not occupy two separate, successive moments in More's career – an early involvement in the world, followed by disillusionment and withdrawal, for example, or even a more complex round of alternating states – but rather are closely bound up with each other throughout his life, while in his greatest works, they are fused with the intensity and power we have encountered in the Holbein painting. This is above all true, of course, of *Utopia*, whose subtle displacements, distortions, and shifts of perspective are the closest equivalent in Renaissance prose to the anamorphic virtuosity of Holbein's art. Like *The Ambassadors*, *Utopia* presents two distinct worlds that occupy the same textual space while insisting upon the impossibility of their doing so. We can neither separate them entirely nor bring them into accord, so that the intellectual gratification of radical discontinuity is as impossible to achieve as the pleasure of wholly integrated form. We are constantly tantalised by the resemblances between England and Utopia – analogous to Dinteville's death's-head brooch in relation to the skull – and as constantly frustrated by the abyss that divides them; and no sooner do we confidently take the measure of the abyss than we perceive a new element that seems to establish the unmistakable link between them. This is more than a case of 'like in some ways, unlike in others', as if we had two distinct objects that we could hold up to each other and compare, for the two worlds in *Utopia* occupy the same space and are in an essentially unstable relation-ship to each other. The division of the work into two books is, in this regard, like one of More's straight-faced jokes, for it invites us to establish a simple order of contrast that the work frustrates: Utopia and its analogues inhabit the world of book I just as England inhabits the world of book II. Similarly, the persona More and Hythlodaeus sit in the same garden and converse with each other, but as in Holbein's painting, they cast shadows in different directions and are, in crucial respects, necessarily blind to each other.

This disquieting internal rupture – this sense within the general frame of the work of incompatible perspectives between which the reader restlessly moves – is mirrored at virtually every level of the text, from its largest units of design to its smallest verbal details. Elizabeth McCutcheon has recently called attention to the significance of the latter in a fine discussion of More's extraordinarily frequent use of litotes, a rhetorical figure 'in which a thing is affirmed by stating the negative of its opposite'.[19] More's use of the figure, she writes, bespeaks 'a tendency to see more than one side to a question'; more important, for our purposes, it compels a mental movement, a psycho-logical passage from one point to another and back again.[20] This restless shifting of perspective is, I would suggest, the close equivalent at the verbal level to the visual technique of anamorphosis, whose etymology itself sug-gests a back-and-forth movement, a constant forming and re-forming.

It would obviously take us too long, even were it in our power, to explicate in detail all of *Utopia*'s anamorphic techniques, but, beyond litotes, we may point to the network of linkages and contradictions worked out with man-darin complexity by Louis Marin in his recent *Utopiques*. Marin demon-strates, with at least partial success, that there are in the smooth surface of Utopian life a series of half-hidden ruptures, ruptures betrayed by subtle inconsistencies and contradictions in topography, economic exchange, the exercise of power, concepts of criminality, and the uses of violence. These ruptures, according to Marin, reveal the presence in the work of the half-effaced signs of its own production, the presence of those sociohistorical forces to which Utopia owes its existence and which it is designed to render invisible. In the midst of Utopian description – timeless, immobile, synchronic, maplike – there survive *traces* of narrative that mark in the finished product the hidden processes by which it was produced. These brief, fragmentary narrative enclaves destroy the structural integrity of the description, tear the canvas, writes Marin, on which the best government is depicted.[21] But where Marin would speak of a canvas torn, I would speak, at least in most of the instances he analyses, of a subtle anamorphic art that constantly questions its own status and the status of the world it pretends to represent. That is, Marin seems to underestimate More's self-consciousness, a self-consciousness for once the match of its Gallic counterparts. If there exist highly significant 'blind spots' in *Utopia* – for example, an urban design that does not seem to allow for the centralised exercise of power that the system nevertheless calls for – they exist like the great, central blind spot in Holbein's *Ambassadors*: as the object of the artist's profound, playful attention.

This playfulness – so easily acknowledged and ignored – deserves special emphasis, for it occupies a central role in both the painting and the book. The arts of mapmaking, calculation, and measurement that figure so prominently in *The Ambassadors* and *Utopia* have important practical functions in everyday life, but they are present here as recreation, the elegant play of distinguished and serious men. This play is not conceived by humanists as an escape from the serious, but as a mode of civility, an enhancement of specifically human powers. As such, the globes and compasses, along with the lute and flutes, sit without contradiction next to the book of merchant's arithmetic, on the one hand, and the book of divine worship, on the other, just as the mock alphabet and maps of *Utopia* are bound up – literally and figuratively – with a searching inquiry into the sources of human misery and the possibilities of human government. The distorted skull in Holbein's painting, for all the grimness of its imagery, is itself an invitation to the viewer to play, while the reader of *Utopia* is invited to enter a carefully demarcated playground that possesses nonetheless a riddling relation to the world outside.[22] That the playfulness in *The Ambassadors* focuses on a skull suggests that the anamorphic technique may derive in part at least from medieval methods of meditation, particularly the concentration upon an object – frequently the death's-head – that enables one to lose the world, to perceive the vanity of human life and the illusory quality of reality.[23] One might argue that Holbein's painting signals the *decay* of such methods, a loss of intensity that can only be partially recuperated through illusionist tricks, but if so, one must conclude that this decay released a magnificent aesthetic byproduct. And while *Utopia* too may owe something to meditative technique, detached from its original purpose, one would be hard pressed from More's works to conclude that the technique was in decay.

In almost all his writings, More returns again and again to the unsettling of man's sense of reality, the questioning of his instruments of measurement and representation, the demonstration of blind spots in his field of vision. In the *Dialogue of Comfort*, Antony challenges Vincent to prove that he is awake and not merely dreaming that he is awake, or dreaming that he has been challenged to prove his wakefulness, or dreaming that he has responded to this challenge by moving his limbs or talking rationally, or dreaming that he is merrily describing such a dream to his friends, or dreaming that he has finally appealed beyond body and words to the unshakable conviction in his soul that he is awake. None of Vincent's responses does anything to arrest the vertiginous fall into an infinite regress of self-mirroring dreams; as with similar games played by Nicholas of Cusa, the mind is driven at once to an acknowledgement of the conjectural status of all its operations and to a profession of faith.[24] In these arguments, Antony says, we must appeal finally to 'the Scripture of God' and 'the common faith of Christ's Catholic Church'.[25] This faith is not, it should be noted, an *answer* to the speculations about sleep and waking; rather it may more fairly be said to license those speculations, to transform into play thoughts that might otherwise lead, as More implies, to suicide or heresy.

We may recall at this point an object in Holbein's painting that until now we barely noted: the crucifix only half visible at the extreme edge of the curtain. This sign is not impervious to effacement – after all, it is turned into a blur, along with everything else, when the skull is brought into focus – yet it may be said to possess a certain cultic imperviousness to the corrosive effects of anamorphosis. In this sense, the marginal presence of the crucifix – symbol of life redeemed from death – sanctions the marginal presence of the skull – emblem of death lurking beneath life. Similarly, Antony's faith is theoretically susceptible to the charge of being a dream, but More refuses to carry the argument that far, for it is precisely faith that invites the speculation even as it closes off the infinite regress. But is there any guarantee of this imperviousness to anamorphic subversion? Not, I think, within the painting or the text themselves: any assurance must be imposed from without, by an individual or by an interpretive community with an interest in establishing a fixed point beyond the ceaseless oscillation of irreconcilable perspectives. Holbein's painting seems deliberately ambiguous about the ultimate origin of this assurance: both the Catholic Church and Lutheran faith are invoked, and we might note that his earlier woodcut series on the Dance of Death was printed, within the space of a few years, by both Catholic and Protestant printers in Lyons.[26] More's *Dialogue of Comfort*, by contrast, is not at all ambiguous: Antony's assurance rests not upon the feeling faith of the individual, but upon the power exercised jointly by the sacred text and by the institution that controls interpretation of that text. The daring of *Utopia* is to be gauged by the extreme marginality of the Scripture of God and the common faith of Christ's Catholic Church: in defence of Utopian principles, Hythlodaeus several times invokes the 'doctrine' and 'authority' of Christ, but the institutional implications of this authority are unspoken. Like Holbein, More had partially pulled the curtain in front of the crucifix.[27]

What unites *Utopia* – enigmatic in its relation to the ultimate authority of the Church – and the *Dialogue of Comfort* – unambiguously committed to that authority – is More's lifelong interest in the ironies that arise from man's confident belief in illusions. The dreamer who insists that he is awake is only one of a network of such ironies that we may trace all the way back to the pageant verses More composed in his youth. 'Old and young, man and woman, rich and poor, prince and page', he writes characteristically in the unfinished *Four Last Things* (1522), 'all the while we live in this world, we be but prisoners, and within a sure prison, out of which there can no man escape', but few of us have ever glimpsed the walls, and we strut about as though we were free. Or again, 'all our whole life is but a sickness never curable, but as one uncurable canker, with continual swaddling and plastering, botched up to live as long as we may, and in conclusion undoubtedly to die of the same sickness, and though there never came other'[28] – but few of us understand our condition, and we strut about as though we were in health.

8

Facing History, or the Anxiety of Reading: Holbein's *The Ambassadors* according to Greenblatt and Lyotard

Jürgen Pieters

'One does not read, one does not hear a painting.'
  Jean-François Lyotard, *Discours, Figure* (Lyotard, 1971: 10)[1]

I

Tradition has it that the last painting made by Holbein before his first departure from Basel to England in 1526 was so realistic that its buyer tried to brush away the small fly which the painter had meticulously represented in one of its lower corners (Baltrušaitis, 1977, p. 99). Whether or not the story is historically sound is of lesser importance than the symbolical, or even allegorical, meaning we have been reading into it over the past centuries. While to Holbein's contemporaries the anecdote illustrated the artist's exceptional craftsmanship, its meaning for late-twentieth-century theoreticians of art will be wholly different. To the latter, the story is taken as a symbolic explanation of the fact that certain images, in a manner that is both immediate and unproblematically causal, call up certain thoughts and words. The image becomes the thought, it becomes the words that it provoked in the first place.

The thoughts which Holbein's fly conjures up are quite straightforward ones: whenever we see a fly on a painting – especially on the sort of paintings made in Holbein's day – there should be no doubt as to the ontological status of the animal. Flies on paintings are real flies, not represented flies. Flies do not belong on paintings, they ruin the aesthetic experience which paintings are supposed to produce. Therefore, they should be driven away. The words and thoughts that will occupy me in the present article, are radically different from the ones described above – at least, so they seem at first sight.

In the course of this essay, I will, however, remain in the company of Holbein and his work. The painting that will be central to my investigation is Holbein's justly famous *The Ambassadors*, now to be seen at the end of room 4 in London's National Gallery.[2] Holbein painted *The Ambassadors* in 1533, one year after he had finally settled in England and some three years before he was appointed court-painter to Henry VIII. It is obvious that *The Ambassadors* is set in the same regal *milieux* to which Holbein was soon to become professionally affiliated. The figures represented on the portrait are two ambassadors visiting Henry's court: they are, to the left, Jean de Dinteville (1504–1565), Seigneur de Polisy, and, to the right, Georges de Selve (1509–1542), later to become Bishop of Lavaur. The former had been sent to Henry's court by the French king François I toward the end of 1532, not only in order to attend Henry's imminent marriage to Anne Boleyn and the subsequent crowning of England's new queen, but also in order to tighten the bonds between the two courts in their joint struggles against the Emperor Charles V. In May 1533, de Dinteville received the company of de Selve.

Even though there is still some quarrel among commentators about the exact date on which the painting was finished,[3] there can be no doubt as to the year of its making. Apart from a number of letters and reports which allow us to reconstruct the major events and dates of de Dinteville's mission, there are two further signals on the painting itself. First, there is the date beneath the artist's signature in the lower left corner; second, the ages of both ambassadors are subtly incorporated in the painting: that of de Dinteville (29) is inscribed on his dagger; that of de Selve (24) can be seen on the book supporting his right arm.

The year of Holbein's painting is a crucial one, both in the history of Henry's court and, by extension, in that of sixteenth-century Europe. In January 1533, Henry secretly married Anne Boleyn, at that time already pregnant with the later Queen Elizabeth;[4] four months later, he divorced Catharine of Aragon without the necessary papal consent. Also in 1533, Thomas Cromwell succeeded Sir Thomas More as the King's secretary and soon set to work in order to draw up the set of regulations that in 1534 would declare Henry head of the Anglican Church. The consequences of this bill, the famous 'Act of Supremacy', were soon to be felt all over Europe.

Holbein's painting not only gives us a number of clues as to the *time* of its production, it also hints at *the place* where it was made. The mosaic of Holbein's masterpiece turns out to be an almost exact copy of the floor in the sanctuary of Westmister Abbey, where Anne Boleyn was crowned on 1 June 1533. The original design of the floor, dating from the thirteenth century, may be considered a symbolical representation of the late medieval world-view. As such, Susan Foister points out (in Foister, Roy and Wyld, 1997, p. 43), it fits well into the general framework of Holbein's painting, with its various symbolical references to contemporary macro- and micro-cosmic theories.[5]

The thoughts produced by the details just listed are, ironically, of a different sort from those conjured up by the little fly with which we began our *exposé*. While at first sight the painted insect seemed to be an obstacle to a coherent interpretation of the work of art of which, eventually, it had to be considered a part, the presence of a great number of straightforwardly referential elements in the ambassadorial portrait turns out to be a precondition for an equally coherent interpretation of the painting. Taken together, they build up a chronological and topographical framework that enables us to read the painting in a satisfactory way. They function as that which Roland Barthes has called the 'studium' of a photograph, the ensemble of data that not only allow the spectator to position him- or herself in a culturally acceptable manner *vis-à-vis* the artefact (Barthes, 1995, p. 1126), but that also serve as the basis of his/her (dis)approval at what (s)he sees. As such, the 'referential' elements in Holbein's painting point the spectator to other pictorial details that are, by extension, also read in terms of their referentiality. Not only do these new elements seem to complete the painting's 'studium', they also confirm what earlier interpretive options the spectator had followed. To these can be said to belong the medallion of the Order of St Michael worn by de Dinteville, the books on the lower shelf of the table in between the two portrayed characters, and several instruments, both musical and scientific ones.[6] All the latter refer without exception to the *quadrivium* of the *artes liberales* (mathematics, geometry, astronomy, and music), while the characters portrayed can be taken to personify the 'trivial' *artes* of rhetoric, grammar and dialectic. As such, the painting builds up, metonymically rather than metaphorically, the time in which it was produced and from which it springs. To be sure, it was a time of religious conflicts, but it was also a time in which scientific and geographical discoveries abounded.[7] It is self-evident that the representation of this potently energetic milieu is in a way a mark of honour to the king himself.

II

What is important about these details for my exposition is not so much *what* they represent as the fact that their presence confirms both our initial reading of the painting and the historicist axioma on which this reading rests. If we want to gain an accurate understanding of this kind of painting, so the theory goes, we will need to understand the historical context out of which it grew and of which it is a manifestation. The more information we can get about this context, the deeper our understanding of its product(s) will be. There are, of course, a number of dangers inherent to this approach. One of these is that we risk taking the artefact to be nothing more than a historical document which, unproblematically and transparently, gives access to the times from which it stems. Apart from the question whether our idea of 'the times from which it stems' is not in itself already the product of the paintings by Holbein and others, it is hardly illusory to imagine that an analysis like the one above may exclude from its reading pictorial details that do not fit in the interpretation initially construed on the basis of the painting's 'studium'.

In and of itself, *The Ambassadors* forms an apt warning against the kind of naïve historicism exemplified in the previous section of this article, a reading-method which treats (artistic) signs in terms of their presupposed one-on-one relationship to phenomena in the outside, historical world. The exact locus of this warning is the strange stain in the lower front area of Holbein's portrait, beginning at the feet of de Dinteville and rising diagonally to the feet of his companion. In Barthes' terminology we could label this stain the 'punctum' of Holbein's painting. Barthes' description of the 'punctum' as a disorderly phenomenon that jumps out of a photograph and wounds the spectator in the face (Barthes, 1995, p. 1126), is an accurate one. Barthes' metaphor becomes literalised in the stain which jumps out of Holbein's painting: the stain is an anamorphotic skull that reveals its true and painful reality only to the spectator who does not assume the rightful position from which to contemplate paintings such as this one – right (i.e. centrally) in front of it and from a certain distance – but who looks at it from a specific angle, in this case to the lower right side of the painting. From that angle, the stain shows itself for what it is: the representation of a regular human skull.

At first sight, Holbein's exercise in anamorphosis can be taken to function as any other skull on late medieval and early-modern *vanitas*-paintings. Thus, death's presence puts into perspective (quite literally) the magnitude of human rationality suggested elsewhere on the painting. Both scientific and geographic discoveries, human prowess and all material riches are returned to their true proportions. In the face of death, they become null and void. In the case of *The Ambassadors*, though, it would seem that there is more at stake. Not only does the painting contain a number of 'normal' *mementi mori*,[8] its 'punctum' is also situated on a different optical plane from that of the painting's regular representations. Seen from that plane, the latter become as fuzzy as the anamorphotic skull is from the painting's normal perspective. In this way, Holbein's painting is not only a comment on the theories of perspective usually associated with the advent of the Renaissance,[9] in its double, mutually exclusive perspectivism, it also throws the *vanitas*-motif back on the acts of looking and reading themselves. The very moment that we acknowledge the painting's thematisation of the *memento mori*, we are faced with the astounding possibility of the ultimate impossibility of capturing and defining what it is exactly that we see; we are faced, in other words, with what J. Hillis Miller has called the 'possibility of the impossibility of unveiling' (Miller, 1991, p. 114).

III

Lately, we have become aware of the problematics that accompany any historicist practice. This is in no small measure thanks to Stephen Greenblatt's New Historicist critique on the limitations of traditional ('Old') historical approaches, a critique which is exemplified in his reading of *The Ambassadors* in *Renaissance Self-Fashioning* (Greenblatt, 1980, pp. 17ff., cf. below). Even though it is not easy to explain briefly what the crucial difference between the Old and the New Historicism really comes down to, any attempt to do so may profit from Greenblatt's assertion that his work grew from a desire 'to speak with the dead'. 'This desire', Greenblatt goes on to write,

> is a familiar, if unvoiced, motive in literary studies, a motive organised, professionalised, buried beneath thick layers of bureaucratic decorum: literature professors are salaried, middle-class shamans. If I never believed that the dead could hear me, and if I knew that the dead could not speak, I was nonetheless certain that I could re-create a conversation with them. Even when I came to understand that in my most intense moments of straining to listen all I could hear was my own voice, even then I did not abandon my desire. It was true that I could hear only my own voice, but my own voice was the voice of the dead, for the dead had contrived to leave textual traces of themselves, and those traces make themselves heard in the voices of the living. (Greenblatt 1988, p. 1)

In itself, Greenblatt's assertion does not seem to lead to a rigid distinction between any two varieties of historicist criticism. Theoretically speaking, all historicist practice ought to result from a desire to speak with the past. What *is* distinctive for the New Historicism, however, is not only that it claims to be aware of the workings of this desire, but also that it incorporates and thematises this awareness. While traditional historicists left the reader with the impression that they were somehow located beyond history, the New Historicists are aware of their own historicity and of the historicity of their hermeneutic desires.[10] Their attention is not drawn by the panoramic overviews (re)presented by the likes of Tillyard and Dover Wilson; it is, rather, fixed on what several of the philosophers with whom Greenblatt likes to affiliate himself (Foucault, de Certeau, Lyotard, ...) have called 'the historical event'. What their respective philosophies aim at is not the singular historical fact which traditional historicists were confident they could procure. The historical event as seen by poststructuralist philosophers has more to do with what Lyotard has termed the 'quod' rather than the 'quid' of historical reality, the fact that things happened rather than what it was that happened, and with the insurpassable distance between that extra-textual 'quod' and its discursive counterparts.[11] A hermeneutic approach that sets itself the task of recovering the event of history, Lyotard writes, takes things as they come. It does not force them into the framework it wants history to adopt. Neither does it believe in the possibility of simply extracting facts from the sources in which they are recounted.

While many of the critical and epistemological principles underlying the philosophy of Lyotard and others are taken for granted these days, it is not always clear whether the full implications arising from such an approach are wholly accepted. The clearest analysis of these, I believe, is to be found in the works of Dominick LaCapra. In several of his writings, LaCapra has pointed out the historigraphical paradox which seems to inform the literary analyses of Greenblatt's New Historicism. This paradox can be summarised as follows: on the one hand, there is the awareness 'that history [has to] be redescribed as a discourse that is fundamentally rhetorical, and that representing the past takes place through the creation of powerful, persuasive images which can be best understood as created objects, models, metaphors, or proposals about reality' (Hans Kellner in Ankersmit and Kellner, 1995, p. 2); on the other hand, there is the permanent urge – not in spite of, but through this awareness – to capture the past in its plenitude and thus to get a grip on what Greenblatt himself has called the text's 'full situation' (Greenblatt, 1982, p. 3).

In the introductory chapter to his *History and Criticism*, LaCapra argues that it is the foremost task of the late-twentieth-century historian to find the exact balance between the two sides of this paradox. 'How to confront the limitations of a documentary model [of historiography, JP] without simply converting all history into metahistory or denying the role of referential uses of language in the past and in the historian's account of it is a complicated issue', LaCapra writes, 'but one the historian is increasingly forced to face' (LaCapra, 1985, p. 21). LaCapra urges the historian to follow what he terms a 'dialogical' approach to history. The idea implies not only an awareness of the fact that, in the historiographical praxis, 'the historian enters into a "conversational" exchange with the past and with other inquirers seeking an understanding of it', but also an awareness of the fundamental *Unheimlichkeit* of this dialogue with the dead, who are, after all, pieced together 'through their textualised remainders' (LaCapra, 1985, p. 36).

LaCapra's image of history-writing as a dialogue with the dead derives to some extent from a well-known passage in a letter written by Machiavelli to Francesco Vettori. Reporting on his daily habit of withdrawing to his study and of setting up a conversation with the people whom he reads about in his books, Machiavelli writes the following:

> On the coming of evening, I return to my house and enter my study; and at the door I take off my every-day clothes, covered with mud and dust, and I put on garments regal and courtly; and, thus reclothed appropriately, I enter the ancient courts of ancient men, where, being lovingly received by them, I feed on that food that alone is mine and for which I was born, where I am not ashamed to speak with them and to ask them the reason of their actions; and they, out of their humanity, answer me; and for four hours of time I feel no boredom, I forget every trouble, I do not fear poverty, death does not terrify me; I am completely transferred into them. (quoted in LaCapra, 1985, p. 15)

The attractiveness of this passage lies in its last sentence, in which LaCapra, somewhat anachronistically of course, finds a reference to Freud's concept of 'transference'. In Freud, so LaCapra argues, the notion refers to the mechanism of 'repetition-displacement of the past into the present' (LaCapra, 1985, p. 72) as it occurs in psychoanalytical sessions. As such, he explains in his essay on 'History and Psychoanalysis', the notion is an interesting one to explain the relationship between the past *wie es gewesen* and the interpretive representations of it in historical discourse (LaCapra, 1989, p. 33). While a documentary approach to historical sources led to the conclusion that the relationship between text and context was one-on-one, a transferential approach will not only allow us to see texts as a displaced and hence differential repetition of an extra-textual reality, it will also call to attention the rhetorical nature of source-materials.

The advantages of such a transferential dialogism to contemporary theories of historiography are in a way similar to those outlined by Freud in his analysis of the use of the concept in early-twentieth-century theories of psychoanalysis. In Freud's opinion the method of transference was primarily meant to serve as a warning against forms of facile *Hineininterpretierung* in the interpretation of patients' dreams. Transferred onto the domain of historiography, the notion turns out to be instrumental in recurrent debates on the alleged objectivity of certain historical (re)constructions. Rather than ridiculing the significance of such debates, it revalorises the very question of historical objectivity by redefining it. From a transferential point of view, objectivity is no longer seen in Ranke's terms of the *wie es eigentlich gewesen*, but rather as '[the] injunction to face facts that may prove embarrassing for the theses one would like to propound or the patterns one is striving to elicit' (LaCapra, 1989, p. 37). LaCapra's call to objectivity does not, in other words, imply a return to 'the simple idea of recounting the past purely in its own terms and for its own sake'; rather, it demands on behalf of the historian some sort of ' "suspended" or "poised" attention [that] would jeopardise the overriding desire [. . .] that leads the historian to "find order in chaos" ' (LaCapra, 1989, p. 39).

IV

The way in which LaCapra voices his appeal for a transferential approach to the remnants of the past, reminds us in more than one way of Greenblatt's *dictum* that literary texts from the past are best treated in terms of a dialogue with the dead. Furthermore, the theory of transference involves a Lyotardian respect for and search of the 'eventness' of history. In what follows, I hope to furnish the missing link between both analogies. What will result from the ensuing confrontation between Greenblatt and Lyotard, is, ironically, a critique of Greenblatt's New Historicism from within the perspective of Lyotard's work. The concrete arena for this confrontation is Holbein's portrayal of the human skull in *The Ambassadors*, as 'read' by Greenblatt in *Renaissance Self-Fashioning* and by Lyotard in *Discours, Figure* (Lyotard, 1971).

Holbein's painting has an important role to play in *Renaissance Self-Fashioning*. Not only is the work reproduced on the front cover of Greenblatt's book, it also features prominently in the first of the six chapters that make up its core. In that chapter, Greenblatt compares Holbein's painting to Thomas More's *Utopia,* the latter being the focal point of the largest section of the chapter. Insisting as they do 'with uncanny pervasiveness, on the fictional character of [the] entire so-called reality and the art that pretends to represent it', both works are, according to Greenblatt, supreme indications of 'the representational power of art, its central role in man's apprehension and control of reality' (Greenblatt, 1980, p. 21). Accordingly, Greenblatt believes that Holbein's painting enables us better to understand what in the initial section of his essay he described as 'More's estrangement' (Greenblatt, 1980, p. 17), the author's ambivalent feeling that on the one hand he did not belong to the social and political milieu in which he had to function, while on the other he felt strangely attracted to the theatricalities of power surrounding him (see Greenblatt, 1980, p. 12). The spirit in which More perceived reality – a spirit to be found in all of his works, Greenblatt contends – is a mixture of 'ambition, ironic amusement, curiosity, and revulsion' (Greenblatt, 1980, p. 13). It not only reveals More's fundamental estrangement from the society in which he lived, but even more so his estrangement from his inner self, a self that turns out to be an empty void, constantly yearning to be filled.

The question whether Holbein's character was marked by a similar problematic is an interesting one, yet it will have to be left outside the scope of this essay.[12] What concerns me here, is the way in which Greenblatt deals with the anamorphotic 'punctum' of Holbein's painting. I want to argue that in his interpretation of this crucial detail, Greenblatt turns out to be an heir of the traditional historicism he has been so adamant to differentiate his own practice from. Greenblatt's analysis of the painting follows the logic of most interpretations of *The Ambassadors*, in that the author insists upon the fact that the painting's harmonious construction – thematised, as we have seen, by the array of objects in the centre of the work – is undermined in its 'punctum', by what Greenblatt ironically describes as an 'unreadable blur'. '[S]lashing across the pavement', he writes, 'intruding upon these complex harmonies and disrupting them, is the extraordinary anamorphic representation of [a] death's head.' The irony of the passage is due to the fact that Greenblatt in one and the same logical movement affirms and denies the unreadability of what has to remain indefinitely other. First the stain is 'unreadable', next it's a 'death's head'. At least, that's what it is to the reader who voluntarily abandons her/his position in front of the painting, assuming the position that reveals the 'true nature' of what at first seemed to be a mere stain. As I have noted before, this new perspective points the reader to a number of other disharmonious features, all of which counterbalance the 'forces of harmony, reconciliation, and confident intellectual achievement embodied elsewhere in the picture's objects and figures' (Greenblatt, 1980, pp. 18–19). Yet, despite Greenblatt's belief that these new forces of disharmony involve an intensification of the 'elusive' and 'disturbing' presence of death in Holbein's painting, his immediate *Gleichschaltung* of the 'unreadable blur' and the 'death's head' results in a reduction of whatever it is both the 'blur' and the 'death's head' are supposed to represent. In other words, by giving death the recognisable contours of a death's head, it is given a face and, hence, a meaning which does not really differ from that which it is given in the sort of traditional, late-medieval *vanitas*-paintings against which Holbein is considered to react. While Greenblatt emphatically argues that Holbein disrupts the 'confidence of a clear perception of things' that characterised these traditional paintings,[13] his analysis of the difference which Holbein's work clearly marks shows that he cannot escape from the oppositional framework set up by the very tradition from which Holbein sought to diverge. Death is personified, it is given a face and a meaning, a meaning that finds its foundation in that which death is not, i.e. life. Moreover, Greenblatt seems to suggest repeatedly that the perspective from the side, which 'reveals' the essence of the skull beyond its anamorphotic appearance, is the privileged vantage-point from which the painting – and hence death itself, that which was earlier said to be forever 'inaccessib[le] and absen[t]' – can best be seen and understood. '[I]f it [the skull, but also death, whose shadow is thrown by the skull upon this painting, JP] can become visible to us, when we take up the appropriate position at the angle of the painting', Greenblatt writes, 'it is manifestly not accessible to the figures in the painting' (Greenblatt, 1980, p. 19, emphasis added). The remark is crudely ironic, since the crux of Holbein's work of art is of course the idea that death can never be accessible, least of all in our hackneyed representations of it. There is, simply, no unitary perspective from which to understand life and death simultaneously. The relationship is one of mutual exclusion and infinite differentiation; it cannot be grasped in the dialectics of opposition from which Greenblatt does not seem able to escape.

V

The question remains, of course, whether there *is* any other way to understand Holbein's skull. The terms in which I have voiced my critique of Greenblatt already point in the direction of the work of Lyotard. Following Bill Readings, I suggest that the greatest accomplishment of Lyotard is to be found in his critique of Saussurean semiotics: according to Lyotard each and every discursive order contains a self-differentiating presence that undermines its workings in the most resolute way possible (Readings, 1991, p. 4; see Lyotard, 1971, p. 75). Lyotard's master thesis, *Discours, Figure*, not only contains an elaborate analysis of this critique, its title also provides Lyotard with a name for the game: 'the figure'. Even though the concept is used in several different ways throughout the book, the first definition which Lyotard gives provides us with a clear idea of the author's purposes. In the introductory notes, the 'figure' is described as 'a spatial manifestation which the linguistic space cannot incorporate without being undermined, something exterior, which it cannot internalise in terms of *signification*' (Lyotard, 1971, p. 13, emphasis his).[14] This definition provides a clue as to Lyotard's critique of Saussurean linguistics. Its basis is Lyotard's belief that there is a contradiction at stake in Saussure's theory of the linguistic sign: according to Lyotard, Saussure on the one hand points out that the linguistic sign derives its function and its value from the oppositional position it assumes in the system of the langue – in other words, 'signification' and 'value' become one – while on the other hand, in several instances in the *Cours de Linguistique Générale* both concepts are radically opposed, in terms of 'vertical versus horizontal' and 'depth versus surface' (Lyotard, 1971, p. 100). Thus, Lyotard argues, Saussure not only misrecognises the crucial notion of 'désignation', he also structures his theory of the linguistic sign in a way that no longer allows for a differentiation between signified and *designatum*. The latter is, as it were, taken in under the umbrella of the former, and language no longer has to concern itself with whatever it is that it refers to (Lyotard, 1971, p. 100).[15]

In Lyotard's opinion, meaning is not merely a function of the structural position taken up by a sign in the linguistic system, it is as much dependent on the situation in which the sign is used. To Lyotard, this is made perfectly clear in the type of words which Emile Benvéniste called 'des indicateurs'. In Lyotard's definition, these words 'await the "content" of their concretisation in a discursive act [and in doing so] open up language to an experience which it cannot store of and by itself, since the experience belongs to the order of the "hic et nunc"' (Lyotard, 1971, p. 39). What is crucial about the linguistic indicator, Lyotard argues further, is that its 'signification (Sinn)' is one with its 'désignation (Bedeutung)': 'what it wants to say is that about which it talks and we cannot give its "signified" independently of its "designatum"' (Lyotard, 1971, p. 39). If only for this reason, deictic words are a perfect counterbalance for what Lyotard calls the 'illusion of the signified', an illusion which has been central to Western thought for centuries and which results, according to Lyotard, from 'some sort of 90-degrees rotation-act which collapses the designatum onto the signified and confounds the latter with the object it stands for' (Lyotard, 1971, p. 100).

In the words of Geoffrey Bennington, Lyotard's analysis of deixis makes clear that the surface of the linguistic system – what Lyotard would call its 'textual plane' – hides the depths of the sensory plane (Bennington, 1988, p. 63). In his wonderful study of Lyotard's work, Bennington argues that the rigorous analysis of the problematics of deixis in *Discours, Figure* is, in fact, the first theoretical anchorage of the further analysis of the concept of the 'figure' (Bennington, 1988, p. 64).[16] At the same time, however, Bennington warns students of Lyotard not to take the latter's critique of Saussure as a mere attempt to re-introduce naïve notions of referentiality in linguistic theory, nor as a simple means of arguing for the importance of bodily perception in the sensory field or the implications of such perceptions on our usage of language. *Discours, Figure* is as much a critique of Merleau-Ponty's phenomenology as it is of Saussure's work (see Lyotard, 1971, p. 69–70). In the same way as he asserted that the seeming stability of the 'textual plane' is undermined by the heterogeneous phenomenological depth which it inherently contains but which it forever tries to hide, Lyotard will argue that the 'sensory plane' contains an incommensurable textual excess which Merleau-Ponty wants to exclude from his phenomenological approach, yet without which the field of perception cannot function.

Surely, it will come as no surprise that this is where the notion of the 'figure' receives its full force. As Bennington puts it, the concept entails a simultaneous 'disruption' of the phenomenological space and of the 'at-homeness of the body in the world' (Bennington, 1988, pp. 70–1).[17] It will be clear why anamorphotic representations such as Holbein's are important to Lyotard's theory. Evidently, the technique is a perfect example of his thesis that two-dimensional representational planes – texts, paintings, ... – always contain different, heterogeneous and incommensurable planes of representation, whose representations can in no way be considered part of the workings of another and whose mutual differences cannot be caught in a unitary framework. Holbein's skull is in a way similar to Mallarmé's typographical experiments in 'Un coup de dés': both are exemplary of the way in which a material signifier, in its very figurality, resists the illusion as though the linguistic sign were a transparent surface that points the reader/spectator unproblematically and directly to what it is the sign can be taken to stand for. In the same way that a letter, to use the example taken by Lyotard, contains a plastic line that turns it into more than a repeatable and recognisable (oppositional) sign, Holbein's signifier can be interpreted in terms of the evidence it provides of the ineradicable presence of the other of representation in representation (Lyotard, 1971, pp. 211 ff.; see also Readings, 1991, p. 20 and Dews, 1984). In other words, in his privileging of the figural Lyotard proves to be aware of the fact that his critique of discursive monopolies can only be made in the medium of the discursive. The solution which Lyotard provides for this problem, one could say, is to act as if there is no problem at all: the 'figure' shows itself *in* the discursive, since language can never destroy the other of which it attempts to be, from a distance, the transparent double. If we want to become fully aware of this, Lyotard argues in his brief analysis of Holbein's painting, it suffices to return the ninety-degrees-rotation mentioned earlier to our perception of Holbein's work. To make this rotation, Lyotard claims, is not only 'an ontological act which inverses the relationship between that which is visible and that which is invisible, between the signifier and that which is represented', it also results in a different attitude toward what we see and toward the nature of what we see. 'When we look the painting right in the face', Lyotard writes,

> our desire to inhabit the scene which it represents, leads us to mistake the screen for what it is, since we break through it as if it were a transparent window which offers us a scene that we can join, something calm, something powerful. If, on the other hand, we take an oblique look at the painting [...] the scene falls apart and the unexpected seal of the earlier view (that was a vision) begins to talk. The painted canvas does not fade away into representation; rather, the representation explodes, it dissolves into enigmatic and senseless traces, drawing lines across the canvas. It is hardly a metaphor, therefore, to say that the death's head *speaks*. (Lyotard, 1971, p. 377, emphasis his)

VI

While the last quotation may serve as an immediate point-of-return to Greenblatt's desire to have the dead speak, its directness is, perhaps, not of the exact nature we would want it to be. In Lyotard's analysis of Holbein's painting the death's head is, of course, speaking; Lyotard says so himself. Yet, while at first sight this could lead us to the conclusion that the projects of both Lyotard and Greenblatt run along similar courses, Lyotard's idea of what it is exactly that the skull is saying, points toward the crucial difference we have been trying to trace. While it is clear that our perspective from aside gives the painting a meaning different from the one produced by a frontal view, this meaning is, ultimately, nothing more than 'absence itself, death, and not a "content"' (Lyotard, 1971, p. 377). The side-way perspective, which, in Greenblatt's analysis, turned out to be the privileged one – laying bare as it did the essence of what was hidden before – results in Lyotard's analysis as much in a representation that can never capture what it is supposed to make present. As such, ironically, it can tell us more about death than Greenblatt's reading of the painting does. Death is, after all, 'absence itself', the unutterable, that to which there can be no direct access.

According to Lyotard, the message of Holbein's anamorphosis can be interpreted as follows: 'reading demands that we stick to representation, to the phantasm of presence [and die because of it]' (Lyotard, 1971, p. 377). Lyotard's sentence is in more than one way ambivalent. On the one hand, it contains an interesting pun, pointing to the inevitable limitations (or the limiting inevitability) of every singular representation;[18] on the other it serves as yet another example of the way in which the meaning of the concepts used by Lyotard gradually changes in the course of his study. At the beginning of *Discours, Figure*, the act of reading ('lire') has clearly perjorative connotations: the verb refers to the mere recognition of what is known and hence to the exclusion of what does not fit in one's fixed frames of reference.[19] In the sentence quoted above, however, the act of reading has become a positive one. Here, to read is to consider representations as such, as representations.[20] For Lyotard, it is only this type of reading which can make us aware of the event-ness of history and of the event-ness of the figural work of art (and of the event-ness of its singular historical receptions, one could add).

VII

In a crucial passage in the chapter significantly entitled 'Opposition and difference', Lyotard forges an explicit connection between the concepts of the 'figure' and that of the 'event'. Interestingly, the passage is followed by an exposition on what Lyotard calls the truth of history: 'Truth is not to be found in the order of knowledge, it is met with in its disorder, as an event' (Lyotard, 1971, p. 135). Opposed to this discursive knowledge, whose domain is, Lyotard writes, 'the space of signification', 'truth arises (e-venit) as that which is out of place' (Lyotard, 1971, p. 135). In the domains of both 'signification' and 'désignation', however, '[e]verything is in its place'. There, everything has its fixed position, a position from which it derives its ultimate meaning. In these domains, Lyotard writes, '[e]verything is set in order to clear away the event and to restore good form and clear and distinct thinking' (Lyotard, 1971, p. 135). It is this restoration which the figural event of Holbein's free-floating anamorphosis disrupts. As such, Lyotard argues, 'this floating movement goes hand in hand with anguish', the anxiety of what is unknown and unexpected. It is the anxiety involved in the experience of the sublime, the feeling of self-alienation resulting from one's encounter with what Greenblatt in several of his later essays has called objects of 'wonder' (see e.g. Greenblatt, 1990, pp. 161–83 and Greenblatt, 1991, passim). The encounter with the wonderful entails a confrontation with the unknown in the self. 'It pulls out and away from myself', Greenblatt writes: it allows one '[to] understand the uncanny otherness of [one's] own voice' (Greenblatt, 1990, p. 8). As such, the experience of wonder has similar consequences as the dialogue with the dead. Both lead to an understanding of the 'way in which all voices come to be woven out of strands of alien experience' (Greenblatt, 1990, p. 8). At the end of the introductory chapter to *Shakespearean Negotiations*, Greenblatt writes that the dream of speaking with the dead must never be abandoned (Greenblatt, 1988, p. 20). It mustn't, of course, though we will have to remind ourselves, permanently, that history is of such stuff as dreams are made of.

In the introduction to *Learning to Curse*, a collection of essays published over a period of some 15 years, Greenblatt explicitly inscribes his own work in the tradition of the aesthetics of *Verfremdung*. 'I am committed', he writes, 'to the project of making strange what has become familiar, of demonstrating that what seems an untroubling and untroubled part of ourselves [...] is actually part of something else, something different' (Greenblatt, 1990, p. 8). In conclusion, we could say that what his reading of Holbein's painting in terms of the idea of the conversation with the dead shows, is that such a project, possibly inevitably so, may at certain points tip over in its contrary: the making familiar of what forever has to remain strange.

Yet, is it really inevitable? Lyotard's analysis of the seismic event of the 'figure' seems to provide us with a way out of the dilemma of the dialectics of *Verfremdung*. While his blatantly a-historic exclamation that the figural logic is the exclusive property of poetic discourse, may seem from a strictly historicist perspective somewhat crude, I believe that a work like *Discours, Figure* can be taken in some respect (the one outlined above, that is) as a corrective to Greenblatt's New Historicism. Lyotard's stubborn emphasis on the event-ness *of* and *within* the order of representation serves as an exemplary critical reading of the (Geertzian) cultural semiotics to which Greenblatt at some point has allied himself. As I hope my example will have made clear, the latter approach at crucial moments in its reading-practice threatens to bypass the theoretical distinction it has made between a sign and its referent and, thus, to take the relationship between them for an immediate link. As a consequence, one could say, Greenblatt treats Holbein's skull in a way similar to the anonymous art-lover who tried to drive away Holbein's fly. Without wanting to suggest that Greenblatt shares with the latter the belief that representations coincide with their referent, his reaction to the anamorphotic death's head is not radically different. The difference is that between driving the thing (*Das Ding*) away and giving it a name and a face, to have it speak.

9

Reading Cultural History

Catherine Belsey

I

In the Rhymney Valley, fifteen miles north of Cardiff, just off the main road to Merthyr Tydfil, stands the manor house of Llancaiach Fawr. It was constructed in the sixteenth century for the ap Richard family, later the Prichards, Welsh gentry who married locally and whose eldest sons were either David or Edward alternately. During the political upheavals of the 1640s Edward Prichard initially pledged his support for the King and was put in command of Royalist forces. Later, he changed his mind: as a devout Puritan, who was being asked to pay more taxes than he liked, and who no doubt saw the way things were going, Prichard changed sides, and in 1646 he held Cardiff Castle for Parliament. On 5 August 1645, at what may well have been a critical moment in Colonel Prichard's struggle with his conscience over these matters, Charles I had dinner at Llancaiach Fawr on his way to Brecon. The reflections of the King's host on the occasion are not recorded.

Llancaiach Fawr is now open to the public, restored with a view to reproducing its condition at that historic moment. The award-winning 'living history museum' invites visitors to experience the past directly, as they are conducted round the house of the absent Prichards by their servants, dressed in seventeenth-century costume and speaking a version of seventeenth-century English. The servants refer only to events and places which could have been known in the period; they cook to recipes from the time, and are unable to recognise the names of any modern dishes that might resemble them; they prescribe herbal remedies for visitors who cough or sneeze. The servant-guides question visitors politely about themselves, and express astonishment that it is possible to travel from Cardiff in such a very short time. There is a good deal of ribaldry, no doubt licensed by the period. And the male servants are all deeply resentful of their absent mistress, Mary Prichard, who is forever, we are led to understand, discontented and peevish, laying claim to higher breeding than her husband, and constantly indisposed.

The house is a domestic museum, and what it puts on display is a seventeenth-century family. It is emblematic of the limitations of the project that the Prichards themselves are away from home: how could the early

modern family be made present, after all, in a heritage spectacle which is in
certain ways quintessentially postmodern? Meanwhile, I am writing a book
about representations of the early modern family, and the family 'itself' will
be no more present in my cultural history than it is in the manor house. In
both cases all we have access to is the trace of past meanings, and since, as
Jacques Derrida explains, meaning itself is no more than a trace, what we can
know of the meanings of the family at a specific moment in history is only
the trace of a trace. But my interest in Llancaiach Fawr is motivated not only
by its thematic overlap with my research, but also by the radical methodological differences between the two projects, its and mine.

'History comes alive at Llancaiach Fawr', the Guide Book announces.
'From the moment that visitors enter the formal gardens, they are surrounded by the sights, smells and sounds of the past.' Some of the sounds
turn out to be tape-recorded: I was astonished to hear invisible horses
stamping in the adjacent stables. But some are not: the peacocks screaming
on the lawn are real. Modern standards of hygiene prohibit the exact
reproduction of the smells. Internal privies at Llancaiach Fawr discharged
into a diverted brook. (To the cultural historian the inclusion of ensuite
privies in a number of relatively modest domestic buildings of the mid-
sixteenth century in England, Scotland and Wales shows a commitment to
privacy considerably earlier than other sources might have led us to expect.)
'Step over the threshold of Llancaiach Fawr', invites a publicity leaflet, 'and
travel back over 350 years.' The servants are happy to discuss the political
situation as it obtains in 1645, and to give their views, not all of them shared.
But above all, the museum centres on domesticity: visitors can try on copies
of clothes from the period, or handle replicas of the kitchenware. In other
words, Llancaiach Fawr encourages us to cross a boundary between present
and past, between one historical moment and another, into a vanished
epoch. The project is to recover the life of an early modern household, to
permit us to encounter cultural history as participant observers, by suspend-
ing our own interests, identities, commitments and convictions. 'In every
respect', the Guide Book affirms, 'it should be an unforgettable experience.'

It is. I mean no disrespect to the Prichard family or their modern 'servants'
if I say that what I found most unforgettable was my own acute embarrassment. This was not attributable to a sense of my superior knowledge of the
period: on the contrary, I learned a lot. Where I did know – or thought
I knew – about the cultural history of the mid-seventeenth century, I could
not fault the account I was given. The problem was rather that I was asked to
cross the boundary in one direction, and irreversibly for the duration, to
enter the past in dialogue where, deprived of any intelligible reference to the
present, I had no secure place to speak from. I felt tongue-tied, unfamiliar
with the conventions of the time and unable to give an account of my own
interest in what I was hearing. (How, for instance, could I possibly explain to

a seventeenth-century steward why I wanted to see (but not to use) the privy in order to chart the emergence of privacy in the period?) They ask where you live; the place does not exist in their world and they shake their heads in bewilderment; alternatively, it does exist, but it is not the same place now as it was in 1645. When they are displayed as exhibits in a glass case in a conventional modern museum, the furniture and pottery of the period are objects of an always conjectural knowledge; conversely, when they are experienced, held, handled, they become irretrievably alien, as do the eating habits and the herbal remedies. To try on the clothes is to be 'dressed up', in costume. This was not 'costume' in the seventeenth century, however, but everyday dress, and people presumably knew how to inhabit it. When the familiar present ceases to be a secure foothold, the past becomes more remote, not less, harder to read, because the only frame of interpretation available to a modern visitor is relegated to a distance, out of reach.

II

If the present is ruled out of order, translation of the past into the terms of the present is not an option. It was precisely in order to challenge the conventional idea of history as a process of translation that 'living history' was devised. Llancaiach Fawr is by no means unique, of course. The everyday life of Plimoth Plantation, where the original Pilgrims landed, is brilliantly replicated on Cape Cod; Colonial Williamsburg reproduces the life of a community in eighteenth-century Virginia. The Holocaust Museum in Washington DC is laid out experientially in chronological order. In the early days, visitors were offered a card which would give them the identity of an inmate of one of the camps. They were invited to insert the card into machines at intervals to find out what stage 'their' story had reached; in the end, they would discover whether 'they' had escaped or died. Meanwhile, the Globe Theatre in London promises the chance to see the plays of Shakespeare and his contemporaries performed in an 'authentic' setting.

Conventional historiography, on the other hand, translates the past into the present. Here too the project is recovery, but the idea is to make the past present to our *understanding*. An earlier epoch exists as a document written in an unfamiliar language for the linguistically competent historian to render in a language we know.[1] Traditional cultural history follows the same pattern. Ideas and beliefs are assembled, material objects decoded, letters and diaries analysed, all in order to offer the modern world an understanding of the values of the past. 'Living history' is synchronic: it isolates a specific moment of the past and erases, ostensibly at least, everything that has happened since. Conventional historiography, by contrast, locates the specific moment diachronically, charts its causes and consequences, and in the

process constructs a story. This narrative, intelligible, as Hayden White
points out, generically, as comedy or tragedy, romance or satire,[2] so that it
'makes sense' to modern readers, effaces its own genre, as well as the present
from which it is recounted, and the interests, convictions and commitments
of the historian. Traditional cultural history, too, constructs a narrative – of
origins and vestiges – in which the arrival of the present constitutes the end
of the story, whether happy or tragic. The more totalising the narrative, the
more readable the history; but the process of translation itself, the act of
making history, is erased. 'That', conventional history affirms, 'is simply how
it was.'

Unlike history, legend draws attention to its own textuality: 'That's what
they say,' it affirms; 'that's what we read'.[3] But at the same time, legend
eliminates the difference of the past: even the most heroic of golden worlds
exists in a kind of synchronic present as a model. History is born at the
moment when textuality is effaced: 'that's what happened,' it says; the past is
apparently recovered in its truth as an object of knowledge. But here too,
paradoxically, since the translation takes the place of the event or the object,
supplants the real and pushes it further away, what is lost is the pastness of
the past, its otherness. This ordered, teleological, generic history can never
resemble the past as it was lived. The project of 'living history', by contrast, is
to recover the experience, to turn the detached analyst into a participant. In
the first case meaning is thought to defer experience; in the second experience
is offered at the expense of meaning.

It seems to me that neither project can deliver what it promises, that
recovery of the past, whether as translation or experience, is not a possibility.
In both instances the present is all too present – apparent as the form into
which the past is translated in one case, and as embarrassment in the other.
Llancaiach Fawr invites us to erase the differences between one historical
period and another, to experience as participants a different moment of
cultural history. I do not believe we can. Instead, I want to define a distinct
practice, which I shall call history at the level of the signifier. This is a form
of cultural history which involves neither translation nor experience, but
depends on reading. Moreover, it is a material practice – as material in its
own way as social history, to which it can be related. But it is not synonymous with social history nor, in my view, subordinate to it.

III

To distinguish history at the level of the signifier from social history is to
make a methodological distinction which 'living history', like life, indeed,
obscures. The kind of cultural history I am putting forward is a history of
representation. An early modern funeral monument to a mother, for ex-

ample, depicts her orphaned children as chubby and vulnerable. A century earlier, children were generally represented on tombs, where they appeared at all, as miniature adults, with no very notable distinguishing features except their smaller size, and even that was not always indicated. This does not imply that in practice children changed shape. On the contrary, what it suggests is that the difference between parents and children now signifies in a new way. A baby on a tomb of 1631 fingers the decoration on her mother's bodice, just as any modern baby might. The inference a cultural historian draws is not that medieval babies did not in practice play with projecting ornaments, but that this habit was not then thought worth representing. Representational priorities change as values change, and history at the level of the signifier records these shifts of value. A textual history of the nuclear family is not to be conflated or confused with its social history. The number of people sharing a house is not what is at stake here; their 'experience' of each other is not accessible. We can, however, discuss and attempt to date the emergence of shared values and the gradual spread of new ideals.

Social history gives priority to describing practices, while cultural history records meanings. It is a relief to be able to differentiate, to know that we no longer have to try to reconcile the sympathy Renaissance plays seem to evoke for young lovers who defy enforced marriage with the widespread early modern practice of arranging partnerships in the interests of property. Lawrence Stone's influential account of *The Family, Sex and Marriage* disappoints to the degree that it fails to distinguish between practice and values. Stone largely ignores fiction. At the same time, the texts he invokes – letters, diaries, legal documents – are treated as broadly transparent. But analysts of texts know that the values a society approves, endorses in letters and diaries, or prescribes by law, may well differ very considerably from its day-to-day practices, just as its practices may differ from the utopian or tragic alternatives defined in fiction.[4] Nor does fiction 'reflect' practice. After all, people did not, Jim Sharpe, the distinguished social historian, once patiently explained to me, commonly take their sisters' hearts to banquets on daggers, as Giovanni does in *'Tis Pity She's a Whore*.

Cultural history records meanings and values, which is to say that its concern is not so much what individuals actually did, but more what people wanted to do, wished they had done, what they cared about and deplored. Not that a society's practices are irrelevant to history at the level of the signifier. As Althusser pointed out, stressing the materiality of ideology, beliefs are inscribed in practices, particularly ritualistic practices.[5] Where practices feature in cultural history, they do so primarily in terms of their meanings – as customs or habits, for example, which demonstrate the values a culture subscribes to. If fiction idealises marrying for love, while the majority of parents resolutely go on arranging the unions of their children, cultural history recognises a conflict between residual and emergent values.

The distinction I am proposing is not a binary opposition: meaning and practice inevitably inform and indeed invade each other. The meaning of the hall in the late medieval house changes as it ceases to be the setting for even ceremonial dinners, and the owners increasingly retreat with the children to a separate and relatively private dining room. It is important to be aware that, even so, 'the family' continues into the seventeenth century to include the servants, whose moral behaviour and religious observances are the responsibility of their master and mistress. Similarly, it helps to know that when Viola asks whether Orsino is still a bachelor, she is not simply identifying a possible husband, but establishing whether she can hope to join his household dressed as a lady, since Olivia's is closed to her. Because Orsino's retainers would be male, an Elizabethan audience would understand, the only opportunities for a woman in his house would take the form of menial work. We misread fiction if we misunderstand the practices of the period. Social and cultural history are thus profoundly interrelated, but we stand to lose if we collapse one into the other, or efface the differences.

For cultural historians practices signify. Culture constitutes the vocabulary within which we do what we do; it specifies the meanings we set out to inhabit or repudiate, the values we make efforts to live by or protest against, and the protest is also cultural. Culture resides primarily in the representations of the world exchanged, negotiated and, indeed, contested in a society. Some of these representations may coincide with existing practices; they may determine or legitimate them; or alternatively, they may challenge them. Representations are not, however, purely discursive: they also have, in my view, their own materiality. That is to say, culture is in its way *lived*.

No sane person would now look to Hollywood movies for the truth of contemporary social practice; any future social historian who saw our advertisements as depicting our actual way of life would be seriously misled. At the same time, the popular appeal of film and advertising, and their corresponding commercial success, depend to a high degree on their inscription of widely shared ideals, fantasies and values. We live our lives in relation to these dreams, in self-congratulation, disappointment or resignation. 'Life', we recognise, is not like fiction; at the same time, however, fiction generates hopes, desires and aspirations, and these too are lived; popular texts affirm norms and proprieties which we adopt, with whatever anxiety, or repudiate. Culture is lived as *a relation to* practice, as commitment or resistance, or as an uneasy alliance between the two, an anxious, undecided ambivalence. If love has become a matter of free choice, is Giovanni entitled to choose to love his sister? And if he can be said to have his true love's heart, what exactly are the limits of that possession?

To affirm the relative independence of cultural history is not, I want to stress, a covert way to denigrate social history. On the contrary, social history is an important and distinguished discipline, with its own scrupulous standards of scholarship and accuracy. We should do well to take account of it, and to emulate its meticulousness. But there may be a substantial gap between the endorsement of a value and its widespread implementation, or between practice and the ambivalences which attend it. This gap is of interest as evidence of conflicting values, but the discipline of cultural history need not depend for confirmation on the research of social historians, any more than it supplants that research. And if this opposition is itself deconstructed in different ways by the brilliant work of Natalie Zemon Davis, Carlo Ginzburg or Stuart Clark, this only goes to show that our methodological distinctions are no more than that, frames which enable us to isolate for study specific aspects of the vast and unfamiliar terrain that constitutes the past.

History at the level of the signifier is decisively textual. Culture is lived, but we have no direct access to early modern 'life'. The materials of cultural history reside in the signifying practices of a society, and these include its fictions,[6] where meanings and values are defined and contested for the delight and instruction of an audience which is expected to understand a proportion, at least, of what is at stake. Meaning is value-laden: we learn the proper attitudes to good and evil as we learn to understand the terms, or to recognise heroes and villains. Culture is learned as well as lived, and we learn to live it as we learn to speak, to follow stories, to read, write, interpret images, obey or repudiate conventions. No human practice takes place out-side it. Birth, reproduction, and death are probably as close to nature as most of us come, but these events are experienced in culture – in all its uncertainties and ambivalences. If we experience them as natural, that only goes to show how thoroughly we have internalised the meanings culture prescribes.

IV

The form of cultural history I am attempting to define acknowledges our distance from the past. In this respect, history at the level of the signifier is both more and less ambitious than 'living history'. Its project is not the recovery of the experience in its imaginary fullness, but the recognition of cultural difference. On the other hand, it asks questions that 'living history' cannot answer. As a historian of family values, I wanted to know more about the nature of the relationship between the politically astute Colonel Prichard and his 'peevish' wife, two of whose four children, both the boys, died young. The servants could not tell me. They could report on the behaviour of the couple when they were together, but this in turn would need to be inter-preted, historicised, before it could become part of a history of the family. The Guide Book includes a photograph of the servants in bed, three of them sharing an attic. I wondered quite what exchanges occurred in that attic after dark. The modern impersonators of the servants might have answered my questions, but I'm not sure I would have trusted them to know any more than I did.

History at the level of the signifier looks at the residues the past has left – its documents, which I take to include fiction, sermons, pamphlets, maps, visual images, ornaments, the allocation of space, architecture, including the opportunities domestic buildings provide for privacy, and sleeping arrangements. To this extent, cultural history self-evidently resembles anthropology: it constructs a culture by reading its artefacts. But it differs from anthropology in its classic mode to the degree that it studies a vanished epoch. Unlike synchronic ethnography, the distance cultural history sets out to bridge is by definition chronological. In this respect it resembles archaeology. History at the level of the signifier interprets the residues of the past explicitly from the present, and emphasises the pastness of the past. It takes for granted that we *make* history, which is to say that we make a story which differs from the one contemporaries would have made.

We do not, that is to say, interpret another culture from what Clifford Geertz calls 'the Native's Point of View'.[7] There is a radical dissimilarity between, on the one hand, sympathetic, imaginative engagement with the perspective of a participant in another culture, a native speaker – or writer – and on the other hand, the abandonment of our own cultural location, and the historically specific knowledges it entails. At Llancaiach Fawr I inspected the privy, once I had finally prevailed on my hosts to allow it, alone and in silence. Only then could I take account of its location on the first floor, and note the ventilation arrangements; only then could I make a mental comparison with the provisions at Chenies Manor in Buckinghamshire and Castle Menzies on Tayside, and give due consideration to the fact that in all these cases the properties belonged to the gentry rather than the aristocracy, if Highland chieftains can be classified at all within this framework. The comparison led me to wonder whether courts of the period might have strong reasons not to cultivate privacy, might positively discourage places of concealment. Few of these inconclusive reflections would have been possible from the native's point of view.

Meanwhile, in my experience at Llancaiach Fawr, dialogue was extremely restricted when I was denied access to my own culture. Dialogue is an exchange between subjects. The subject is what speaks or writes, and it does so in a language which is the inscription of certain knowledges – of a culture. As subjects, we have learnt to signify in a specific society, since signification always precedes us as individuals, and meanings pertain at a specific historical moment. To speak or write is to reproduce, however differentially, the meanings we have learnt. We participate in dialogue from our own moment, and it follows that we understand, if at all, from where we are. We interpret the past and its subjects from the present, since we have nowhere else to interpret from, and it follows that 'our situation can allow us to be familiar with their situation in ways other than their own ways'.[8] We read the documents of the past in order to produce the possible range of their meanings, which is not the same as the range of meanings that could consciously have been identified at the time. Cultural history does not inhabit the past and it does not share its frame of reference. We interpret, inevitably, from the present, and the present necessarily informs our account of a past that cannot speak for itself. In a conventional museum we understand the objects in the glass cases to the degree that we are able to frame them with a knowledge, constituted in the present, of their purpose and use. 'Living history', by contrast, shows these same objects to be precisely unfamiliar: we have to learn in the present to handle them. Documents offer information which historians now sift, filter and reconstitute as narrative. The present disrupts the subject-object couple of empiricist knowledge: there is no 'objective' account of the past.

V

Does it follow, then, if 'objectivity' is not an option, that we not only make history, but we also make it up? Certainly, fiction (etymologically, 'making') invades the realm of 'fact'. Llancaiach Fawr is theatrical and the theatricality is part of the experience: we are guided round the manor house by actors, who play roles in a performance and interact with the audience of visitors. The visit itself is offered not only as instruction but also as recreation, a suitable activity for holiday-makers or family outings. But in this respect, as education in the form of entertainment, it hardly differs from conventional museums, television documentaries, popular history magazines, or the accounts of the past that feature in the book-review pages of the Sunday papers. Public anniversaries memorialising historic events, however solemn, are also recreational as well as theatrical, and the occasions themselves construct to a degree the nature of the memory they reaffirm.

Moreover, the historical documents too are already the effect of 'making' in this sense, so that even the material on which history is based is not entirely independent of the fictional process. Written records from the period select, however innocently, the information worth preserving, to the degree that they choose what to exclude: even the most apparently indiscriminate chronicle leaves out a good deal more than it recounts. In an age of photoopportunities we are conscious of the degree to which portraits and photographs from the past are also 'staged'. Self-representation is very often a 'performance': wills stand as monuments to the deceased, as well as dispositions of property; letters are exchanged not only within the framework of the epistolary conventions of the moment, but also in the light of expectations about what the recipient might want to know; diaries may present an image of the self to gratify or appal the reader, even when this reader is understood to be the author at a future date. And in turn the process of representation inevitably invades the historian's narrative: the vocabulary in which it is written is necessarily value-laden; the story itself is told according to the conventions of narrative in general and a generic pattern in particular, whether the genre is comic or tragic.

Some empiricist historians take the view that to query the transparency of their work is synonymous with proposing that there is no difference between fact and fiction. Poststructuralist theory, they affirm, urges that we might as well read a novel as a work of history, or that history itself is pure invention.[9] It would be odd indeed if a theory which turns on difference should set out to erase differences. I take it for granted that the real exists, as distinct from invention, and that the past happened in a sense that the events of *Middlemarch* did not. Its residues testify in their stubborn otherness to the previous existence of a world that is more than the product of our current imagination. The texts, the documents, the material remains do not in practice always confirm our expectations. On the contrary, they surprise us, and elicit a corresponding modification of what we thought we knew. Familiar with the quite different arrangements in courts and palaces of the period, I had not expected to find ensuite privies lower down the social scale.

In other words, the problem of history is not the real, but our account of it, our record of its past, which is always delimited by the signifier. We cannot know the past outside the residues it leaves, and these remains are always subject to our interpretation. Reflection, judgment, narration have no purchase outside language, and we have no independent guarantee that the differences inscribed in language map on to differences in the real. In consequence, while we owe it to the past to read as meticulously, assess as scrupulously and record as faithfully as we can, these virtuous practices, however rigorously carried out, cannot ensure the impartiality, the independence, in short, the truth, of the stories we tell. We have no direct access to a past that exists outside the construction we put on it in the present.

To the degree that the present informs our account of the past, we make history *out of a relation, which is always a relation of difference, between the present and the past*. I put it in these terms because I want to stress two points. First, a relation of difference is not full; it is not a thing; it has no content. Cultural history as a relation between present and past is neither a recovery of the past nor an affirmation of the present, but an acknowledgement of the gap that divides them from each other. And second, if the kind of cultural history I am proposing is not in consequence empty, a blank sheet, or a self-proclaimed fiction, that is because we *make* a relation, in both senses of that term, out of *our* reading practices and *their* documents. We produce, that is to say, a past, which is both the consequence of our analysis and its motive. I take it for granted that the real existed then as now; but I take it equally for granted that the real was no more knowable then than it is now. All we can analyse is the signifier, in which not only the real, but meaning too, while not simply lost, is forever differed and deferred, relegated by signifying practice itself to uncertainty and undecidability, difficult, recalcitrant, evasive. Meanings do not, in other words, present themselves as fully formed, discrete objects of knowledge. Indeed, they do not *present* themselves at all. The idea, intelligibility, what we imagine as the concept, does not exist independent of the signifier itself, which both precedes and relegates the supposed pure signified.[10] The signifier, the place where meanings are made and also supplanted, is the material of our study – the signifier precisely in its materiality.

VI

History at the level of the signifier treats signifying practices – maps, houses, clothing, tombs – as texts. Such 'documents' from the past are both substantial and legible. We can read them, as much as we can ever read anything, to the degree that we are familiar with the signifying practices of their moment. And since signifying practice in general, like language in particular, is in the first instance public, conventional, shared, learned, there is no reason why we should not learn to read the meanings of the past by immersing ourselves in the documents, even though we shall never understand them as native speakers.[11]

If we are to make history at the level of the signifier, we shall need to pay all the documents in question extremely close attention. While I unreservedly welcome the rereading taking place in English departments, under headings like gender studies, queer theory, postcolonial analysis, I am uneasy about the predominantly thematic character of much of this work. I regret, that is to say, what I see as a neglect of the signifer, the basic material of the hermeneutic practice I am proposing. The decline of close reading is the result, of course, of a reaction against American New Criticism and practical criticism in the UK. I do not want to return to either of these activities, but I am occasionally unconvinced by some of the interpretations that are put forward in the name of recent approaches. At the end of the introduction to an anthology of new historicism and cultural materialism, Kiernan Ryan makes the point in these terms:

Radical historicist criticism is undoubtedly the poorer for its reluctance to meet the complex demands of a text's diction and formal refinements; for in the end only a precise local knowledge of the literary work, acquired through a 'thick description' of decisive verbal effects, will allow the critic to determine how far the work's complicity with power truly extends, and how far beyond our own horizon it may already have reached.[12]

Theory is often blamed for bad reading habits, but it does not follow from the undecidability of meaning that inattentive readings are just as good as any others. The prime exponent of undecidability, Jacques Derrida, reads minutely, demonstrating in his mode of analysis a precision that would put many literary critics to shame. Exactly because meaning is not present to itself or the reader, because all we have is the signifier, we need to tease out, by detailed attention to the textuality of the text, its nuances and equivocations, its displacements and evasions, the questions posed there and the anxieties on display about the answers proffered.

What is at stake is not an empty formalism. But it is in my view imperative, if we are to make good cultural history, to take account of the modes of address of the texts we analyse. In written works it matters who addresses whom, in what situation and with what authority.[13] When the works in question are fictional, it matters that we differentiate between the fictional speaker and the text. The views of the villain are probably contrary to what the audience is invited to believe: Iago's racism and misogyny, for example, should not necessarily be taken for the play's. There is a pragmatics of the utterance within the world of the fiction: Hamlet, say, invites Horatio to endorse the promptings of his conscience; but the dialogue between them also sets up a relationship between the play and the spectators, and the nature of the ethical invitation there is altogether more elusive, not least because we have no access to the historical audience's reaction. Genre also delimits what is affirmed. A domestic conduct book sets out to overcome the anxieties about marriage that motivate its publication; a play, by contrast, foregrounds anxieties to sustain the plot for five acts, and a happy ending does not necessarily dispel them entirely. Moreover, in fictional practice genres are rarely pure. A familiarity with fairy tales might protect us from reading substantial areas of Shakespeare mimetically.

Difference is once again the critical term. In addition to their attention to the formal differences within and between texts, the readings we make in the practice of history at the level of the signifer will also give full weight, I hope, to the reading process itself as a relation of difference. They will not claim, that is to say, access to the truth of the text, or the single, correct interpretation. They will acknowledge their own motivation and their own partiality and know that reading takes place from a position in the present. And they will also recognise the difference *within* the past and *within* the text: conflicts and inconsistencies of meaning that both reproduce and motivate debate, disagreement and struggle in the world at large.

VII

Current theory permits us to see meaning as heterogeneous to the point where an affirmation and its opposite, power and resistance, may share the same inscription. Dissension, in other words, inhabits discursive practice, characterises it, and at the same time destabilises it. Texts take issue with other texts, but they also differ from themselves, inscribe the conflicts they take part in. It is perhaps too easily assumed that other epochs were somehow simpler than our own, or that the cultural history of former periods is appropriately represented as ultimately unified. Our world, we allow, is divided, full of debate, culturally diverse and intellectually stratified, but nostalgia still tempts us to imagine a previous culture as a consensual realm, in which the important meanings and values could be taken for granted as shared, despite distinctions of language, class or gender. This seductive account of the past seems to me fundamentally misguided, and nowhere more so than as an interpretation of the early modern period, where virtually every topic was matter for dispute, much of it passionate, some of it violent. In my view, the century between 1550 and 1650 in England was one long moment of dissension, where radical shifts in economic and political relations were both the condition and the effect of fundamental challenges at the level of ideas, and these challenges in turn were the result of cultural exchanges between the present and a recovered classical past, among the emerging European 'nations', and between the Old World and the New.

But it is also, I believe, misguided, however tempting, to identify difference simply with conflict. Sometimes difference is synonymous with indifference. As I see it, the Renaissance was also a period when knowledges that were self-evident in one genre of writing might well be entirely ignored in another. Medical advice might be contrary to clerical instruction, for instance. Sometimes conflicting knowledges would compete for supremacy; but in other cases cognitive dissonance simply subsisted without closure. Incompatible convictions, rationalist on the one hand and magical on the other, profoundly sceptical in one instance and deeply sentimental in another, might survive alongside each other, sometimes contesting the same ground, sometimes without ever coming into contact. We do the period an injustice, I increasingly believe, if we try to make its meanings and values fit together to form an internally consistent totality, expect physiological knowledge to 'explain' Shakespearean comedy, for instance, especially if to explain is to efface or resolve the discordant elements within the texts.[14] At the very least, physiology and comedy are different genres, addressed to different audiences, on different occasions.

Everyday meanings are elusive, contradictory or undecidable. This implies a version of cultural history which takes account of the resistances, as well as the regularities, of the past. Like political, social or economic history, though in its own way, cultural history can be a record of oppressions inadequately imposed and proprieties acknowledged and then evaded. The project is not an account of a coherent 'world picture', but a record of the difficulties that arise when societies attempt to bring their members into line.

Dissent is the reason why things change, or one of them, at least: the one that is open to our appropriation, as the blind mechanisms of the market are mostly not. And the instabilities of cultures are the pressure points for change. If the future is also our concern, as current interest in gender studies, queer theory and postcolonial studies presumably implies, we need a version of cultural history that acknowledges incoherences and offers evidence that things change, so that we have grounds for hoping that in the long term injustice might be significantly reduced. Otherwise, there is no point in complaining. We need, in other words, a theory and practice of reading that foregrounds dissent.

Nowhere is cognitive dissonance more evident than in fiction. Part of our awareness of the density of some of Shakespeare's plays, part of their ability to make a sense, however varying, to succeeding generations or from distinct political positions, may be the effect of a conjunction within them of different knowledges, which precisely do not cohere into a single, decipherable, decodable, thematic *message*. Fiction, which may have no design on its audience but to entertain, can afford to mingle the propositions currently in circulation, without any obligation to rationalise them. As a space of play, where some of the prohibitions of the symbolic Law are temporarily suspended, fiction can permit inconsistency without irritable reaching after resolution. Fiction, then, and Shakespeare's fiction no less than any other, is a crucial element in the cultural history we produce.

It follows from my interest in dissent that there are certain critical differences between the form of cultural history I am proposing and the practice of new historicism. I value the break new historicism has made with a literary paradigm that no longer challenged us in its own terms, and I share its commitment to extending our attention beyond the purely literary, but the highly sophisticated work of Stephen Greenblatt and his colleagues differs from the model I am putting forward in three specific ways. First, new historicism seems to me to treat texts as relatively transparent: not, that is, to look for the inconsistencies and instabilities of meaning which are my primary concern. In consequence, second, the cultural moments it depicts are seen as more unified, more harmonious, more homogeneous than they are in my account. New historicism reproduces in its homogenising impulse the values of American functionalism, which implies that the local features of a society all work in the last analysis to maintain the social order as a whole. In my own view, derived from Foucault's, power is always and necessarily coupled with resistance as its defining difference. Third, and closely linked with my reservations about functionalism, it is important to me that I tell a story. New historicism takes over from anthropology an inclination to isolate synchronic moments, rather than situate them in a differential relation to what came before and after. In this respect, too, new historicist practice differs radically from the work of Foucault, to whose influence it is so widely attributed. Foucault commonly contrasts one epoch with another. My own interest, like his, is in the reasons why certain cultural values, and certain cultures, indeed, do not survive, or survive only with difficulty, by effacing their own internal differences.

VIII

Any essay in cultural history is subject to the inadequacy of all interpretation. The limitations of cultural history are not, or not only, however, a matter of ignorance, but also an effect of representation: the past necessarily exceeds our depiction of it. Meanwhile, we too are participants in our own continuing history. The presence of our historical moment in the processes of both interpretation and representation means that we are necessarily implicated in the stories we tell, to a degree that neither 'living history' nor conventional historiography are able to acknowledge. There is no place outside history from which to make what sense we can of the past.

10

Theses on the Philosophy of History

Walter Benjamin

I

The story is told of an automaton constructed in such a way that it could play a winning game of chess, answering each move of an opponent with a countermove. A puppet in Turkish attire and with a hookah in its mouth sat before a chessboard placed on a large table. A system of mirrors created the illusion that this table was transparent from all sides. Actually, a little hunchback who was an expert chess player sat inside and guided the puppet's hand by means of strings. One can imagine a philosophical counterpart to this device. The puppet called 'historical materialism' is to win all the time. It can easily be a match for anyone if it enlists the services of theology, which today, as we know, is wizened and has to keep out of sight.

II

'One of the most remarkable characteristics of human nature,' writes Lotze, 'is, alongside so much selfishness in specific instances, the freedom from envy which the present displays toward the future.' Reflection shows us that our image of happiness is thoroughly coloured by the time to which the course of our own existence has assigned us. The kind of happiness that could arouse envy in us exists only in the air we have breathed, among people we could have talked to, women who could have given themselves to us. In other words, our image of happiness is indissolubly bound up with the image of redemption. The same applies to our view of the past, which is the concern of history. The past carries with it a temporal index by which it is referred to redemption. There is a secret agreement between past generations and the present one. Our coming was expected on earth. Like every generation that preceded us, we have been endowed with a *weak* Messianic power, a power to which the past has a claim. That claim cannot be settled cheaply. Historical materialists are aware of that.

III

A chronicler who recites events without distinguishing between major and minor ones acts in accordance with the following truth: nothing that has ever happened should be regarded as lost for history. To be sure, only a redeemed mankind receives the fullness of its past – which is to say, only for a redeemed mankind has its past become citable in all its moments. Each moment it has lived becomes a *citation à l'ordre du jour* – and that day is Judgment Day.

IV

> Seek for food and clothing first, then
> the Kingdom of God shall be added unto you.
>   Hegel, 1807

The class struggle, which is always present to a historian influenced by Marx, is a fight for the crude and material things without which no refined and spiritual things could exist. Nevertheless, it is not in the form of the spoils which fall to the victor that the latter make their presence felt in the class struggle. They manifest themselves in this struggle as courage, humour, cunning, and fortitude. They have retroactive force and will constantly call in question every victory, past and present, of the rulers. As flowers turn toward the sun, by dint of a secret heliotropism the past strives to turn toward that sun which is rising in the sky of history. A historical materialist must be aware of this most inconspicuous of all transformations.

V

The true picture of the past flits by. The past can be seized only as an image which flashes up at the instant when it can be recognised and is never seen again. 'The truth will not run away from us': in the historical outlook of historicism these words of Gottfried Keller mark the exact point where historical materialism cuts through historicism. For every image of the past that is not recognised by the present as one of its own concerns threatens to disappear irretrievably. (The good tidings which the historian of the past brings with throbbing heart may be lost in a void the very moment he opens his mouth.)

VI

To articulate the past historically does not mean to recognise it 'the way it really was' (Ranke). It means to seize hold of a memory as it flashes up at a moment of danger. Historical materialism wishes to retain that image of the past which unexpectedly appears to man singled out by history at a moment of danger. The danger affects both the content of the tradition and its receivers. The same threat hangs over both: that of becoming a tool of the ruling classes. In every era the attempt must be made anew to wrest tradition away from a conformism that is about to overpower it. The Messiah comes not only as the redeemer, he comes as the subduer of Antichrist. Only that historian will have the gift of fanning the spark of hope in the past who is firmly convinced that *even the dead* will not be safe from the enemy if he wins. And this enemy has not ceased to be victorious.

VII

Consider the darkness and the great cold
In this vale which resounds with mysery.
                    Brecht, *The Threepenny Opera*

To historians who wish to relive an era, Fustel de Coulanges recommends that they blot out everything they know about the later course of history. There is no better way of characterising the method with which historical materialism has broken. It is a process of empathy whose origin is the indolence of the heart, *acedia*, which despairs of grasping and holding the genuine historical image as it flares up briefly. Among medieval theologians it was regarded as the root cause of sadness. Flaubert, who was familiar with it, wrote: '*Peu de gens devineront combien il a fallu être triste pour ressusciter Carthage.*' ('Few will be able to guess how sad one had to be in order to resuscitate Carthage.') The nature of this sadness stands out more clearly if one asks with whom the adherents of historicism actually empathise. The answer is inevitable: with the victor. And all rulers are the heirs of those who conquered before them. Hence, empathy with the victor invariably benefits the rulers. Historical materialists know what that means. Whoever has emerged victorious participates to this day in the triumphal procession in which the present rulers step over those who are lying prostrate. According to traditional practice, the spoils are carried along in the procession. They are called cultural treasures, and a historical materialist views them with cautious detachment. For without exception the cultural treasures he surveys have an origin which he cannot contemplate without horror. They owe their existence not only to the efforts of the great minds and talents who have created them, but also to the anonymous toil of their contemporaries. There is no document of civilisation which is not at the same time a document of barbarism. And just as such a document is not free of barbarism, barbarism taints also the manner in which it was transmitted from one owner to another. A historical materialist therefore dissociates himself from it as far as possible. He regards it as his task to brush history against the grain.

VIII

The tradition of the oppressed teaches us that the 'state of emergency' in which we live is not the exception but the rule. We must attain to a conception of history that is in keeping with this insight. Then we shall clearly realise that it is our task to bring about a real state of emergency, and this will improve our position in the struggle against Fascism. One reason why Fascism has a chance is that in the name of progress its opponents treat it as a historical norm. The current amazement that the things we are experiencing are 'still' possible in the twentieth century is *not* philosophical. This amazement is not the beginning of knowledge – unless it is the knowledge that the view of history which gives rise to it is untenable.

IX

Mein Flügel ist zum Schwung bereit,
ich kehrte gern zurück,
denn blieb ich auch lebendige Zeit,
ich hätte wenig Glück.
   Gerhard Scholem, 'Gruss vom Angelus'

(My wing is ready for flight, / I would like to turn back. / If I stayed timeless time, / I would have little luck.)

A Klee painting named 'Angelus Novus' shows an angel looking as though he is about to move away from something he is fixedly contemplating. His eyes are staring, his mouth is open, his wings are spread. This is how one pictures the angel of history. His face is turned toward the past. Where we perceive a chain of events, he sees one single catastrophe which keeps piling wreckage upon wreckage and hurls it in front of his feet. The angel would like to stay, awaken the dead, and make whole what has been smashed. But a storm is blowing from Paradise; it has got caught in his wings with such violence that the angel can no longer close them. This storm irresistibly propels him into the future to which his back is turned, while the pile of debris before him grows skyward. This storm is what we call progress.

X

The themes which monastic discipline assigned to friars for meditation were designed to turn them away from the world and its affairs. The thoughts which we are developing here originate from similar considerations. At a moment when the politicians in whom the opponents of Fascism had placed their hopes are prostrate and confirm their defeat by betraying their own cause, these observations are intended to disentangle the political worldlings from the snares in which the traitors have entrapped them. Our consideration proceeds from the insight that the politicians' stubborn faith in progress, their confidence in their 'mass basis', and, finally, their servile integration in an uncontrollable apparatus have been three aspects of the same thing. It seeks to convey an idea of the high price our accustomed thinking will have to pay for a conception of history that avoids any complicity with the thinking to which these politicians continue to adhere.

XI

The conformism which has been part and parcel of Social Democracy from the beginning attaches not only to its political tactics but to its economic views as well. It is one reason for its later breakdown. Nothing has corrupted the German working class so much as the notion that it was moving with the current. It regarded technological developments as the fall of the stream with which it thought it was moving. From there it was but a step to the illusion that the factory work which was supposed to tend toward technological progress constituted a political achievement. The old Protestant ethics of work was resurrected among German workers in secularised form. The Gotha Program[1] already bears traces of this confusion, defining labour as 'the source of all wealth and all culture'. Smelling a rat, Marx countered that '... the man who possesses no other property than his labour power' must of necessity become 'the slave of other men who have made themselves the owners....' However, the confusion spread, and soon thereafter Josef Dietzgen proclaimed: 'The saviour of modern times is called work. The ... improvement ... of labour constitutes the wealth which is now able to accomplish what no redeemer has ever been able to do.' This vulgar-Marxist conception of the nature of labour bypasses the question of how its products might benefit the workers while still not being at their disposal. It recognises only the progress in the mastery of nature, not the retrogression of society; it already displays the technocratic features later encountered in Fascism. Among these is a conception of nature which differs ominously from the one in the Socialist utopias before the 1848 revolution. The new conception of labour amounts to the exploitation of nature, which with naïve complacency is contrasted with the exploitation of the proletariat. Compared with this positivistic conception, Fourier's fantasies, which have so often been ridiculed, prove to be surprisingly sound. According to Fourier, as a result of efficient cooperative labour, four moons would illuminate the earthly night, the ice would recede from the poles, sea water would no longer taste salty, and beasts of prey would do man's bidding. All this illustrates a kind of labour which, far from exploiting nature, is capable of delivering her of the creations which lie dormant in her womb as potentials. Nature, which, as Dietzgen puts it, 'exists gratis', is a complement to the corrupted conception of labour.

XII

We need history, but not the way a spoiled loafer
in the garden of knowledge needs it.
    Nietzsche, *Of the Use and Abuse of History*

Not man or men but the struggling, oppressed class itself is the depository of historical knowledge. In Marx it appears as the last enslaved class, as the avenger that completes the task of liberation in the name of generations of the downtrodden. This conviction, which had a brief resurgence in the Spartacist group,[2] has always been objectionable to Social Democrats. Within three decades they managed virtually to erase the name of Blanqui, though it had been the rallying sound that had reverberated through the preceding century. Social Democracy thought fit to assign to the working class the role of the redeemer of future generations, in this way cutting the sinews of its greatest strength. This training made the working class forget both its hatred and its spirit of sacrifice, for both are nourished by the image of enslaved ancestors rather than that of liberated grandchildren.

XIII

Every day our cause becomes clearer and people get smarter.
    Wilhelm Dietzgen, *Die Religion der Sozialdemokratie*

Social Democratic theory, and even more its practice, have been formed by a conception of progress which did not adhere to reality but made dogmatic claims. Progress as pictured in the minds of Social Democrats was, first of all, the progress of mankind itself (and not just advances in men's ability and knowledge). Secondly, it was something boundless, in keeping with the infinite perfectibility of mankind. Thirdly, progress was regarded as irresistible, something that automatically pursued a straight or spiral course. Each of these predicates is controversial and open to criticism. However, when the chips are down, criticism must penetrate beyond these predicates and focus on something that they have in common. The concept of the historical progress of mankind cannot be sundered from the concept of its progression through a homogeneous, empty time. A critique of the concept of such a progression must be the basis of any criticism of the concept of progress itself.

XIV

Origin is the goal.
   Karl Kraus, *Worte in Versen*, Vol. I

History is the subject of a structure whose site is not homogeneous, empty time, but time filled by the presence of the now [*Jetztzeit*].[3] Thus, to Robespierre ancient Rome was a past charged with the time of the now which he blasted out of the continuum of history. The French Revolution viewed itself as Rome reincarnate. It evoked ancient Rome the way fashion evokes costumes of the past. Fashion has a flair for the topical, no matter where it stirs in the thickets of long ago; it is a tiger's leap into the past. This jump, however, takes place in an arena where the ruling class gives the commands. The same leap in the open air of history is the dialectical one, which is how Marx understood the revolution.

XV

The awareness that they are about to make the continuum of history explode is characteristic of the revolutionary classes at the moment of their action. The great revolution introduced a new calendar. The initial day of a calendar serves as a historical timelapse camera. And, basically, it is the same day that keeps recurring in the guise of holidays, which are days of remembrance. Thus the calendars do not measure time as clocks do; they are monuments of a historical consciousness of which not the slightest trace has been apparent in Europe in the past hundred years. In the July revolution an incident occurred which showed this consciousness still alive. On the first evening of fighting it turned out that the clocks in towers were being fired on simultaneously and independently from several places in Paris. An eye-witness, who may have owed his insight to the rhyme, wrote as follows:

   Qui le croirait! on dit, qu'irrités contre l'heure
   De nouveaux Josués au pied de chaque tour,

Tiraient sur les cadrans pour arrêter le jour.

(Who would have believed it! we are told that new Joshuas at the foot of every tower, as though irritated with time itself, fired at the dials in order to stop the day.)

XVI

A historical materialist cannot do without the notion of a present which is not a transition, but in which time stands still and has come to a stop. For this notion defines the present in which he himself is writing history. Historicism gives the 'eternal' image of the past; historical materialism supplies a unique experience with the past. The historical materialist leaves it to others to be drained by the whore called 'Once upon a time' in historicism's bordello. He remains in control of his powers, man enough to blast open the continuum of history.

XVII

Historicism rightly culminates in universal history. Materialistic historiography differs from it as to method more clearly than from any other kind. Universal history has no theoretical armature. Its method is additive; it musters a mass of data to fill the homogeneous, empty time. Materialistic historiography, on the other hand, is based on a constructive principle. Thinking involves not only the flow of thoughts, but their arrest as well. Where thinking suddenly stops in a configuration pregnant with tensions, it gives that configuration a shock, by which it crystallises into a monad. A historical materialist approaches a historical subject only where he encounters it as a monad. In this structure he recognises the sign of a Messianic cessation of happening, or, put differently, a revolutionary chance in the fight for the oppressed past. He takes cognisance of it in order to blast a specific era out of the homogeneous course of history – blasting a specific life out of the era or a specific work out of the lifework. As a result of this method the lifework is preserved in this work and at the same time cancelled;[4] in the lifework, the era; and in the era, the entire course of history. The nourishing fruit of the historically understood contains time as a precious but tasteless seed.

XVIII

'In relation to the history of organic life on earth,' writes a modern biologist, 'the paltry fifty millennia of *homo sapiens* constitute something like two seconds at the close of a twenty-four-hour day. On this scale, the history of civilised mankind would fill one-fifth of the last second of the last hour.' The present, which, as a model of Messianic time, comprises the entire history of mankind in an enormous abridgment, coincides exactly with the stature which the history of mankind has in the universe.

A

Historicism contents itself with establishing a causal connection between various moments in history. But no fact that is a cause is for that very reason historical. It became historical posthumously, as it were, through events that may be separated from it by thousands of years. A historian who takes this as his point of departure stops telling the sequence of events like the beads of a rosary. Instead, he grasps the constellation which his own era has formed with a definite earlier one. Thus he establishes a conception of the present as the 'time of the now' which is shot through with chips of Messianic time.

B

The soothsayers who found out from time what it had in store certainly did not experience time as either homogeneous or empty. Anyone who keeps this in mind will perhaps get an idea of how past times were experienced in remembrance – namely, in just the same way. We know that the Jews were prohibited from investigating the future. The Torah and the prayers instruct them in remembrance, however. This stripped the future of its magic, to which all those succumb who turn to the soothsayers for enlightenment. This does not imply, however, that for the Jews the future turned into homogeneous, empty time. For every second of time was the strait gate through which the Messiah might enter.

11

Camus' *The Plague*, or a Monument to Witnessing

Shoshana Felman

I

What we call history we usually conceive of as a discipline of inquiry and as a mode of knowledge. What we call narrative we usually conceive of as a mode of discourse and as a literary genre. The relationship between narrative and history has been posited, time and again, both in theories of narrative and in theories of history. I will define here narrative, along with Barbara Herrnstein Smith, as 'verbal acts consisting of *someone telling someone else that something happened*'.[1] That 'something happened' in itself is history; that 'someone is telling someone else that something happened' is narrative. If narrative is basically a verbal act that functions as a historiographical report, history is, parallelly but conversely, the establishment of the facts of the past through their narrativisation.

Between Narrative and History

'The term history,' writes Hegel in his *Lectures on the Philosophy of History*, 'unites the objective and the subjective side, and denotes...not less what *happened* than the *narration*[2] of what happened. This union of the two meanings we must regard as of a higher order than mere outward accident; we must suppose historical narrations to have appeared contemporaneously with historical deeds and events.'[3] Although this classical philosophy of history, which claimed to unravel history, on the one hand, as the manifestation of a definite principle of progress and, on the other, as the materialisation of a universal, overarching meaning, was, as one historian puts it, 'consumed in the holocaust of two world wars',[4] contemporary theorists of history still by and large subscribe, on different grounds, to the view of the necessity of historical narrativisation and of the inherent relationship between history and narrative. 'Historians', writes Louis Mink, 'generally claim that they can give at least partial explanations of past events.' But historical explanation requires a certain perspective. 'The insistence on

127

historical perspective seems to be more than a mere recommendation of the attitude of objectivity. . . . It is at least in part a claim that for the historical understanding of an event one must know its consequences as well as its antecedents; that the historians must look before *and* after . . . ; that in *some* sense we may understand a particular event by locating it correctly in a narrative sequence.'[5] History is thus contingent on interpretive narrativisation. 'And it is these [*interpretive* hypotheses] which historians generally believe in some way distinguish history as *interpretive narrative* from chronology on the one hand and "science" on the other' (p. 36). 'The major point of difficulty in attempting to transform history into a cumulative science', argues Mink, 'is not one of the *logic of evidence* but one of the *meaning of conclusions*' (p. 39). Detachable conclusions are possible in science, but not in history: 'despite the fact that an historian may "summarise" conclusions in the final chapter, it seems clear that these are seldom or never detachable conclusions; not merely their validity but their meaning refers back to the ordering of evidence in the total argument. The significant conclusions, one might say, are ingredient in the argument itself, . . . in the sense that they are *represented by the narrative order itself*' (p. 39).

The question I would like to address in the present essay is the following: If narrative is defined by a claim to establish a certain history, and if history is defined by a claim to explain events through their narrativisation, is the mode of operation of these mutual claims (from history to narrative and from narrative to history) itself subject to history? Has contemporary history – with its cataclysm of the Second World War and the Holocaust – left intact the traditional shuttle movement between narrative and history? If not, what is the impact of the Holocaust on the mutual claims of history and narrative and the manner in which they are implicated in each other? Can contemporary narrative historically bear witness, not simply to the impact of the Holocaust but to the way in which the impact of *history as holocaust* has modified, affected, shifted the very modes of the relationship between narrative and history?

Under Western Eyes, or the Contemporary Witness

As an initial textual approach, I will attempt to search for answers to these questions in the postwar narrative writings of Albert Camus.

Why Camus?

Because Camus, I would maintain, exemplifies the way in which traditional relationships of narrative to history *have changed* through the historical necessity of involving literature in action, of creating a new form of *narrative as testimony* not merely to record, but to rethink and, in the act of its rethinking, in effect *transform history* by bearing literary witness to the Holocaust. I will argue that Camus does indeed exemplify this literary witness to the

Holocaust and this new, transformational relationship between narrative and history,[6] even though it is by no means clear or obvious that his texts in any way refer to, or claim to deal with, the Holocaust as such.

'There is no such thing as a literature of the Holocaust, nor can there be', writes Elie Wiesel.[7] The fact that the author of this statement is himself the best-known writer of the Holocaust adds sharpness to the paradox of its pronouncement. I would like, however, to take this statement of impossibility seriously, and to explore the implications of its paradox in a different sense. What if we did not know what a literature of the Holocaust is, or might be? What if we did not know what the Holocaust is, or might be? What if, by reading, we could only try to find out, leaving the space of such a question open?

Granting that it might well be that 'there is no such thing as a literature of the Holocaust, nor can there be', I propose to test the impact of the Holocaust on narrative (on the relationship of narrative to history) precisely in a writer who *does not* present himself, and *is not officially identified as*, a writer of (about) the Holocaust.

I wish, moreover, to explore the meaning of the Holocaust for a specifically *non-Jewish* European writer, one who, in his fate as Frenchman, was nonetheless immediately implicated in the cataclysm of the Second World War.

Historically, Camus' artistic productivity extends from 1942 to 1960, that is, from the last phase of the Second World War through the decade and a half that form the war's immediate aftermath. During those postwar years, Camus held a position of intellectual leadership attested by the 1957 Nobel Prize for literature he was awarded (at the age of 43, three years before his accidental death in a car crash) for illuminating, as the prize citation goes, 'the problems of the human conscience in our time'. I will argue that, by virtue of his intellectual leadership and of the ethical stance he occupied throughout the war and after it, Camus' work indeed exemplifies 'the problems of the human conscience in our time' as the problems of a radical and necessary transformation: the radical and necessary transformation of the very categories both of ethics and of history, in their relation to the function of the writer. 'The writer's function', said Camus in his Nobel acceptance speech, 'is not without its arduous duties. By definition, he cannot serve today those who make history; he must serve those who are subject to it.' What does it mean to be subject to history? What is the historic specificity of our being subject to the history of our times? Why and how does the contemporary writer serve, not the making of, but the subjection to (the state of being subject to) history? I propose here to explore the impact of history as holocaust on those *subjects of history* who were, however, neither its perpetrators nor its most immediate and most devastated victims, but its historic *onlookers*: its *witnesses*.

In light of those concerns, I will study the relationship of narrative to history as it evolves in two novels by Camus, crucially situated at the beginning and at the end of his career as writer: *The Plague* (1947) and *The Fall* (1956). Both those novels, although separated by a nine-year interval (an interval whose historical and narrative significance I will try to ponder) were written subsequent to the trauma of the Second World War. Both, I would maintain, are endeavouring, each in its own way, to assimilate the trauma. Both are explicitly preoccupied by the very possibilities – and impossibilities – of dialogue between history and language.

The Historic Resonances of the Plague

Promptly after the war's end, Camus published *The Plague*, the story of a town stricken by a ravaging bubonic epidemic. I would like to start meditating on the book by listening, first, to the particular resonance of a few quotations. When the first signs of the Plague have been discovered in the city, the narrator of the novel, a doctor in his profession, tries to envision the forthcoming horror of the spread of the contagion.

> There have been as many plagues as wars in history; yet always plagues and wars take people by surprise. (p. 35)

> Figures floated across his memory, and he recalled that some thirty or so great plagues known to history had accounted for nearly a hundred million deaths. But what was a hundred million deaths? When one has served in a war, one hardly knows what a dead man is, after a while. And since a dead man has no substance unless one has actually seen him dead, a hundred million corpses broadcast throughout history are no more than a puff of smoke in the imagination. (pp. 36–7)

It is obviously not any war that is here implicitly evoked by Camus' narrator, but one whose historical atrocities are quite specific. How is it possible, indeed, to read about a hundred million corpses in connection with the singularly chosen metaphor of 'a puff of smoke' without immediately associating it with the millions of corpses that were literally transformed into smoke in the Nazi death camps' crematoria?

> The doctor remembered the plague in Constantinople that... caused ten thousand deaths in a single day. Ten thousand dead made about five times the audience in a biggish cinema. Yes, that was how it should be done. You should collect the people at the exits of five picture-houses, you should lead them to a city square and make them die in heaps if you wanted to get a clear notion of what it means. Then at least you could add

some familiar faces to the anonymous mass. But naturally that was impossible to put into practice; moreover, what man knows ten thousand faces? (p. 37)

It is not hard to understand why it has become, indeed, a commonplace to read the novel as an allegory of the Second World War: the horror of the epidemic constantly suggests that of the war through the Plague's potential for a massive killing. What the Plague, above all, means is a *mass murder* of such scope that it deprives the very loss of life of any tragic impact, reducing death itself to an anonymous, depersonalised experience, to a statistical *abstraction*.

'No,' Rambert said bitterly, 'you can't understand. . . . You live in a world of abstractions.'
  The doctor glanced up at the statue of the Republic, then said . . . he knew he was using the language of the facts as everybody could see them . . . but was [Rambert] right in reproaching him, Rieux, in living in a world of abstractions? Could that term 'abstraction' really apply to those days he spent in his hospital while the Plague was battening on the town, raising the death-toll to five hundred victims a week? Yes, an element of abstraction, of a divorce from reality, entered into such calamities. Still when abstraction sets to killing you, you've got to get busy with it. (pp. 82–3)

If the Plague is as murderous, as dehumanising as the war, the specific situation of the *town under quarantine* which, in its isolation from the outside world, is enclosed within its own contagious, deadly space and abandoned to its fear and desperation, is reminiscent of the situation of a concentration camp.

There were other camps of much the same kind in the town, but the narrator, for lack of first-hand information and in deference to veracity, has nothing to add about them. This much, however, he can say: the mere existence of these camps, the smell of crowded humanity coming from them, the baying of their loud-speakers in the dusk, the air of mystery that clung about them, and the dread these forbidden places inspired told seriously on our fellow-citizens' morale and added to the general nervousness and apprehension. (p. 226)

On the other hand, the organisation of the 'volunteers' who, at the risk of their lives, offer themselves as medical helpers in the desperate fight against the plague, evokes the struggle of European resistance movements throughout Europe against the overpowering forces of Nazism.

To recognise in the dramatic allegory of the epidemic the recent history of
the struggle against Nazism, readers did not need to know that Camus was
himself during the war a member of the French Resistance, that he edited the
French underground newspaper *Combat*, and that a long extract of *The
Plague* had appeared clandestinely in Occupied France in a collection of
Resistance texts. But in the context of the question of the dialogue between
history and narrative, it is instructive to take notice of the fact that the novel
was initially produced as an underground testimony, as a verbal action of
resistance which, as such, is not a simple *statement* or description of the
historical conflict it narrates, but an actual intervention in this conflict.
Camus' narrative intends to be not merely a historic witness, but a participant in the events it describes.

The Project of Recording History

Emerging out of the very urgency of history, *The Plague* nonetheless presents
itself as a pure 'chronicle', an objective reproduction of historical events.
Thus, the opening chapter reads:

> The unusual events described in this chronicle occurred in 194 – at Oran.
> (p. 3)

> ...Our fellow citizens had not the faintest reason to apprehend the
> incidents that took place in the spring of the year in question and were
> (as we subsequently realised) premonitory signs of the grave events we are
> to chronicle. To some, these events will seem quite natural; to others, all
> but incredible. But obviously, a narrator cannot take account of these
> differences of outlook. *His business is only to say: this is what happened*,
> when he knows that it actually did happen, that it affected the life of a
> whole populace, and that there are *thousand of eyewitnesses* who can
> appraise in their hearts the truth of what he writes.
>   In any case the narrator ... would have little claim to competence for a
> task like this, had not chance put him in the way of *gathering much
> information*, and had he not been, by the force of things, closely involved
> in all that he proposes to narrate. *This is his justification for playing the
> part of the historian*. Naturally, a historian, even an amateur, always has
> data, personal or at second hand, to guide him. The present narrator has
> *three kinds of data*: first, *what he saw himself*; secondly, *the accounts of
> other eyewitnesses* (thanks to the part he played, he was enabled to learn
> their personal impression from all those figuring in this chronicle); and
> lastly, *documents* that subsequently came into his hands. (p. 6)

In this opening chapter of *The Plague*, the relationship of narrative to
history seems to be direct and entirely unproblematic: if history is of the

order of a 'happening' – of an 'acting' and a 'seeing' – and if narrative is of the order of a 'telling', the two orders are conflated in the discourse of the *testimony*, through which language is transmitting the direct experience of 'eyewitnessing'. As testimony, the account of *The Plague* is thus itself a first-hand document, situated at the level of primordial data, closely adhering to historical perception. Joining events to language, the narrator-as-eyewitness is the testimonial *bridge* which, mediating between narrative and history, guarantees their correspondence and adherence to each other. This bridging between narrative and history is possible since the narrator is both an *informed* and an *honest* witness ['témoin fidèle']. Once endowed with language through the medium of the witness, *history speaks for itself.* All the witness has to do is to *efface himself*, and let the *literality of events* voice its own *self-evidence*. 'His business is only to say: *this is what happened,* when he knows that it actually did happen.' The 'subject of history' can thus voice its presence to the history of which it was a part in articulating, in a single, unified and homogeneous utterance, history's presence to itself.

II

A Missing Literality, or an Event Without a Referent

If the narrative is testimony, a historiographical report whose sole function is to say 'This is what happened', why, however, does Camus have recourse to the metaphor of the plague? If the *literality* of a historical event is what is here at stake, why not designate this historical event by its literal, referential name? Why not refer directly to the Second World War as the explicit subject of the testimony?

A superficial answer to this question could invoke the political necessity of disguise stemming from the initial underground testimonial status of the first published excerpt of the novel, that sees the light still under Nazi occupation. But beyond this circumstantial explanation, what is striking in Camus' choice of metaphor in lieu of the historic referent is that the Plague designates not simply a metaphorically substitutive event, but an event that is *historically impossible: an event without a referent.* 'It is impossible', say the doctors at the first signs of the plague, 'everybody knows that it has vanished from the Western world' (p. 36, TM).[8]

There is thus a certain tension, a certain aporia that inheres between the allegorical and the historical qualities of the event: the allegory seems to name the *vanishing of the event* as part of its *actual historical occurrence*. The literality of history includes something which, from inside the event, makes its literality vanish. Camus' testimony is not simply to the literality of history, but to its *unreality*, to the historical vanishing point of its unbelievability. In much the same way as the doctors think the Plague historically impossible because it does not fit into the frame of reference of their science (their knowledge of medical history), the victims of the plague do not believe in the foreshadowing disaster because it contradicts their 'humanism', their ideological beliefs and expectations.

> In this respect our townsfolk were like everybody else, wrapped up in themselves; in other words they were humanists: they disbelieved in pesti-lences. A pestilence isn't a thing made to man's measure; therefore we tell ourselves that pestilence is a mere bogy of the mind, a bad dream that will pass away. But it doesn't always pass away and, from one bad dream to another, it is men who pass away, and the humanists first of all, because they have not taken their precautions. Our townsfolk...thought that everything still was possible for them; which presupposed that pestilences were impossible. (p. 36)

The Plague (the Holocaust) is disbelieved because it does not enter, and cannot be framed by, any existing frame of reference (be it of knowledge or belief). Because our perception of reality is moulded by frames of reference, what is outside them, however imminent and otherwise conspicuous, remains historically invisible, unreal, and can only be encountered by a systematic disbelief.

In much the same way as Camus' victims of the epidemic, the victims of the Holocaust in turn did not believe in the information that was forthcoming about the Nazis' final aims. 'The majority of Jewish leaders in Eastern Europe did not yet realise that this was the beginning of a systematic campaign of destruction. The whole scheme was beyond human imagination; they thought the Nazis incapable of the murder of millions. ... If the information about the "final solution" had been believed it would have reached every corner of Poland within a few days. But it was not believed. After July 1942 (the deportations from Warsaw) it is more and more difficult to understand that there still was widespread confusion about the Nazi designs among Jews in Poland, and that the rumours were not recognised for what they were – certainties. Any rational analysis of the situation would have shown that the Nazi aim was the destruction of all Jews. But the psychological pressures militated against rational analysis and created an atmosphere in which wish-ful thinking seemed to offer the only antidote to utter despair... Most Jews in Europe, and many non-Jews, had at the very least heard rumours about some horrible events in Western Europe... But they were either not believed or it was assumed that "it cannot happen here". Only a relatively small minority tried to hide or to escape, aware that deportation meant death.'[9]

The unreality that strikes, thus, the event before and during its occurrence through the victims' own refusal to believe in its historic referentiality, is matched and re-enacted on another level by the way in which the relief at the war's end is immediately accompanied by a denial and forgetfulness of the war's horrors. As soon as the quarantined town finds itself liberated from the Plague,

> these ecstatic couples, locked together . . . proclaimed in the midst of the tumult of rejoicing, with the proud egoism and injustice of happy people, that the plague was over, the reign of terror ended. Calmly they *denied, in the teeth of evidence, that we had ever known a crazy world* in which men were killed off like flies, or that precise savagery, that calculated frenzy of the plague . . . In short, they denied that we had ever been that hag-ridden populace a part of which was daily fed into a furnace and went up in oily fumes. (pp. 276–7)

Paradoxically enough, the event historically occurs through its disappearance as an historic actuality and as a referential possibility. It is as though the vanishing point of its literality ('Everybody knows that it has vanished from the Western world') is what constitutes, precisely, the historical particularity of the event before and after its occurrence. The event (the Plague –, the Holocaust) occurs, in other words, as what is not provided for by the conceptual framework we call 'History', and as what, in general, has no place in, and therefore cannot be assimilated by or integrated into, any existing cultural frame of reference. Since we can literally witness only that which is within the reach of the conceptual frame of reference we inhabit, the Holocaust is testified to by *The Plague* as an event whose specificity resides, precisely, in the fact that *it cannot, historically, be witnessed.*

> One could not imagine plague or could imagine it only along misleading lines (La peste ne s'imaginait pas ou s'imaginait faussement). (p. 39, *TM*)

Literature as Testimonial Breakthrough

It is precisely because history as holocaust proceeds from a *failure to imagine*, that it takes an *imaginative* medium like the Plague to gain an insight into its historical *reality*, as well as into the attested historicity of its unimaginability.

What, however, is the nature of the failure to imagine and what is the imaginative breakthrough that Camus requires of the testimony for the act of witness to become truly historical, or historically insightful?

We may feel our way toward an answer to this question in the dialogue between Dr Rieux, Camus' narrator, and Rambert, a visiting journalist to the town. Rambert's Parisian newspaper had commissioned him to make a report on the living conditions prevailing among the Arab population.

Rieux replied that these conditions were not good. But, before he said any more, he wanted to know if the journalist could tell the truth.

'Certainly,' Rambert replied.

'I mean,' Rieux said, 'would you be capable of pronouncing a *total condemnation?*' [pouvez-vous porter une condemnation totale]

'Total? Well, no, I must admit. But surely such a condemnation would be unfounded?'

Rieux said quietly that it would in effect be unfounded; but that he had put the question solely to find out if Rambert's *testimony* could or couldn't be an *unqualified* one '*I've no use for testimonies that are not unqualified*', he added. [Je n'admets que les témoignages sans reserve] 'That is why I shall not support your testimony with my information.' (pp. 11–12, *TM*)

Normally, it is the journalist who, by profession, is considered the historical *witness* of society and culture, the bearer of historic testimony. And yet, Camus' narrator is suggesting that the testimony he himself enacts by the very telling of *The Plague* (playing 'the part of the historian') is by no means a journalistic testimony, but something else. If 'his business is only to say: this is what happened', he does not say it in the manner of a journalist, because his is an *unqualified testimony* which, as such, implies 'a total condemnation'.

A Total Condemnation

What, however, does Rieux exactly mean by 'unqualified testimony' and by 'total condemnation', and in what way are the two related? In the initial dialogue between the doctor and the journalist, both these concepts that Rieux states as his narrative and testimonial standards remain somewhat elliptical and enigmatic. They can be clarified, however, by the later dialogue between the two protagonists in their next encounter. Rambert seeks to leave the quarantined town so that he can rejoin a beloved woman whom he had left behind in Paris.[10] Since the gates of the town are locked by decree of the medical authorities, Rambert comes to plead with Rieux.

He had explained that his presence in Oran was purely accidental, he had no connection with the town and no reasons for staying in it; that being so, he surely was entitled to leave . . . The official told him he quite appreciated his position, but no exception could be made . . .

'But, confound it,' Rambert exclaimed, I'm not from here '[je ne suis pas d'ici] . . .

'Quite so. Anyhow, let's hope the epidemic will soon be over.' Finally, he tried to console Rambert by pointing out that, as a journalist he had an excellent subject to his hand in Oran . . .

Whereat Rambert had shrugged his shoulders...

When Rieux said nothing [Rambert] continued:...'All I wanted to know was whether you couldn't possibly give me *a certificate stating that I haven't got this damned disease*'...

'Please don't doubt I understand you,' Rieux said, 'but you must see your argument doesn't hold water. *I can't give you that certificate, because I don't know whether you have the disease or not*, and even if I did, how could I certify that between the moment of leaving my consulting-room and your arrival at the Prefect's Office you wouldn't be *infected?* And even if...I gave you a certificate, it wouldn't help.'

'Why not?'

'Because there are thousands of people placed as you are in this town, and there can't be any question of allowing them to leave it'...

'But *I'm not from here.*'

'Unfortunately, *from now on you will be from here*, like everybody else.' (pp. 80–2, *TM*)

This episode implicitly recalls the very first encounter between the journalist and the physician: the enigmatic 'total condemnation' of which Rieux had spoken as the touchstone of an 'unqualified' discursive (testimonial) truth – a 'total condemnation' which Rambert, however, could perceive only as a theoretical, unreal question and which, in his capacity as witness (journalist), he therefore could not (would not) utter, here turns out to be, ironically, Rambert's own total condemnation – to the Plague and to the quarantine, his inescapable implication in a situation which condemns him absolutely to imprisonment and to contagion. The adjective *total*, which was precisely what Rambert could not conceive of, thus turns out to have two meanings: 'total' in the sense that the condemnation is without the possibility of a remission or exception; 'total', also, in the sense that the condemnation *implicates* its bearer, *contaminates* the witness, *includes* the onlooker. Rambert wishes to prevent precisely this inclusion: to testify as an outsider, to exclude himself both from the condemned and the condemning situation to which he testifies. This is why his testimony is not 'unqualified'.

But a 'total condemnation' is a situation from which one cannot choose to exclude oneself, except by self deception. And it is precisely his attitude of self-exclusion from the condemnation which condemns Rambert, in making him unwittingly participate in the historical death sentence inflicted upon others, while maintaining his own blindness with respect to his own situation as condemned.[11]

Rambert does not believe in the reality of a 'total condemnation', as people failed to believe in the reality of gas chambers. This is why Camus' own testimony, as opposed to the journalist's, cannot be simply referential

but, to be truly historical, must be *literary*. If the failure to imagine out of
which history as holocaust proceeds stems, precisely, from the witnesses'
failure to imagine their own implication and their own inclusion in the
condemnation, Camus' own literary testimony must, above all, wrench the
witnessing away from this historical failure of imagination. Literature bears
testimony not just to duplicate or to record events, but to make history
available to the imaginative act whose historical unavailability has
prompted, and made possible, a holocaust.

Bearing Witness to the Body

The specific task of the literary testimony is, in other words, to open up in
that belated witness, which the reader now historically becomes, the imaginative capability of perceiving history – what is happening to others – *in one's
own body*, with the power of sight (of insight) usually afforded only by one's
own immediate physical involvement.[12]

It is thus that the literary testimony of *The Plague* offers its *historical
eyewitnessing in the flesh*. Rambert has to learn on his body what a holocaust
– a situation of 'total condemnation' – is: a situation which does not – cannot –
except the witness; an experience that requires one to live through one's own
death, and paradoxically, bear witness to that living through one's dying; a
death experience which can be truly comprehended, witnessed only from
inside (from inside the witness' own annihilation); a radical experience to
which no outsider can be witness, but to which no witness can be, or remain,
outsider.

Having been an involuntary witness to the Plague, Rambert finds himself,
in the course of time, radically transformed by the very process of his
witnessing. Ultimately, he decides to stay in town of his own accord so as
to join the medical volunteers:

> 'Doctor,' Rambert said, 'I'm not going. I want to stay with you.'
> ... Rieux seemed unable to shake off his fatigue.
> 'And what about her?' ...
> Rambert said he'd thought it over very carefully, and his views hadn't
> changed, but if he went away, he would feel ashamed of himself, and that
> would embarrass his relations with the woman he loved.
> Showing more animation, Rieux told him that was sheer nonsense; there
> was nothing shameful in preferring happiness.
> 'Certainly,' Rambert replied. 'But it may be shameful to be happy by
> oneself.'
> Tarrou, who had not spoken so far, now remarked, without turning his
> head, that if Rambert wished to take a share in other people's unhappi-
> ness, he'd have no time left for happiness. So the choice had to be made.

Testimony as a Crisis

'That's not it,' Rambert rejoined. 'Until now I always felt a stranger in this town, and that I'd no concern with you people. *But now that I have seen what I have seen, I know that I'm from here* [je sais que je suis d'ici], whether I want it or not. This business is everybody's business.' [cette histoire nous concerne tous] (p. 174, *TM*)

Bearing witness to the way in which 'this history concerns us all', *The Plague* partakes of an *apprenticeship in history* through an apprenticeship in witnessing. The relationship of narrative to history is not, however, as unproblematic as the opening chapter seemed to indicate, since the witness – or the witnessing – which joins the two is *not a given*. The historical apprenticeship takes place only through a *crisis in*, and a consequent *transformation of*, the witness. And it is only through the medium of that crisis that the event can speak, and that the narrative can lend its voice to history. If the narrative is truly *claimed* by history, it is by virtue of that radical discontinuity, that radical change the witness has undergone:

If only he could put the clock back and be once more the man who, at the outbreak of the epidemic, had had only one thought and one desire: to escape and return to the woman he loved! But that, he knew, was out of the question now; he had changed too greatly. The plague had forced on him a detachment which, try as he might, he couldn't think away, and which like a formless fear haunted his mind. Almost he thought the plague had ended too abruptly, he hadn't had time to pull himself together. Happiness was bearing down on him full speed, the event outrunning expectation. (pp. 273–4)

'Almost he thought the event had ended too abruptly, he hadn't had time to pull himself together.' The event outrunning expectation, history outruns the narrative, as though the narrative did not quite have the time to catch its breath and to catch up with history, to catch up with the full significance as well as the abruptness, the overwhelming aspect of the crisis and of the change that history has meant.

Knowledge and Memories

Nevertheless, the narrative is testimony to an apprenticeship of history and to an apprenticeship of witnessing insofar as this historical crisis of the witness brings about a certain form of *cognition*. 'Now that I have seen what I have seen,' said Rambert, '*I know* that I'm from here.' However anguishing and ground shaking, seeing leads to knowing, a knowing that, in some ill-understood way, might be ground breaking. Rieux, in turn, in his double role as a doctor (involved witness) and as a narrator (a 'historian', witness of the other witnesses), *learns something* from the witnessing and from the telling, and his testimony takes stock of this knowledge:

> Tarrou had 'lost the match', as he put it. But what had he, Rieux, won? No more than the experience of *having known* plague and remembering it, of *having known* friendship and remembering of, of *knowing* affection and being destined one day to remember it. So all a man could win in the conflict between plague and life was *knowledge* and memories...
>
> Knowing meant that: a living warmth, and a picture of death [Une chaleur de vie et une image de mort, c'était cela la connaissance]. (pp. 270–1)

The task of the testimony is to impart that knowledge: a firsthand, carnal knowledge of victimisation, of what it means to be 'from here' (from quarantine), wherever one is from; a firsthand knowledge of a historical passage through death, and of the way life will forever be inhabited by that passage and by that death; knowledge of the way in which 'this history concerns us all', in which 'this business' of the Plague 'is everybody's business'; knowledge of the way in which history is the body's business; knowledge of a 'total condemnation'.

To Speak for All

It is from this communal knowledge that the authority of the witness, that is, the truth claim of the narrative, proceeds, when Rieux finally emerges from his anonymity to name himself as the narrator. The maintained narrative veil of anonymity that only the end unveils embodies, on the one hand, the narrator's objectivity (his self-effacement) and, on the other hand, his shared vulnerability to death and to the Plague (in the course of the account, we do not know if Rieux, as others, will survive since we do not know until the very final pages who is the narrator, who is the survivor). And it is by virtue of this shared vulnerability, and on the grounds of his communal knowledge, that Rieux has earned his historical vocation, his obligation – and his right – to speak for all:

> This chronicle is drawing to an end, and this seems to be the moment for Dr Bernard Rieux to confess that he is the narrator... His profession put him in touch with a great many of our townspeople while plague was raging, and he had opportunities of hearing their various opinions. Thus he was well placed for giving a *true account* of all he saw and heard...
>
> *Summoned to give evidence* [appelé à témoigner] regarding what was a sort of crime, he has exercised the restraint that behooves a *conscientious*

witness [un témoin de bonne volonté]. All the same, following the dictates of his heart, *he has deliberately taken the victim's side* and tried to share with his fellow citizens the only certitudes they had in common – love, exile, and suffering. Thus he can *truly say* there was not one of their anxieties in which he did not share, no predicament of theirs that was not his.

To be an *honest witness* [témoin fidèle], it was for him to confine himself mainly to what people did or said and what could be gleaned from documents. Regarding his personal troubles and his long suspense, his duty was to hold his peace . . . *Thus, decidedly, it was up to him to speak for all.* (pp. 280–1)

The Physician's Witness

It is, of course, not a coincidence that the key-witness whose position appoints him to speak for all is a physician. Not only is the doctor's stance designated naturally and symbolically for the most insightful *body-witnessing* of history; but, by virtue of his job – his professional struggle against death – the doctor's testimonial stance is, of necessity, at once one of *resistance* (to the Plague) and one of *preservation* (of life, as well as of its memory): in much the same way the physician wishes to preserve life, the historian in Rieux wishes to preserve events. It is thus in the midst of the oblivious joy of liberation from the Plague – joy in which Rieux cannot fail but witness the crowd's immediate forgetfulness of history as holocaust – that Rieux decides to 'compile his chronicle', so as to rescue from the death of an oblivion not just the evidence of the survival, but the evidence – the knowledge – of its cost. Mediating between life and death as well as between past and future, the testimonial stance of the physician incorporates, indeed, this further knowledge which the crowd does not possess, that the *cost* of the survival has not been paid once and for all, but will be paid again; that history might once again claim the price of such a testimony; that the experience of survival is by no means in itself immune to a future plague.

> He knew what those jubilant crowds did not know but could have learnt from books: that the plague bacillus never dies or disappears for good; that it can lie dormant for years and years . . . and that perhaps the day would come when, for the bane and the enlightenment of men, it would rouse up its rats again and send them forth to die in a happy city. (p. 287)

> From the dark harbour soared the first rocket of the firework display organised by the municipality, and the town acclaimed it with a long-drawn sign of delight. Cottard, Tarrou, the men and the women Rieux had loved and lost – all alike, dead or guilty, were forgotten . . . And it was in the midst of shouts rolling against the terrace wall in massive waves that

waxed in volume and duration, while cataracts of coloured fire fell thicker through the darkness, that Dr Rieux resolved to compile this chronicle, so that he should not be one of those who hold their peace but should bear witness in favour of those plague-stricken people; so that some memorial of the injustice and outrage done them might endure...

Nonetheless, he knew that the tale he had to tell could not be one of a final victory. It could be only the record of what had to be done, and what assuredly will have to be done again in the never-ending fight against terror and its relentless onslaughts, despite their personal afflictions, by all who, while unable to be saints but refusing to bow down to pestilences, strive their utmost to be healers. (pp. 286-7)

III

An Age of Testimony

The story of the Plague amounts, thus, to the historical determination to bear witness, a determination that is lived at once as an artistic and as a political decision, and that functions at the novel's end not as a true closure, but as a signature, of Camus' work. 'If the Greeks invented tragedy, the Romans the epistle and the Renaissance the sonnet,' as Elie Wiesel has put it, 'our generation invented a new literature, that of testimony. We have all been witnesses and we feel we have to bear testimony for the future.[13] Without quite yet exhausting its significance, the ending of *The Plague* announces the new awareness and the new moral and political imperative of an *Age of Testimony*: an age whose writing task (and reading task) is to confront the horror of its own destructiveness, to attest to the unthinkable disaster of culture's breakdown, and to attempt to assimilate the massive trauma, and the cataclysmic shift in being that resulted, within some reworked frame of culture or within some revolutionised order of consciousness. 'It is true that consciousness is always lagging behind reality', writes Camus in one of his editorials in *Combat* (1948): 'History rushes onward while thought reflects. But this inevitable backwardness becomes more pronounced the faster History speeds up. The world has changed more in the past fifty years than it did in the previous two hundred years.'[14] The 'literature of testimony' is thus not an art of leisure but an art of urgency: it exists *in time* not just as a memorial but as an artistic promissory note, as an attempt to bring the 'backwardness' of consciousness to the level of precipitant events. 'As everybody knows', writes Camus, 'political thought today lags more and more behind events. Thus the French fought the 1914 war with 1870 methods and the 1939 war with the methods of 1918.'[15] The literature of testimony, therefore, is not simply a statement (any statement can but lag behind events), but a performative *engagement* between consciousness and history, a struggling act of readjustment between the integrative scope of words and the unintegrated impact of events. This ceaseless engagement between consciousness and history *obliges* artists, in Camus' conception, to transform words into events and to make *an act* of every publication; it is what keeps art in a state of *constant obligation.* 'To tell the truth, it is not easy', says Camus, 'and I can understand why artists regret their former comfort':

> Indeed, history's amphitheatre has always contained the martyr and the lion. The former relied on eternal consolations and the latter on raw historical meat. But until now the artist was on the sidelines. He used to sing purposely...to encourage the martyr and make the lion forget his appetite. But now the artist is in the amphitheatre. Of necessity, his voice is not quite the same; it is not nearly so firm.
> It is easy to see all that art can lose from such a *constant obligation.* Ease, to begin with, and that divine liberty so apparent in the work of Mozart. It is easier to understand why our works of art have a drawn, set look and why they collapse so suddenly. It is obvious why we have more journalists than creative writers... The period of the revered master, of the artist with a camellia in his buttonhole, of the armchair genius, is over. To create today is to create dangerously. *Any publication is an act, and that act exposes one to the passions of an age that forgives nothing...*
> The problem is more complex...as soon as it becomes apparent that the battle is waged within the artist himself.... The doubt felt by the artists who preceded us concerned their own talent. The doubt felt by artists of today concerns the necessity of their art....
> The questioning of art by the artist has many reasons.... Among the best explanations is the feeling the contemporary artist has of lying or of indulging in useless words if he pays no attention to history's woes.[16]

A Debt of Silence

Contemporary writing is testimonial to the extent that it exists in a state of *referential debt,* of 'constant obligation' to the 'woes of history', and to its dead. Thus, Rieux must testify because Tarrou's death has entrusted him with the testimonial legacy of the latter's notebooks. The age of testimony is the age of the transferral of a writing debt:

> 'And your colleague, doctor, how's he getting on?'
> 'He's dead.' Rieux was listening to his patient's rumbling chest.
> 'Ah, really?' The old fellow sounded embarrassed.
> 'Of plague,' Rieux added.

'Yes,' the old man said after a moment's silence, 'it's always the best who go. That's how life is. But he was a man who knew what he wanted.'

'Why do you say that?' The doctor was putting back his stethoscope.

'Oh, for no particular reason. Only – well, *he never talked just for talking's sake*...All those folks are saying: "It was plague. We've had the plague here." You'd almost think they expected to be given medals for it. But what does that mean – "plague"? Just life, no more than that.' (p. 285)

If Rieux's writing is indebted to Tarrou's, it is to the extent that 'Tarrou never talked just for talking's sake', never made of Plague a claim or an entitlement for moral or emotional profiteering. Thus, the writing debt is not so much a debt of words as it is a debt of silence.

And it is as much a debt of knowledge as of acknowledging the unpayability of the debt of knowledge. 'And how, in effect, is it possible to accept not to know?' asks Maurice Blanchot in his contemporary meditation on the relationship between writing and disaster: 'We read the books on Auschwitz. The vow of everybody there, the last vow: know what has happened, do not forget, and at the same time: you will never know.'[17]

Thus, the literature of testimony is at once a performance of its obligation and a statement of its falling short of cancelling its referential debt. 'This is why I write certain things rather than others,' says Elie Wiesel: 'to remain faithful.'

Of course, there are times of doubt for the survivor, times when one would...long for comfort. I hear a voice within me telling me to stop mourning the past. I too want to sing of love and of its magic.... I would like to shout, and shout loudly: 'Listen, listen well! I too am capable of victory, do you hear? I too am open to laughter and joy! I want to stride, head high, my face unguarded, without having to point to the ashes over there on the horizon'... One feels like shouting this, but the shout changes into a murmur. One must make a choice; one must remain faithful... This sentiment moves all survivors: they owe nothing to anyone, but everything to the dead.

I owe them my roots and memory. I am duty-bound to serve as their emissary, transmitting the history of their disappearance, even if it disturbs, even if it brings pain. Not to do so would be to betray them... And since I feel incapable of communicating their cry by shouting, I simply look at them. I see them and I write....

All those children, those old people, I see them. I never stop seeing them. I belong to them.

But they, to whom they belong?[18]

A Question of Belonging

The literature of testimony puts into effect, puts into action a question of belonging. To whom do the dead belong? And consequently, on whose side must the living (the surviving) be? Is it possible to *belong with* Plague? 'I'm not from here', says Rambert at first; but his experience as a witness to the Plague makes him cross the inner boundary of the very concept of belonging: 'Now that I have seen what I have seen, I know that I'm from here.' This is, as we have remarked, the thrust of Camus' radical concept of 'total condemnation', in its correlation with the demand for 'unqualified testimony'. Neither the condemnation of contemporary history, nor the testimony of contemporary writing, is any longer bound by conventional limits of belonging, or by the commonsensical limits that ensure the separation between life and death. But the purpose of the testimony is, precisely, to cross these lines in an opposite direction to the way the condemnation cancels them out: *to come out on the other side* – of death, of life, of the limits of belonging, of history as total condemnation. To come out on the other side of language: 'the concentration camp language', writes Elie Wiesel, 'negated all other language and took its place. Rather than link, it became wall. Can the reader be brought to the other side?'[19]

The Other Side

But to bring the reader to the other side of language, one must first come out on the other side of death: one must *survive* in order to bear witness, and one must bear witness in order to affirm one's survival, one's own crossing of the line of death. 'Survival and bearing witness become reciprocal acts', notes profoundly Terrence Des Pres.[20] Tied up with survival, bearing witness is then not just a linguistic, but an existential[21] stance. 'Rejected by mankind', writes Elie Wiesel, 'the condemned...persist in surviving – not only to survive, but to testify. The victims elect to become witnesses.' In Camus' testimonial work, it is also the reverse that could be said: the witnesses elect to become victims. Or rather, in the impossibility of being, in Camus' utopian terms, *Neither Executioners nor Victims*, and faced with the historical necessity of choosing between those two contemporary roles, Camus' witnesses elect to *side with* the targets of victimisation. This is the quintessence of the historical, ethical and existential choice that constitutes their unqualified testimonial stance.

> Summoned to testify [appelé à témoigner] regarding what was a sort of crime, [Rieux] had exercised the restraint that behooves a conscientious witness. All the same, following the dictates of his heart, *he has deliberately taken the victims' side* and tried to share with his fellow citizens the only

certitudes they had in common – love, exile and suffering. Thus he can truly say there was not one of their anxieties in which he did not share, no predicament of theirs that was not his.... Thus, decidedly, it was up to him to speak for all.

The Sniper

But there was at least one of our townsfolk for whom Dr Rieux could not speak...It is fitting [il est juste] that this chronicle should end with some reference to that man, who had an ignorant, that is to say, lonely, heart.

On turning out of the main thoroughfares where the rejoicings were in full swing...Dr Rieux was held up by a police cordon...

'Sorry, doctor,' a policeman said, 'but I can't let you through. There's a crazy fellow with a gun, shooting at everybody. But you'd better stay; we may need you'...

'It's Cottard!' Grand's voice was shrill with excitement. 'He's gone mad!' (pp. 281–5)

'It is fitting [*juste*, judicious] that this chronicle should end with some reference to that man.' How to account for this residue of violence and madness? Even though *The Plague* ends with the healer's vow to testify – to do justice to history – it is *juste*, judicious, right, the narrator tells us, that the narrative should terminate with this incongruent episode of the sniper. Why is such an ending '*juste*'? There is more to justice, and more to doing justice to history, than the doctor's testimony can account for: 'But there was at least one of our townsfolk for whom Dr Rieux could not speak.' Perhaps the most profound feature of Camus' testimony is that, in the very midst of its monumental effort to take the victims' side from the perspective of the healer, it acknowledges this residue, this failure of the healer's testimonial stance to encompass all of Plague, to 'speak for all', to say all.

The Plague's testimony to the Holocaust, 'unqualified' though it may be, nonetheless leaves out the 'judicious' residue of a radical and self-subversive question:

In a holocaust, is a healer's testimony truly possible? Can a healer's testimony exhaust the lesson of history as plague?

It will take Camus nine years to be able to address – and to articulate – this question, which he will dramatise in his last novel.

12

Why Bother with History?

Keith Jenkins

I start with some comments by Geoffrey Bennington which I hope will help me to make the two points that I want to consider in this paper. My first point is that postmodern ways of thinking probably signal the end of history/historiography as 'we' have known it in its modernist upper case (metanarrative) and in its lower case (professional/academic) forms. And that as a consequence, this capsizal of History/history carries with it not only a reconsideration of the nature(s) of the discursive phenomena which have lived under these signs, but also raises the ethical question of whether or not we still need, in these postmodern times, to reconsider them at all. Maybe we can just 'forget history'; maybe we can now lead lives within grammatical formulations which have no reference to a past tense articulated in ways which are, as it were, 'historically' familiar to us.

My second, subordinate point, refers to lower case professional/academic historiography more particularly and the ways its peculiar methods of appropriating/consuming the past are also fatally problematicised by postmodernism. I think most people would agree that in the bulk of the literature it is the capsizal of metanarrative constructions which has received most attention: it would seem that few people believe in such teleological fantasies any more. And yet, for many people (for many proper/professional historians), that metanarrative collapse seems to have left lower case historiography intact; indeed, the collapse of its 'rival' seems to have served only to bolster its claims to be 'proper' history. But my point is that I think this evaluation is a mistaken one. For as I read it, the specificities of the fall-out occasioned by the capsizal of the upper case have caused fatal collateral damage to the lower, the result being the effective end of the whole (modernist) History/history ensemble. And at this juncture I refer back to my first, major point, that under the impact of postmodernism, modernist constructions as we have gotten used to them are not only no longer viable, but that the need to bother with the past at all – not least for ethical purposes – is questionable: that perhaps we don't need what we might call a 'historical consciousness' any more. In effect, I suppose that what I'm going to be running here is a sort of 'end of history' argument. Let me begin doing so then, taking as my 'way in' the comments by Bennington I've already mentioned I'll be using.

In his article, 'Demanding History', which appeared in the volume *Post-structuralism and the Question of History* (1987) (edited by D. Attridge, R. Young and Bennington himself), Bennington argued that traditional (modernist) historiography is characterised by two demands. First of all, *history itself demands*. That is to say, 'it' demands that 'we' do certain things: that we do its bidding, that we come to know it so to become 'familiar' with it, that we obey its laws, lay down before its evidence, and so on. Secondly, *history is demanded*. It's demanded by us. We want it. We demand that it performs, say, the role of the great pedagogue, delivering up its secrets, its meanings, its reality and its ethics, so that we can 'learn lessons from it', orientate ourselves within it, find and legitimate our identities, and thus benefit from its study: either way, consciousness of the demanding/demanded past – a historical consciousness – is considered to be 'a good thing'.

Now, these two ways of positioning history (history demands – history is demanded) are part of an interesting opening move in Bennington's own essay. But, rather than follow him further here, I merely want to dwell for a little while on the observations I've just mentioned and extend them in ways which – though I'm sure Bennington is aware of them – he hasn't bothered to do himself. I have three points to make that are germane to my own double-faceted argument.

First, *vis-à-vis* the statement *history demands*, I think we need to make the (expected) qualifying distinction between upper and lower case historiography/historians; that is, between metanarrative type upper case and professional/academic lower case demands. Thus, upper case historiography has suggested and occasionally still suggests that 'we' (we objects of the historical process, 'we' who are *subjected* to it) do the bidding of a history which has its own *raison d'être*... its own immanent meaning(s), its own trajectory and teleology... this is a history which is going somewhere irrespective of whether we know it or not, so that the best we can do is to try and 'discover' its 'objective' journey/destination not, normally, to resist it, but to become its (increasingly 'historically conscious') bearers; its fellow-travellers. Typically this capitalised History has got, of course, its own capitalised Ontology, its own preferred way of making itself known (Epistemology) its own Method, and (and this is crucial) its own substantive Ethic... for it is this ethical dimension which makes this history's demands not only necessary to comply with but necessarily good; in this construal to be at one with the march of history is to be with the angels – as it were.

Obviously, I could go on describing the characteristics of such a metanarrative history for some time, but I'm sure this type of construction and its various expressions are familiar. Of course, the very fact that, historically, there have been so many expressions of upper case history's demands, might make us immediately consider the idea that these demands are actually just our own interpretative desires. But, 'historically' speaking, this fact – of one past but many metanarratives – has overwhelmingly served to convince adherents of them that, strange though it may seem, their preferred interpretation is not really an interpretation at all but 'the truth'. Thus we have witnessed various foundational Marxisms, Whiggisms, Fascisms, etc.; metanarratives ultimately of the essentialist 'ends justify the means' type; metanarratives which demand that we recognise that we *all* belong to a history that is bigger, better, more prioritising, more compelling and, indeed, more demanding, than our own, personal histories; that it is to 'it' that our first loyalties lie.

Now, the demands issuing out of such upper case histories are, in some ways at least, very different from the demands made on us by history in the professional/academic lower case. But that's not to say that the lower case is any more permissive; any less 'normative'. Lower case professional/academic historiography insists with as much conviction as any upper case history ever did that it (and it alone) really is 'proper' history, and that a 'proper' understanding of the past can only be achieved if its strictures are jealously followed. Though the demands made by history in the lower case may be less overtly (and less theoretically) formulated, they are no less certaintist (and in fact no less theoretical) for that. Lower case professional/academic historiography – a historiography every bit as local, as temporally located and as ideologically positioned as any other demanding construct – really does think that its own peculiar *species* of historiography is identical to its *genus*; that it 'truly' is history *per se*. Accordingly, and as indicated, this type of historiography has its own (arbitrary) demands. For example. 'It' demands that we study it for its own sake (own-sakism) as opposed to studying it (explicitly) for the sake of, say, the proletariat, the bourgeoisie, or women. 'It' insists that only dis-interested, objectivist study, will make it reveal the way it really was (as distinct from how we would like it to have been) – the past 'in and for itself' – the 'only past worth having'. 'It' insists on, at least, epistemological if not ontological realism. 'It' insists that its 'facts' can be best discovered and authenticated empirically (and not 'theoretically' – as if empiricism wasn't just another theory). 'It' valorises its original sources and especially its documents (documentarism). 'It' refuses to go along with the idea, common to poststructuralism/postmodernism, that language is not some sort of (modernist) reflection of the world it somehow captures in words, but is constitutive of that world. 'It' just won't let us recognise that language is anterior to the world it shapes; that what we experience as reality is a linguistic construct, the effect (the 'reality effect') of the specific language system we inhabit, structuring it 'like a language' according to its own rules of signification. 'It' refuses to let us admit that there is no world that is not ordered as a language: as textuality. 'It' refuses to let us happily bask in the knowledge that there is nothing meaning-full 'outside of the text'. 'It' demands that historians accept that whilst its truth(s) may never be absolutely/transparently known, to find those truth(s) – 'its' truths – is the only legitimate function of the 'proper' historian.

Moreover, the fact that this last aim cannot ever be achieved – the fact that lower case historiography is obviously 'interpretative' – indeed, the fact that a 'true interpretation' is very obviously an oxymoron (I mean, you can have a 'true truth' and an 'interpretive interpretation' but not the two together) is, Job-like, transformed from a weakness into a strength. For whilst in lower case historiography various interpretations are held, in principle, to be capable of a synthesis (one past so in principle one account . . .) unsynthesisable interpretations just are a fact of 'professional' life. Out of necessity then, such interpretative 'openness' has to be re-articulated back into, and normalised as a welcome feature of professional historiography, its 'open nature' and its 'tolerance' of the 'different' (of difference) being embraced; here, lower case historiography gains credit for its liberal pluralism and for its championing of academic freedom as opposed to the suffocating closures of the (ideologically fixated) upper case. The historicised past studied under these (its) demands, then, constitutes proper, normative, professional history: this is what must be done. This is the only sort of 'real' history there is . . . as the various Introductions and Primers to professional/academic history absolutely insist, this is the only way to proceed; this is how history ought to be; this is how history *per se* must be 'practised' (Elton, 1969; Tosh, 1991; Marwick, 1989; Stanford, 1994).

I turn now to the second point I want to make, which is, to recall, to develop Bennington's idea that not only does History/history make demands on us (of the type I've mentioned) but that we make demands on it: that *we demand history*. That we demand that it gives us – again to recall – trajectories, meanings, legitimitations, 'practices' and ethics which we can learn from and so 'place ourselves' in a past-backed-up-present (and future). But after having put the matter that way, I don't think it should take us too long to realise the rather obvious point that it is these sorts of demands (the demands we make of history) which have actually constructed and thus constituted the (reciprocal) demands we have pretty much taken thus far as issuing *independently* from history (from the past) itself. My second point is simply this then: that those upper and lower case histories which demanded/ demand that we did or do their bidding *do not independently exist and never have done*. Their demands are always only ours. Those 'demanding' histories are mere figments of, projections of (at this point in our 'actuality'), the Modernist imagination. In so far as we have thought that there really is a history (a past) that has its own demands, then we have forgotten that we've merely been throwing our voice. As soon as you think about it, the idea of a historicised past existing independent of our variously present-day constitutive concerns, is an absurd one. At which point Bennington's dualism –

Bennington's interesting binary opposition – can be 'deconstructed'. *All* the characteristics alleged to belong to 'the past' belong to us. *All* the demands allegedly from the past are demands we make of the past. Accordingly, we now recognise – and more importantly (and threateningly) some of us now act in the 'knowledge' – that there never has been, and there never will be, any such thing as an upper case past that is expressive of some kind of demanding/commanding essence, whilst the ridiculous idea (demand) that the only legitimate/proper study of the past is lower case own-sakism is recognised for what it is, as simply the mystifying way in which a modernist bourgeoisie conveniently articulated and still articulates its own professional code, its own guild practices, *as if* these issued not from 'it' at all, but from out of the past itself. Accordingly, the whole modernist upper/lower case ensemble now appears as an ultimately self-referencing, problematic expression of our various interests, an ideological discourse *per se* without any real access to the past as such, unable to engage in a dialogue with anything other than an 'always already' historiographically constituted historicised past. In summary form we might thus say that the past as constituted by its existing traces is always apprehended and appropriated textually through the sedimented layers of our previous interpretations and through the reading habits and categories developed by our previous/current methodological practices. And whilst we suspect that there may well be a 'real past' (an actual past) metaphorically underlying all our disparate versions of it, we 'know' that that past, that 'real referent', is ultimately inaccessible, and that all we have are our versions . . . but that that hardly matters, since versions are all we've ever had. Accordingly, the notion of a putative 'history-before-all-historiography' (like the putative 'world-before-all-versions-of-the-world') is, as Richard Rorty has put it, 'one well lost' (Rorty in McHale, 1992, p. 5). Or, put another way, historiography *per se* now appears to be just one more foundationless positioned expression in a world of foundationless positioned expressions as we collapse the 'referent into representation'.

Staying with the demise of lower case professional/academic historiography for just a moment longer and then going on from it, the idea of a past 'in itself' to be studied for its 'own sake' really is a hopeless ambition. For postmodernists 'know' (and in saying this they are not susceptible to the favourite modernist charge of committing a performative contradiction) . . . postmodernists know that the past has neither rhyme nor reason in it. That it is unfathomable, sublime, shapeless, formless. Consequently, postmodernists recognise that to give to something formless a form, to give to something shapeless a shape, to give to the non-storied the form of a narrative structure as if such a narrative corresponded to the structures of real stories lived in the past (narrativity after Hayden White) (White, 1973, 1987, pp. 1–25) to do all these things is to realise that historiography – despite its sometime empirical features – is, in the forming of its 'narrative substances' (Ankersmit,

1983, 1994) an aestheticising practice. Accordingly, because aesthetics are
not subject to true/false interrogation – I mean, what is the truth of a shape –
such a discourse cannot logically support true/false 'significations' beyond
the level of the statement or the chronicle, nor, and *I want to concentrate
from now on this,* can it provide any grounds for ethical judgements. Thus,
postmodernism ushers in the spectre of the severing of any necessary connection between any kind of historiography and any kind of ethical system.
Consequently, one of the main reasons why traditional historians of both
cases have said they study the past – to learn 'its' lessons, to learn from 'its'
mistakes, and to morally legitimate current desires and identities – is something that the past/history/historiography just cannot do. Yet despite this, I
think it is pretty much taken for granted that a historical consciousness is,
ethically speaking, still a 'good thing' to have. But how can it be? For if it is a
notion of goodness which defines the desired type of consciousness; that is, if
a 'good historical consciousness' is anything the definer defines as good
(which it is) then because today there are so many explicit, competing
notions of good with no neutral (foundational) criteria for adjudication
between them, so not only does the ultimate closure of 'the good' become
endlessly deferred, but the idea of what constitutes a 'good historical consciousness', or indeed a 'good history', is similarly affected: we now have no
clear sense of what a 'good historical consciousness' is. Nothing can be
gained ethically from a study of the past if that past is unavailable to us 'in
itself' (i.e., as a self-constituting thing with its own ethics and not those we
have ourselves put into it). For if we only get from the past the ethics (the
lessons, the 'guides to action') which we put into it (which we do) then why
bother with this circumvolution? Why not just have 'ethics talk' and leave the
temporal dimension out of it: why not just 'forget history' and historians?

But then, why not forget ethics too? Here a little bit of arbitrary defining
(there is no other) may be useful. For the problem of ethics is that normally
we link up that notion with the idea of a system: an ethical system. Such an
idea of an ethical system (say Kant's) has, at its 'centre', the further notion of
universalism; that is to say, an ethical system is one which, if universalised,
would allow ethical judgements to be made about all and every contingent
situation when one has to make a choice – when one has to decide what one
ought to do. But such a total (transcendental) system is impossible and, in
the event that this should be held should not be the case, not ethical. For if
there was such a thing as a total ethic so that in every situation one only had
to apply it, then one would not be making a choice at all but merely applying
a rule – in which case the implementation of such a rule absolves the subject
from actually making a decision. Consequently, there is no ethics (choice)
involved here, merely the application of a necessity. But if – as I am assuming
– 'morality' involves choice in such a way that a system of 'ethical necessities'
would not be 'moral' at all, then free choice, untrammelled by reference back

to any 'system', would just have to be subjective, contingent, situationist, pragmatic, aleatory and thus always ultimately unsystematisable; ungroundable. It is this situation, the situation where every moral choice is ultimately 'undecidable' but where such choices still have to be made (the situation we are in today) which makes Derrida talk about the 'madness of the decision', Baudrillard talk about the 'radical illusion of morality' and Laclau talk about the 'philosophy of the decision' (Mouffe, 1996). The upshot being – to cut a long story very short – that we are now left within an unbounded space, with nothing certaintist to fall back upon and no fixed horizons to guide us; with no ultimate ethical stabilisers – least of all any stabilisers which we may have thought issued from the past constructed historiographically by us but in such a way so to render forth the illusion that the past was constituting itself for us – to help us. Consequently, that radical illusion now made transparent, so the suggestion that we forget 'history and ethics' now forces itself upon us – or rather, we now force it upon ourselves.

There are, I think, many additional reasons to those I have just mentioned, to make me think that 'ethically speaking' forgetting history and ethics might be an interesting move to make (I'm thinking here of the sorts of arguments which would jack up the linguistic register and the arguments I'm using several notches; say, arguments such as Derrida's play on the notion of the gift and the consequent idea of full presence and absence/lack which runs as a leitmotif throughout Western metaphysics [Bennington and Derrida, 1996]; of Levinas' critique of that same metaphysics as the history of our committing 'ontological violence' on the object [Levinas, 1985]; of Baudrillard's critique [1996] of our pathetic susceptibility to being seduced by the object/'reality' which runs, again, throughout Western metaphysics until our postmodern escape into a happy, carefree acceptance of a non-essentialising simulacra as the beginning and end of Truth, Reality, Meaning, and so on and so forth [Mouffe, 1996]). But I want to remain, for now, in the rather mundane register I have chosen to use and to come to my third and final set of comments – comments to strengthen my argument that, *the demands of history* being collapsed into *our demands for history*, so we might forget history and sort out our present problems in the present. I have two comments to make *vis-à-vis* this third point.

The first comment to underline the futility of going to the past for ethical/moral lessons as variously used and deployed within historiography – and which I've already hinted at – is because that past is utterly promiscuous: it will go with anybody – Marxists, Whigs, racists, feminists, phenomenologists, structuralists, empiricists, Eltonists, Foucauldians, 'postists' – anybody. And this is because, as we have seen, the past has no resistance of its own; the past as such doesn't exist *historically* outside of historians' textual constitutive appropriations, consequently, being constructed by them it has no independence to resist them at the aesthetic 'level of signification'.[1] The historicised past *itself* thus contains nothing independent of us that we *have* to be loyal to; nothing we *have* to feel guilty about, no facts we *have* to respect; no truth we *have* to find, no problems we *have* to solve – for the past doesn't have any problems – only historians have those as they *displace* current ideological problematics from the present into the past as if, once removed, they become amenable to resolution; that if we 'understand' the 'historical conditions' of 'this and that' then the problems of 'this and that' can be some way to being solved. But obviously this displacement is illusory. Given that it is the historians who have the problems not the past, the solutions to their problems lie in them and their present, not in history. In that sense the past doesn't 'actually enter into it' – except rhetorically.

This conclusion – that 'historical' problems and 'historical' solutions are always *historians'* problems and conclusions, leads to my second and final point in this third and final comment. Which is this. Given that history is constituted by the work of historians (historiography) the idea that we can 'learn lessons from the past/history', actually translates out as simply, 'we can learn lessons from historians'. At which point the fairly obvious question arises as to how many of us would trust historians as 'moral guides', as 'lesson givers', and as providers of and legitimators of our identities, any further than we could, how can I put it, throw them? The reification[2] of historians' work as the work of 'history'; the designation of historians' problems as 'historical' problems, the habit of thinking in terms of 'historical' ontologies, 'historical' epistemologies and 'historical' methodologies rather than 'historians', all these ideas, to re-use Rorty's phrase, are ones 'well lost'. The collapse of Bennington's dualism, the absorption of *history's demands* into *our demands*, should firmly lay these particular sleights of hand to rest.

To sum up. I began by saying that a working of Bennington's couplet *history demands/we demand history*, may lead us to the point where we not only re-think the 'nature' of history, but also whether we still need a history at all: what is the point of going to the historicised past? And I said that, in saying this, maybe I was talking about a version of the 'end of history'. And I suppose I've now given some reasons why this is possibly the case. The idea that there really is a past-as-history that makes upper and/or lower case (normative) demands on us, as distinct from 'the fact' that we simply project on to the past our own (normative) desires as if they were not ours at all, is an interesting modernist trick which postmodernists feel under no obligation to continue with. Postmodernism therefore does, I think, signal the end of history as modernists have construed it – and maybe the way in which we need to bother construing it at all. By which I don't mean, it almost goes without saying, that actual life is ending; that there won't (probably) be a tomorrow and a next year. Nor do I mean, again it almost goes without saying, that ethical/moral problems and discussions about ethically/morally positioned representations of the past may not continue, the point being, however, that postmodern implications have so transformed the concepts of History/history and ethics/morality that they are now no longer the same; that traditional ways of posing (and therefore of allegedly answering) the questions no longer make much sense. What I want to say, then, is that today we seem to be living through the last years of the peculiar ways in which modernist historians *conceptualised* the past; the (illusory) way that they tried to make ethical and moral sense of it in upper and lower case forms... the idea that, separate from us, the past 'itself' (as if the past had a 'self') could make normative demands on us and that, separate from it, we could make normative demands on it which it would understand, and respond to, if only we got its 'number'... a dualism now happily collapsed, and which collapse maybe signals the end of 'history demands'/'we demand history' altogether. To end with a few words from Freud suitably jumbled up: for those particular illusions there may well have been a past; it is problematic, however, if there is now much of a future.

13
Writings and Histories

Michel de Certeau

'Studious and charitable, tender as I am for the dead of the world...thus I roamed, from age to age, always young and never tired, for thousands of years.' The open road – 'my road' – seems to take hold of the text of this traveller on foot: 'I went, I wandered...I ran along my path...I went...as a bold voyager.' Walking and /or writing is a labour knowing no rest, 'by the force of desire, pricked by an ardent curiosity that nothing could restrain'. Michelet multiplies his meetings, with 'indulgence' and 'filial fear' in respect to the dead who are the inheritors of a 'strange dialogue', but also with the assurance 'that never could anyone ever stir up again what life has left behind'. In the sepulchre which the historian inhabits, only 'emptiness remains'.[1] Hence this 'intimacy with the other world poses no threat':[2] 'This security made me all the more charitable toward those who were unable to harm me.' Every day he even becomes 'younger' by getting acquainted over and over again with this world that is dead, and definitely other.

After having successively passed through the *History of France*, the shadows 'have returned less saddened to their tombs'.[3] Discourse drives them back into the dark. It is a deposition. It turns them into *severed souls*. It honours them with a ritual of which they had been deprived. It 'bemoans' them by fulfilling the duty of filial piety enjoined upon Freud through a dream in which he saw written on the wall of a railway station, 'Please close the eyes'.[4] Michelet's 'tenderness' seeks one after another of the dead in order to insert every one of them into time, 'this omnipotent decorator of ruins: O Time beautifying of things!'[5] The dear departed find a haven in the text *because* they can neither speak nor do harm anymore. These ghosts find access through *writing* on the condition that they remain *forever silent*.

Another, graver mourning is added to the first. The People are also the separated. 'I was born of the people. I had the people in my heart. ...But I found their language inaccessible. I was unable to make it speak.'[6] It is also silent, in order to become the object of this poem that speaks of it. Surely, only this language 'authorises' the historian's writing, but, for the same reason, it becomes history's absent figure. An *Infans*, this Voice does not speak. It exists only outside of itself, in Michelet's discourse, but it allows him to become a 'popular' writer, to 'jettison' pride and, becoming 'rough and barbaric', to 'lose . . . what I had owned of literary subtlety'.[7]

The other is the phantasm of historiography, the object that it seeks, honours, and buries. A labour of separation concerning this uncanny and fascinating proximity is effected. Michelet stakes himself at this border where, from Virgil to Dante, *fictions* were erected that were not yet *history*. This place points to the question that scientific practices have been articulating ever since, and that a discipline has assigned itself to solve. Alphonse Dupront has said, 'The sole historical quest for "meaning" remains indeed a quest for the Other',[8] but, however contradictory it may be, this project aims at 'understanding' and, through 'meaning', at hiding the alterity of this foreigner; or, in what amounts to the same thing, it aims at calming the dead who still haunt the present, and at offering them scriptural tombs.

THE DISCOURSE OF SEPARATION: WRITING

Modern Western history essentially begins with differentiation between the *present* and the *past*. In this way it is unlike tradition (religious tradition), though it never succeeds in being entirely dissociated from this archaeology, maintaining with it a relation of indebtedness and rejection. This rupture also organises the content of history within the relations between *labour* and *nature*; and finally, as its third form, it ubiquitously takes for granted a rift between *discourse* and the *body* (the social body). It forces the silent body to speak. It assumes a gap to exist between the silent opacity of the 'reality' that it seeks to express and the place where it produces its own speech, protected by the distance established between itself and its object (*Gegen-stand*). The violence of the body reaches the written page only through absence, through the intermediary of documents that the historian has been able to see on the sands from which a presence has since been washed away, and through a murmur that lets us hear – but from afar – the unknown immensity that seduces and menaces our knowledge.

A structure belonging to modern Western culture can doubtless be seen in this historiography: *intelligibility is established through a relation with the other*; it moves (or 'progresses') by changing what it makes of its 'other' – the Indian, the past, the people, the mad, the child, the Third World. Through these variants that are all heteronomous – ethnology, history, psychiatry, pedagogy, etc. – unfolds a problematic form basing its mastery of expression upon what the other keeps silent, and guaranteeing the interpretive work of a science (a 'human' science) by the frontier that separates it from an area awaiting this work in order to be known. Here modern medicine is a decisive figure, from the moment when the body becomes a *legible* picture that can in turn be translated into that which can be *written* within a space of language.

Thanks to the unfolding of the body before the doctor's eyes, what is seen
and what is known of it can be superimposed or exchanged (be translated
from one to the other). The body is a cipher that awaits deciphering. Between
the seventeenth and the eighteenth century, what allows the seen body to be
converted into the known body, or what turns the spatial organisation of the
body into a semantic organisation of a vocabulary – and vice versa – is the
transformation of the body into extension, into open interiority like a book,
or like a silent corpse placed under our eyes.[9] An analogous change takes
place when tradition, a lived body, is revealed to erudite curiosity through a
corpus of texts. Modern medicine and historiography are born almost
simultaneously from the rift between a subject that is supposedly literate,
and an object that is supposedly written in an unknown language. The latter
always remains to be decoded. These two 'heterologies' (discourses on the
other) are built upon a division between the body of knowledge that utters a
discourse and the mute body that nourishes it.

First of all, historiography separates its present time from a past. But
everywhere it repeats the initial act of division. Thus its chronology is
composed of 'periods' (for example, the Middle Ages, modern history,
contemporary history) between which, in every instance, is traced the *decision* to become different or no longer to be such as one had been up to that
time (the Renaissance, the French Revolution). In their respective turns,
each 'new' time provides the *place* for a discourse considering whatever
preceded it to be 'dead', but welcoming a 'past' that had already been
specified by former ruptures. Breakage is therefore the postulate of interpretation (which is constructed as of the present time) and its object (divisions organising representations that must be reinterpreted). The labour
designated by this breakage is self-motivated. In the past from which it is
distinguished, it promotes a selection between what can be *understood* and
what must be *forgotten* in order to obtain the representation of a present
intelligibility. But whatever this new understanding of the past holds to be
irrelevant – shards created by the selection of materials, remainders left aside
by an explication – comes back, despite everything, on the edges of discourse
or in its rifts and crannies: 'resistances', 'survivals', or delays discreetly
perturb the pretty order of a line of 'progress' or a system of interpretation.
These are lapses in the syntax constructed by the law of a place. Therein they
symbolise a return of the repressed, that is, a return of what, at a given
moment, has *become* unthinkable in order for a new identity to *become*
thinkable.

Far from being self-evident, this construction is a uniquely Western trait.
In India, for example, 'new forms never drive the older ones away'. Rather,
there exists a 'stratified stockpiling', Louis Dumont has noted. The march of
time no more needs to be certified by distances taken from various 'pasts'
than a position needs to establish itself by being sectioned off from 'heresies'.

A 'process of coexistence and reabsorption' is, on the contrary, the 'cardinal fact' of Indian history.[10] And, too, among the Merina of Madagascar, the *tetiarana* (former genealogical lists), then the *tantara* (past history) form a 'legacy of ears' (*lovantsofina*) or a 'memory by mouth' (*tadidivava*): far from being an 'object' thrown behind so that an autonomous present will be possible, the past is a treasure placed in the *midst* of the society that is its memorial, a food intended to be chewed and memorised. History is the 'privilege' (*tantara*) that must be remembered so that one shall not oneself be forgotten. In its own midst it places the people who stretch from a past to a future.[11] Among the Fô of Dahomey, history is *remuho*, 'the speech of these past times' – speech (*ho*), or presence, which comes from upriver and carries downstream. It has nothing in common with the conception (apparently close to it, but actually of ethnographical and museological origin) that, in *dissociating* current time from tradition, in thus imposing a break between a present and a past, and in actually upholding the Western relation whose terms it simply reverses, defines identity through a return to a past or marginalised 'negritude'.[12]

It would be senseless to multiply the examples, beyond our historiography, that bear witness to another relation with time or, in what amounts to the same thing, another relation with death. In the West, the group (or the individual) is legitimised by what it excludes (this is the creation of its own space), and it discovers its faith in the confession that it extracts from a dominated being (thus is established the *knowledge* based upon, or of, the other: human science). It comes of realising how ephemeral is every victory over death: inevitably, the reaper returns and cuts his swath. Death obsesses the West. In this respect, the discourse of the human sciences is pathological: a discourse of *pathos* – misfortune and passionate action – in a confrontation with this death that our society can no longer conceive of as a way of living one's life. On its own account, historiography takes for granted the fact that it has become impossible to believe in this presence of the dead that has organised (or organises) the experience of entire civilisations; and the fact too that it is nonetheless impossible 'to get over it', to accept the loss of a living solidarity with what is gone, or to confirm an irreducible limit. What is *perishable* is its data; *progress* is its motto. The one is the experience which the other must both compensate for and struggle against. Historiography tends to prove that the site of its production can encompass the past: it is an odd procedure that posits death, a breakage everywhere reiterated in discourse, and that yet denies loss by appropriating to the present the privilege of recapitulating the past as a form of knowledge. A labour of death and a labour against death.

This paradoxical procedure is symbolised and performed in a gesture which has at once the value of myth and of ritual: *writing*. Indeed, writing replaces the traditional representations that gave authority to the present with a representative labour that places both absence and production in the same area. In its most elementary form, writing is equivalent to constructing a sentence by going over an apparently blank surface, a page. But isn't historiography also an activity that recommences from the point of a new time, which is separated from the ancients, and which takes charge of the construction of a rationality within this new time? It appears to me that in the West, for the last four centuries, 'the making of history' has referred to writing. Little by little it has replaced the myths of yesterday with a practice of meaning. As a practice (and not by virtue of the discourses that are its result) it symbolises a society capable of managing the space that it provides for itself, of replacing the obscurity of the lived body with the expression of a 'will to know' or a 'will to dominate' the body, of changing inherited traditions into a textual product or, in short, of being turned into a blank page that it should itself be able to write. This practice of history is an ambitious, progressive, also utopian practice that is linked to the endless institution of areas 'proper', where a will to power can be inscribed in terms of reason. It has the value of a scientific model. It is not content with a hidden 'truth' that needs to be discovered; it *produces* a symbol through the very relation between a space newly designated within time and a *modus operandi* that fabricates 'scenarios' capable of organising practices into a currently intelligible discourse – namely, the task of 'the making of history'. Indissociable from the destiny of writing in the modern and contemporary West until now, historiography nonetheless has the qualities of grasping scriptural invention in its relation with the elements it inherits, of operating right where the *given* must be transformed into a *construct*, of building representations with past materials, of being situated, finally, on this frontier of the present where, simultaneously, a past must be made from a tradition (by exclusion) and where nothing must be lost in the process (exploitation by means of new methods).

HISTORY AND POLITICS: A PLACE

By taking for granted its distancing from tradition and the social body, in the last resort historiography is based upon a power that in effect distinguishes it from the past and from the whole of society. 'The making of history' is buttressed by a political power which creates a space proper (a walled city, a nation, etc.) where a will can and must write (construct) a system (a reason articulating practices). In the sixteenth and seventeenth centuries, by being established spatially and by being distinguished by virtue of an autonomous will, political power also occasions restriction of thought. Two tasks are necessary and especially important from the standpoint of the historiography that they are going to transform through the intermediary of jurists and 'politicists'. On the one hand, power must be legitimised, it must attribute to its grounding force an authority which in turn makes this very power credible. On the other hand, the relation between a 'will to produce history' (a subject of the political operation) and the 'environment' (into which is carved a power of decision and action) calls for an analysis of the variables thrown into play through any intervention that might influence this relation of forces – that is, an art of manipulating complexity as a function of objectives, hence a calculus of possible relations between a will (that of the prince) and a set of coordinates (the givens of a situation).

These are two features of the 'science' constructed between the sixteenth and the eighteenth century by 'historiographers'. Mostly jurists and magistrates, they were provided by the prince – and in his service – with a privileged 'place' whence it was necessary, for the 'utility' of the state and 'the common good', to bring into accord the truth of the letter and the efficacy of power – 'the first dignity of literature' and the capacity of a 'man of government'.[13] On the one hand, this discourse 'legitimises' the force that power exerts; it provides this force with a familial, political, or moral genealogy; it accredits the prince's current 'utility' while transforming it into 'values' that organise the representation of the past. On the other hand, the picture that is drawn from this past, which is the equivalent of current prospective 'scenarios', formulates *praxeological* models and, through a series of situations, a typology of feasible relations between a concrete will and conjunctural variants; by analysing the failures and successes, this discourse sketches a science of the practices of power. In this way, it is not satisfied with historical justification of the prince through offering him a genealogical blazon. The prince receives a 'lesson' provided by a technician of political management.

Since the sixteenth century – or, to take up clearly marked signs, since Machiavelli and Guichardin[14] – historiography has ceased to be the representation of a providential time, that is, of a history decided by an inaccessible Subject who can be deciphered only in the signs that he gives of his wishes. Historiography takes the position of the subject of action – of the prince, whose objective is to 'make history'. The historiography gives intelligence the function of mobilising possible moves between a power and the realities from which it is distinguished. Its very definition is furnished through a policy of the state; in brief, its purpose is to construct a coherent discourse that specifies the 'shots' that a power is capable of making in relation to given facts, by virtue of an art of dealing with the elements imposed by an environment. This science is strategic because of its object, political history; on other grounds, it is equally strategic through the method it uses in handling given facts, archives, or documents.

It is through a sort of fiction, however, that the historian is accorded this place. In fact, the historians are not the agents of the operation for which they are technicians. They do not make history, they can only engage in the making of histories: the partitive usage indicates the role they play in a position that does not belong to them, but without which a new kind of historiographical analysis would not have been possible.[15] They are solely 'around' power. Thus they receive the directives, in more or less explicit form, that in every modern country burden history – from theses to textbooks – with the task of educating and mobilising. Its discourse will be magisterial without being that of the master, in the same way that historians will be teaching lessons of government without knowing either its responsibilities or its risks. They reflect on the power that they lack. Their analysis is therefore deployed 'next to' the present time, in a staging of the past which is analogous to that which, drawn also through a relation to the present, the prospectivist produces in terms of the future.

Thus located in the vicinity of political problems – but not in the place where political power is exercised – historiography is given an ambivalent status which shows forth most visibly in its modern archaeology. It is in a strange situation, at once critical and fictive. The fact is evident with particular clarity in Machiavelli's *Discorsi* and *Istorie fiorentine*. When the historian seeks to establish, for the place of power, the rules of political conduct and the best political institutions, he *plays the role* of the prince that he is not; he analyses what the prince *ought* to do. Such is the fiction that gives his discourse an access to the space in which it is written. Indeed, a fiction, for it is at once the discourse of the master and that of the servant – it is legitimised through power and drawn from it, in a position where, withdrawn from the scene, as a master thinker, the technician can replay the problems facing the prince.[16] The historiographer depends on 'the prince in fact', and he produces 'the virtual prince'.[17] Therefore he must act *as if* effective power fell under the jurisdiction of his teaching even while, against all probability, his teaching expects the prince to insert himself into a democratic organisation. In this way his fiction puts in question – and makes chimerical – the possibility that political *analysis* would find its extension in the effective *practice* of power. Never will the 'virtual prince', a construct of discourse, be the 'prince in fact'. Never will the gap separating reality from discourse be filled; to the very degree that this discourse is rigorous, it will be destined for futility.[18]

An originary frustration that will make the effectiveness of political life a fascinating question for historians (just as, inversely, the political man will be led to take the historian's position and to play back what he has done, in order to reflect upon it and accredit it), this fiction is also betrayed in the fact that the historian analyses *situations* whereas, for a power, it was at the time a question of *objectives* to be sought. The historian receives, as already realised by another, what the political man should do. Here the past is the consequence of a lack of articulation over 'making history'. The unreal is insinuated into this science of action, with the fiction which consists of acting as if one were the subject of the operation – or with this activity which reproduces politics in laboratory conditions, and substitutes the subject of a historiographical operation for the subject of a historical action. Archives make up the world of this technical game, a world in which complexity is found, but sifted through and miniaturised, therefore made capable of being formalised. A precious space in every sense of the term: I would see in it the professionalised and scriptural equivalent of what games represent in everyone's common experience; that is, practices by which every society makes explicit, puts in miniature, and formalises its most fundamental strategies, and thus acts itself out without the risks or responsibilities of having to make history.

In the case of historiography, fiction can be found at the end of the process, in the product of the manipulation and the analysis. Its story is given as a staging of the past, and not as the circumscribed area in which is effected an operation characterised by its gap in respect to power. Such was already the case of the *Discorsi:* Machiavelli offers them as a commentary on Livy. In fact, the historical figure is only a dummy. The author knows that the principles in whose name he is erecting the model of Roman institutions 'fragment' the tradition and that his enterprise is 'without precedent'.[19] Roman history, a common reference and an agreeable subject in Florentine discussions, furnishes him with a public arena where he can deal with politics instead of the prince. The past is the area of *interest* and *pleasure* that situates beyond the current problems the prince is facing – within the field of 'opinion' or public 'curiosity' – the scene where the historian can play his role as the prince's technician-substitute. The gap in respect to present events delimits the space where historiography is manufactured, around the prince and near the public. It plays between what one *does* and what *pleases* the other, yet it can be identified neither with the one nor the other. Thus the past is the fiction of the present. The same holds true for all veritable historiographical labours. The explication of the past endlessly marks distinctions between the analytical apparatus, which is present, and the materials analysed, the documents concerning curiosities about the dead. A rationalisation of practices and the pleasure of telling legends of former days ('the charm of history', Marbeau used to say)[20] – the techniques that allow the complexity of current times to be managed, and the poignant curiosity surrounding the dead members of the 'family' – are combined within the same text in order to produce both scientific 'reduction' and narrative techniques turning the strategies of power into metaphors belonging to current times.

The real which is written in historiographical discourse originates from the determinations of a place. A *dependency* in respect to a power established from elsewhere, a *mastery* of techniques dealing with social strategies, a *play* with symbols and references that represent public authority: such are the effective relations that appear to characterise this space of writing. Placed next to power, based upon it, yet held at a critical distance; holding in its hands – mimicked by writing itself – the rational instruments of operations modifying the balance of forces in the name of a conquering will; rejoining the masses from afar (from behind political and social separation, which 'distinguishes' it from them) by reinterpreting the traditional references that are invested in them: in its near totality, modern French historiography is bourgeois and – not astonishingly – rationalist.[21]

This given situation is written into the text. The more or less discreet dedication (the fiction of the past must be upheld so that the scholarly play of history can 'take place') bestows upon discourse its status of being *indebted* in respect to the power that, beforehand, belonged to the prince, and that today, by the way of delegation, characterises the scientific institution of the state or its eponym, the *patron* (or thesis director). This 'envoy' designates the legitimising place, the referent of an organised force, inside of which and through which analysis has its place. But the *story* itself, a body of fiction, through the methods it uses and the content it takes up, also marks on the one hand a distance in respect to this debt, and on the other, the two foundations that allow for this deviation: through a technical labour and a public interest historians receive from current events the means for their research and the context for their interests.

By virtue of this triangular structuring, historiography therefore cannot be thought of in terms of an opposition or an adequacy between a subject and an object; that is nothing more than the play of the fiction that it constructs. Nor could anyone believe, as much as historiography might tend to have us believe, that a 'beginning' situated in a former time might explain the present: each historian situates elsewhere the inaugural rupture, at the point where his or her investigations stop; that is, at the borders demarcating a specialisation within the disciplines to which he or she belongs. In fact, historians begin from present determinations. Current events are their real beginning. Lucien Febvre already noted this fact in his own style: 'The Past', he wrote, 'is a reconstitution of societies and human beings engaged in the network of human realities of today.'[22] That this place prohibits the historian from speaking in the name of Man is what Febvre would never have admitted. He felt historical work to be exempt from the law that would submit it to the logic of a *site* of production, and not just to the 'mentality' of a period in a 'progress' of time. But, like all historians, he knew that *to write* is to meet the death that inhabits this site, to make death manifest through a representation of the relations that current time keeps with its other, and to struggle against death through the work of intellectually controlling the connection of a particular will to the forces facing it. Through all of these aspects, historiography stages the conditions of possibility of production, and it is itself the subject on which it endlessly writes.

PRODUCTION AND / OR ARCHAEOLOGY

Production is indeed historiography's quasi-universal principle of explanation, since historical research grasps every document as the symptom of whatever produced it. Clearly, it is not so easy to do as Jean Desanti has said, to 'learn from the very product to be deciphered and to read the concatenation of its generative acts'.[23] On a first level of analysis, we can state that production names a question that appeared in the West with the mythic practice of writing. Up until then, history was developed by introducing a cleavage everywhere between *materia* (facts, the *simplex historia*) and *ornamentum* (presentation, staging, commentary).[24] It aimed at recovering a truth of facts under the proliferation of 'legends', and in thus instituting a discourse conforming to the 'natural order' of things, at the point where mixtures of illusion and truth were proliferating.[25] The problem is no longer advanced in the same way from the time when the 'fact' ceases to function as the 'sign' of a truth, when 'truth' changes its status, slowly ceasing to be what is manifest in order to become what is produced, thereby acquiring a scriptural form. The idea of production transposes the ancient conception of a 'causality' and separates two kinds of problems: on the one hand, reference of the 'fact' to what *made it possible*; on the other, a *coherence* or a 'concatenation' among observed phenomena. The first question is translated in terms of genesis, and endlessly bestows privilege upon what occurs 'before'; the second is expressed in the form of series whose makeup calls for an almost obsessive worry on the part of historians over filling lacunae and maintaining, more or less metaphorically, an order of structure. Often reduced to being no more than a filiation and an order, the two elements are combined in the quasi-concept of temporality. In this respect, it is true, as Desanti says, that it is 'solely at the time when a specific concept of temporality is at hand and fully elaborated that the problem of *History* can be approached'.[26] Meanwhile, temporality can designate the necessary linkage of the two problems, and expose or represent in the same text the ways by which the historian meets the double demand of expressing what existed beforehand and filling lacunae with facts. History furnishes the empty frame of a linear succession which formally answers to questions on *beginnings* and to the need for *order*. It is thus less the result obtained from research than its condition: the web woven a priori by the two threads with which the historical loom moves forward in the single gesture of filling holes. For lack of being able to transform the postulate of their study into its object, historians, Gérard Mairet says, 'replace an acquaintance with time with the knowledge of *what* exists within time'.[27]

In this respect, historiography would simply be a philosophical discourse that is unaware of itself; it would obfuscate the formidable questions that it bears by replacing them with the infinite labour of doing 'as if' it were responding to them. In fact, this repressed dimension returns endlessly in its labours; it can be seen, among other signs, in that which inscribes into it the reference to a 'production' and/or in the questioning that can be placed under the sign of an 'archaeology'.

So that, through 'production', we will not be limited to naming a necessary but unknown relation among known terms – in other words, to designating what supports historical discourse but which is not the object of analysis – we must recall what Marx noted in his *Theses on Feuerbach*, to the effect that 'the thing, reality, sensuousness' must be grasped '*as a human sensuous activity*', as a '*practice*'.[28] A return to fundamentals: 'Life involves, before everything else, eating and drinking, habitation, and many other things. The first historical fact [*die erste geschichtliche Tat*] is thus the production [*die Erzeugung*] of the means to satisfy these needs, the production [*die Produktion*] of material life itself. And this is a historical fact [*geschichtliche Tat*], a fundamental condition [*Grundbedingung*] of all history, which today, as thousands of years ago, must daily and hourly be fulfilled.'[29] From this base, production diversifies according to needs that are or are not easily satisfied, and according to the conditions under which they are satisfied. Production is everywhere, but '*production in general* is an abstraction': 'When we speak of production, we always have in mind production at a definite stage of social development, of the production by individuals in society. ... For example, no production is possible without an instrument of production. ... It is not possible without past, accumulated labors. ... Production is always a particular branch of production.' 'Finally, not only is production particular production, but it is invariably only a definite social corpus, a social subject, that is engaged in a wider or narrower totality of production spheres.'[30] Thus the analysis returns to needs, to technical organisations, to social places and institutions in which, as Marx notes of the piano manufacturer, only that labour which produces capital is productive.[31]

I emphasise and underscore these classical texts because they specify the interrogation that I have encountered by beginning from a so-called history of ideas or mentalities: what relation can be established among definite *places* and the *discourses* that are produced therein? Here it has seemed to me that it might be possible to transpose what Marx calls productive labour in the economical sense of the term to the extent that 'labour is productive only if it produces its opposite', that is, capital.[32] Discourse is doubtless a form of capital, invested in symbols; it can be transmitted, displaced, accrued, or lost. Clearly this perspective also holds for the historian's 'labour' that uses discourse as its tool; and in this respect, historiography also clearly pertains to what it must study: the relation among a *place*, a *labour*, and this 'increase of capital' that can constitute *discourse*. That for Marx discourse falls into the category of what is generated by 'improductive labour' does not impede us from envisaging the *possibility* of treating in these terms the questions placed before historiography, and the questions posed by it.

Perhaps it is a question of giving a specific content already to the 'archaeology' that Michel Foucault has surrounded with new prestige. For my part, born as a historian within religious history, and formed by the dialect of that discipline, I asked myself what role religious productions and institutions might have had in the organisation of the modern 'scriptural' society that has replaced them by transforming them. Archaeology was the way by which I sought to specify the return of a repressed, a system of Scriptures which modernity has *made* into an absent body, without being able to eliminate it. This 'analysis' allowed me also to recognise in current labours a 'past, accumulated' and still-influential labour. In this fashion, which made continuities and distortions appear within systems of *practice*, I was also the subject of my own analysis. That analysis has no autobiographical interest, yet by restoring in a new form the relation of production that a place keeps with a product, it led me to a study of historiography itself. The subject appears within his own text: not with the marvellous liberty that allows Martin Duberman to become in his discourse the interlocutor of his absent characters and to tell of himself by telling of them,[33] but in the manner of an unassailable lacuna that brings to light a lack within the text and ceaselessly moves and misleads him, or indeed *writes*.

This lacuna, a mark of the place within the text and the questioning of the place through the text, ultimately refers to what archaeology designates without being able to put in words: the relation of the *logos* to an *archè*, a 'principle' or 'beginning' which is its other. This other on which it is based, which makes it possible, is what historiography can place always 'earlier', go further and further back to, or designate as what it is within the 'real' that legitimises representation but is not identical to it. The *archè* is *nothing* of what can be said. It is only insinuated into the text through the labour of division, or with the evocation of death.

Thus historians can write only by combining within their practice the 'other' that moves and misleads them and the real that they can represent only through fiction. They are historiographers. Indebted to the experience I have had of the field, I should like to render homage to this writing of history.

Summaries and Notes

1. TAMSIN SPARGO, INTRODUCTION: PAST, PRESENT AND FUTURE PASTS

Notes

1. Karl Marx, *Selected Writings*, ed. D. McLellan (Oxford, 1977), p. 300.
2. See Paul Hamilton, *Historicism* (London, 1996).

2. LESZEK KOLAKOWSKI, 'EMPEROR KENNEDY LEGEND: A NEW ANTHROPOLOGICAL DEBATE'
(From *Salmagundi*, 72 (Fall 1986), 211–17.)

Summary

The essay tells the story of an academic dispute at a future meeting of the Academy of Science about the interpretation of source material which forms the basis of a legend about an Emperor called Kennedy. Conflicting interpretations by a structuralist (Dr Rama), a psychoanalyst (Dr Gama), and a Marxist (Dr Ngama), are presented in turn, after which the members of the Academy vote to decide on the truth. After four ballots with no clear majority, Dr Gama's explanation is declared the winner of a fifth ballot and the psychoanalytic theory is scientifically established as true.

3. CAROLYN STEEDMAN, 'THE WATERCRESS SELLER'
(From *Past Tenses: Essays on Writing, Autobiography and History* (London, 1992), pp. 193–202.)

Summary

'The Watercress Seller' reads the encounter between the nineteenth-century journalist and social investigator Henry Mayhew and a working-class eight-year-old girl as an opening to exploring issues of history, the use of the past, sexuality and representation. Evidence offered by, and about, children in the past throws into relief general problems of historical interpretation. Steedman's pursuit of Mayhew's perception of the little girl who defied his theories of childhood and of working-class life leads to a consideration of historical practice's romance of finding the past, in this instance the little girl. Steedman concludes by calling for greater attention to the effects of

Romantic and post-Romantic models of childhood, and for understanding of the role our own childhood plays in our intellectual and psychic life.

Notes

1. This piece of writing has been through a lot. Here is the text of the earliest and shortest version, given as a paper with the title 'Henry Mayhew and the Problem of Transference' to a Conference on the Ethnography of Childhood held at King's College, Cambridge, in July 1986. I presented a longer version of it to the Birmingham Polytechnic English Faculty Lecture in March 1987, under the title of 'Images of Childhood'. The most recent (and I hope final) working through of what it is proper to call an obsession with the Watercress Seller, will be found in my *Strange Dislocations. Childhood and the Idea of Human Interiority, 1780–1930* Cambridge, MA, 1995), pp. 117–27, 171–4. The reader should be aware that I knew a lot more about her – it – in 1995 than I did nine years before (and in the discussion that is reproduced here) not least that the Little Watercress Girl never 'really' existed. For some account of this kind of obsession with a figure in a text, the reader may care to look at (some of) the Introduction to *Past Tenses. Essays on Writing, Autobiography and History* (Rivers Oram Press, 1992), pp. 1–18. 'The Watercress Seller' was first published in this collection.
2. This work was published in *Childhood, Culture and Class in Britain. Margaret McMillan, 1860–1931* (New Brunswick, NJ, 1990).
3. The publication history of *Life and Labour* is complex in the extreme. The publication of the *Morning Chronicle* inquiry in weekly parts in 1851 included material that made up Henry Mayhew, *Life and Labour of the London Poor, Volume I, The London Street Folk. Parts, with Answers to Correspondents, Bound*, and parts of Volumes 2 and 3 (George Woodfall, 1851), pp. 150–1. Later the same material formed parts of Volumes 1, 2 and 3 of the four volume edition of 1861–2. Henry Mayhew, *London Labour and the London Poor*, Four Volumes, 1861–1862 (Griffin Bohn, 1861). The edition of 1851 is made up of Nos 1–63 of the weekly parts issued by Mayhew. His crucial *Answers to Correspondents* are bound with them in the British Library copy. The only full series of *Answers* extant is bound at the end of the copy of Volume 3 of *London Labour and the London Poor* in the Bibliotèque Nationale, Paris (R. 43429). The British Library's series (bound with Volume I) has several *Answers* missing. See Steedman (1995), *Strange Dislocations*, pp. 112–48; and Bertrand Taithe, *The Essential Mayhew. Representing and Communicating the Poor* (Rivers Oram Press, 1996).
4. Deborah Gorham, 'The "Maiden Tribute of Modern Babylon" Re-examined: Child Prostitution and the Idea of Childhood in Late Victorian England', *Victorian Studies*, 21:3 (Spring 1978), 353–79.
5. Reports of the Commissioners on the Employment of Children in Trades and Manufactures Not Already Regulated by Law, PP 1863, xviii; 1864, xxii; 1865, xx; 1866, xxiv; 1867, xvi. Report of the Commissioners of Inquiry into the Employment of Women and Children in Agriculture, PP 1867–8, xvii.
6. John Ruskin, 'Humility', from 'Time and Tide' (1867), *The Library Edition of the Works of John Ruskin*, vol. 17 (1906), pp. 405–9.
7. Elizabeth Gaskell, *Mary Barton* (1848) (Harmondsworth, 1970), pp. 49–53.
8. Richard Hoggart, *The Uses of Literacy* (London, 1957), pp. 32–8. I have recently explored these moments (and this rug) in very great detail. See Carolyn Steedman, 'What a Rag Rug Means', *Journal of Material Culture*, 3:3 (1998), 259–81.

9. Steven Marcus, 'Freud and Dora: Story, History, Case-History', in *Representation: Essays on Literature and Society* (New York, 1976), pp. 247–310.
10. Gorham, 'The "Maiden Tribute"', p. 365.
11. See 'Dudley Street, Seven Dials' (Plate facing p. 158) and 'The Organ in the Court' (facing p. 176) in Gustave Doré and Blanchard Jerrold, *London. A Pilgrimage* (1872) (New York, 1970).
12. John Thomson, and Adolphe Smith, *Street Life in London*, privately printed (London, 1877).
13. The source book for all the photographs discussed here is Graham Ovenden and Robert Melville, *Victorian Children* (Academy Editions, 1972); on which, see below.
14. Jacqueline Rose, *The Case of Peter Pan, Or, The Impossibility of Children's Fiction* (London, 1984), p. 30. M. Linklater, '"Victorian" Photos Faked', *Sunday Times*, 19 November 1979.
15. For coldness and childhood, see 'Maps and Polar Regions. A Note on the Presentation of Childhood Subjectivity in Fiction of the Eighteenth and Nineteenth Centuries', Steve Pile and Nigel Thrift (eds), *Mapping the Subject. Geographies of Cultural Transformation* (London, 1995), pp. 77–92. Dealing with obsessions takes a long time.
16. This topic has been most throughly explored by Hugh Cunningham in *The Children of the Poor. Representations of Childhood since the Seventeenth Century* (Oxford, 1991).
17. Dominick LaCapra, *History and Criticism* (Ithaca, NY, 1985), pp. 71–94.

4. ROBERT DARNTON, 'WORKERS REVOLT: THE GREAT CAT MASSACRE OF THE RUE SAINT-SÉVERIN'
(From *The Great Cat Massacre and Other Episodes in French Cultural History* (Harmondsworth, 1984), pp. 79–101.)

Summary

Darnton examines a story by a print worker about ritual cat killing in Paris in the 1730s. While the writer claimed that the event was one of the funniest things to have happened in the printing shop, modern readers are not amused. The essay attempts to 'get the joke' as a key to that culture by attempting an ethnological textual analysis. The account is a fictionalised narrative in the tradition of printers' autobiographical writings of the period. As such, it provides shape to the stuff of experience and assumes certain responses and associations on the part of its readers. Darnton connects the narrative first with economic and social changes in the working conditions of printers and labour relations in the period, then with the different history of rituals, carnivals and charivaris that frequently featured cat torture and ceremonies particular to the print craft or trade. He concludes that the cat massacre was part of a popular theatre in which the workers turned the tables on their bourgeois employer by working with a wide range of symbols and ceremonies that mocked his pretensions and his wife. The massacre was symbolic horseplay taken to the edge of open rebellion.

Notes

1. Nicolas Contat, *Anecdotes typographiques où l'on voit la description des coutumes, moeurs et usages singuliers des compagnons imprimeurs*, ed. Giles Barber (Oxford,

1980). The original manuscript is dated 1762. Barber provides a thorough description of its background and of Contat's career in his introduction. The account of the cat massacre occurs on pp. 48–56.

2. Contat, *Anecdotes typographiques*, p. 53.

3. Ibid., pp. 52 and 53.

4. See, for example, Albert Soboul, *La France à la veille de la Révolution* (Paris, 1966), p. 140; and Edward Shorter, 'The History of Work in the West: An Overview' in *Work and Community in the West*, ed. Edward Shorter (New York, 1973).

5. The following discussion is derived from Henri-Jean Martin, *Livre, pouvoirs et société à Paris au XVIIᵉ siècle (1598–1701)* (Geneva, 1969); and Paul Chauvet, *Les Ouvriers du livre en France, des origines à la Révolution de 1789* (Paris, 1959). The statistics come from investigations by the authorities of the Old Regime as reported by Martin (II, 699–700) and Chauvet (pp. 126 and 154).

6. For a more detailed discussion of this material, see Robert Darnton, 'Work and Culture in an Eighteenth-Century Printing Shop', an Englehard lecture at the Library of Congress to be published by the Library of Congress.

7. Contat, *Anecdotes typographiques*, pp. 68–73.

8. Christ to STN, Jan. 8, 1773, papers of the Société typographique de Neuchâtel, Bibliothèque de la Ville de Neuchâtel, Switzerland, hereafter cited as STN.

9. STN to Joseph Duplain, July 2, 1777.

10. STN to Louis Vernange, June 26, 1777.

11. Joseph Duplain to STN, Dec. 10, 1778.

12. Contat, *Anécdotes typographiques*, pp. 30–1.

13. Ibid., p. 52.

14. For a recent overview of the vast literature on folklore and French history and bibliographic references, see Nicole Belmont, *Mythes et croyances dans l'ancienne France* (Paris, 1973). The following discussion is based primarily on the material collected in Eugène Rolland, *Faune populaire de la France* (Paris, 1881), IV; Paul Sébillot, *Le Folke-lore de France* (Paris, 1904–7), 4 vols, especially III, 72–155 and IV, 90–8; and to a lesser extent Arnold Van Gennep, *Manuel de folklore français contemporain* (Paris, 1937–58), 9 vols.

15. In Germany and Switzerland, *Katzenmusik* sometimes included mock trials and executions. The etymology of the term is not clear. See E. Hoffmann-Krayer and Hans Bächtold-Stäubli, *Handwörterbuch des deutschen Aberglaubens* (Berlin and Leipzig, 1931–32), IV, 1125–32 and Paul Grebe et al., *Duden Etymologie: Herkunftswörterbuch der deutschen Sprache* (Mannheim, 1963), p. 317.

16. Information on the cat burning in Saint Chamond comes from a letter kindly sent to me by Elinor Accampo of Colorado College. The Metz ceremony is described in A. Benoist, 'Traditions et anciennes coutumes du pays messin', *Revue des traditions populaires*, XV (1900), 14.

17. Contat, *Anecdotes typographiques*, pp. 30 and 66–7; and Chauvet, *Les Ouvriers du livre*, pp. 7–12.

18. Contat, *Anecdotes typographiques*, pp. 65–7.

19. Ibid., pp. 37–41, quotation from pp. 39–40.

20. A good example of the genre, *La Misère des apprentis imprimeurs* (1710) is printed as an appendix to Contat, *Anecdotes typographiques*, pp. 101–10. For other examples, see A. C. Cailleau, *Les Misères de ce monde, ou complaintes facétieuses sur les apprentissages des différents arts et métiers de la ville et faubourgs de Paris* (Paris, 1783).

21. The classic study of this process is Arnold Van Gennep, *Les Rites de passage* (Paris, 1908). It has been extended by subsequent ethnographic research, notably that of Victor Turner: *The Forest of Symbols: Aspects of Ndembu Ritual* (Ithaca, NY, 1967) and *The Ritual Process* (Chicago, 1969). Jerome's experience fits the Van Gennep–Turner model very well, except in a few respects. He was not considered sacred and dangerous, although the chapel could fine journeymen for drinking with him. He did not live outside adult society, although he left his home for a makeshift room at the edge of the master's household. And he was not exposed to secret *sacra*, although he had to acquire an esoteric lingo and to assimilate a craft ethos after a great deal of tribulation climaxed by a communal meal. Joseph Moxon, Thomas Gent, and Benjamin Franklin mention similar practices in England. In Germany the initiation rite was much more elaborate and had structural similarities to the rites of tribes in Africa, New Guinea, and North America. The apprentice wore a filthy headdress adorned with a goat's horns and a fox's tail, indicating that he had reverted to an animal state. As a *Cornut* or *Mittelding*, part man, part beast, he underwent ritual tortures, including the filing of his fingertips. At the final ceremony, the head of the shop knocked off the hat and slapped him in the face. He then emerged newborn – sometimes newly named and even baptised – as a full-fledged journeyman. Such at least was the practice described in German typographical manuals, notably Christian Gottlob Täubel, *Praktisches Handbuch der Buchdruckerkunst für Anfänger* (Leipzig, 1791); Wilhelm Gottlieb Kircher, *Anweisung in der Buchdruckerkunst so viel davon das Drucken betrifft* (Brunswick, 1793); and Johann Christoph Hildebrand, *Handbuch für Buchdrucker-Lehrlinge* (Eisenach, 1835). The rite was related to an ancient popular play, the *Depositio Cornuti typographici*, which was printed by Jacob Redinger in his *Neu aufgesetztes Format Büchlein* (Frankfurt-am-Main, 1679).
22. Contat, *Anecdotes typographiques*, pp. 65–6.
23. The text does not give Jerome's last name, but it stresses the name change and the acquisition of the 'Monsieur': 'It is only after the end of the apprenticeship that one is called Monsieur; this quality belongs only to journeymen and not to apprentices' (p. 41). In the wage book of the STN, the journeymen always appear with their 'Monsieur', even when they were called by nicknames, such as 'Monsieur Bonnemain'.
24. The black cat in Manet's *Olympia* represents a common motif, the animal 'familiar' of a nude. On Baudelaire's cats, see Roman Jakobson and Claude Lévi-Strauss, 'Les Chats de Charles Baudelaire', *L'Homme*, II (1962), 5–21; and Michel Riffaterre, 'Describing Poetic Structures: Two Approaches to Baudelaire's *Les Chats*', in *Structuralism*, ed. Jacques Ehrmann (New Haven, CT, 1966).
25. Mary Douglas, *Purity and Danger: An Analysis of Concepts of Pollution and Taboo* (London, 1966); and E. R. Leach, 'Anthropological Aspects of Language: Animal Categories and Verbal Abuse', in *New Directions in the Study of Language*, ed. E. H. Lenneberg (Cambridge, MA, 1964).
26. Cervantes and Zola adapted traditional cat lore to the themes of their novels. In *Don Quixote* (part II, ch. 46), a sack full of howling cats interrupts the hero's serenade to Altisidora. Taking them for devils, he tries to mow them down with his sword, only to be bested by one of them in single combat. In *Germinal* (part V, ch. 6), the symbolism works in the opposite way. A mob of workers pursues Maigrat, their class enemy, as if he were a cat trying to escape across the rooftops. Screaming 'Get the cat! Get the cat!' they castrate his body 'like a tomcat' after he

falls from the roof. For an example of cat killing as a satire on French legalism, see Friar John's plan to massacre the Furry Lawcats in Rabelais' *Gargantua and Pantagruel*, book V, ch. 15.

27. Mikhail Bakhtin, *Rabelais and His World*, trans. Helene Iswolsky (Cambridge, MA, 1968). The most important literary version of cat lore to appear in Contat's time was *Les Chats* (Rotterdam, 1728) by François Augustin Paradis de Moncrif. Although it was a mock treatise aimed at a sophisticated audience, it drew on a vast array of popular supersitions and proverbs, many of which appeared in the collections of folklorists a century and a half later.

28. C. S. L. Davies, *Peace, Print and Protestantism* (St Albans, Herts, 1977). The other references come from the sources cited in note 14. Among the many dictionaries of proverbs and slang, see André-Joseph Panckoucke, *Dictionnaire des proverbs françois et des façons de parler comiques, burlesques, et familières* (Paris, 1748) and Gaston Esnault, *Dictionnaire historique des argots français* (Paris, 1965).

29. Rolland, *Faune populaire*, p. 118. See note 14 for the other sources on which this account is based.

30. Emile Chautard, *La Vie étrange de l'argot* (Paris, 1931), pp. 367–8. The following expressions come from Panckoucke, *Dictionnaire des proverbes françois*; Esnault, *Dictionnaire historique des argots français*; and *Dictionnaire de l'Académie française* (Paris, 1762), which contains a surprising amount of polite cat lore. The impolite lore was transmitted in large measure by children's games and rhymes, some of them dating from the sixteenth century: Claude Gaignebet, *Le Folklore obscène des enfants* (Paris, 1980), p. 260.

31. Sébillot, *Le Folk-lore de France*, III, 93–4.

32. Panckoucke, *Dictionnaire des proverbes françois*, p. 66.

33. This and the following quotations come from Contat's account of the cat massacre, *Anecdotes typographiques*, pp. 48–56.

34. According to Giles Barber (ibid., pp. 7 and 60), the actual Jacques Vincent for whom Contat worked began his own apprenticeship in 1690; so he probably was born about 1675. His wife was born in 1684. Thus when Contat entered the shop, the master was about 62, the mistress about 53, and the bawdy young priest in his twenties. That pattern was common enough in the printing industry, where old masters often left their businesses to younger wives, who in turn took up with still younger journeymen. It was a classic pattern for charivaris, which often mocked disparities in age among newly-weds as well as humiliating cuckolds.

35. Pierre Caron, *Les Massacres de septembre* (Paris, 1935).

5. SUSAN WILLIS, 'ERUPTIONS OF FUNK: HISTORICISING TONI MORRISON'
(From *Specifying: Black Women Writing the American Experience* (London, 1987), pp. 83–96, 105–9.)

Summary

'Eruptions of Funk' explores the ways in which sexuality converges with history as a register for the experience of change in Toni Morrison's writing. Morrison's metaphoric rendition of past experience is not nostalgic but represents a way of trying to maintain Afro-American culture, separated by time and space from the black rural

South. Her novels, which each focus on a particular strategic moment in African-
American history, explore social and psychological aspects of the lived experience of
historical transition as exemplified in the migration north and the encounter with
white bourgeois society. A key experience is alienation, which affects men and women
differently in both economic and sexual terms. 'Funk' is Willis's term for that which
disrupts the repression of sensuality in bourgeois culture and for the past as it erupts
into the present. It is associated with Morrison's utopian vision of an alternative
social world that is juxtaposed with the historical realities of domination and dependency. This juxtaposition is read by Willis as a North American variant of magic
realism that represents unresolved contradictions between historical and critical,
mythic and pleasurable.

Notes

1. Much of the criticism of Morrison's work is done from a sociological point of
   view. See, for example, Joan Bischoff, 'The Novels of Toni Morrison: Studies in
   Thwarted Sensitivity', *Studies in Black Literature* 6, 3 (1975), 21–3; Phyllis Klot-
   man, 'Dick-and-Jane and the Shirley Temple Sensibility in *The Bluest Eye*', *Black
   American Literature Forum*, 13 (1979), 123–5; Barbara Lounsberry and Grace
   Anne Hovet, 'Principles of Perception in Toni Morrison's *Sula*', *Black American
   Literature Forum*, 13 (1979), 126–9. These studies focus on the erosion of the
   individual's sensitivity by white cultural domination, on the one hand, and ordering mechanisms within the black neighbourhood on the other. The critics tend to
   agree that, although Morrison regrets the loss of sensitivity, she favours a practical
   and pragmatic point of view.
      Without denying the objective social fact or the importance of literary studies
   that document the social in literature, I am more interested in how texts subvert the
   limitations within which they are written. The focus of this study is, thus, on those
   instances in Morrison's writing in which the literature does something more than
   simply monitor and confirm social fact.
2. The surrealist metaphors of the negritude poets resist being read in the way we can
   read through Morrison's metaphors, progressively constructing their referents and
   meaning. An example from Aimé Césaire's *Cahier d'un Retour au Pays Natal*, in
   Aimé Césaire, trans. Clayton Eshleman and Annette Smith (Berkeley, CA, 1983)
   exemplifies the difference between the poetics of negritude and Morrison's use of
   metaphor.
   Conjuring up the Congo, Césaire depicts a rich natural setting:

   où l'eau fait
   likouala – likouala (p. 50)

'Where the water goes likouala – likouala.' This is followed by one of the most
complex and condensed examples of surrealist metaphor:

   où l'éclair de la colère lance sa hache verdâtre
   et force les sangliers de la putréfaction dans
   la belle orée violente des narines (p. 50)

Reading the metaphor produces something like this: 'Where the lightning bolt of
anger hurls its green axe and forces the wild boars of putrefaction over the
beautiful and violent edge of the nostrils.'
   Overall, the image evokes the powerful and driving force of nature and the hunt.
Individual words are themselves metaphors, linked together to form a total

metaphoric image whose meaning does not reside in a particular referent, but in the myriad cross-references pulled into the whole.

The 'lightning bolt of anger' captures the essence of the poem as a whole, for it voices the enraged outcry of black people and reverses the image of the meek, long-suffering 'comical and ugly nigger' ('un nègre comique et laid', pp. 62–3) produced by colonialism. The image of 'wild boars pouring over the nostrils' (like snot) extends the notion of putrefaction, which is itself a code word for the effects of colonialism. This is developed at length in the poem's opening pages where the Antilles are portrayed not as a tropical island paradise but as a degraded, diseased, and decayed speck of land:

Ici la parade des risibles et scrofuleux bubons, les poutures des microbes très étranges, les poisons sans alexitère connu, les sanies de plaies bien antiques, les fermentations imprévisibles d'éspèces putrescibles. (p. 38)

Right here the parade of laughable and scrofulous buboes, the forced feedings of very strange microbes, the poisons without known alexins, the sanies of really ancient sores, the unforeseeable fermentations of putrescible species. (p. 39)

Bodily orifices, too, are in more than one instance related to the visage of colonialism. But these observations do not translate what the metaphor says; rather, they are embraced by it. There is no single, comprehensive way to decipher Césaire's metaphor as there is for Morrison's. This is because, although history infuses the image, the metaphor resists being tied to any specific referent or set of referents. The effect is finally an explosion of meanings, created out of the convergence of many possible interpretations, as opposed to Morrison's revelation of meaning, made possible by linking images to referents.

3. Harriette Arnow's *The Dollmaker* (New York, 1973), an account of an Appalachian family's migration to Detroit during World War II, is very similar to Morrison's portrayal of black Southern migration. Notably, it documents the initial experience and assimilation to wage labour, the erosion of folk culture, and the fragmentation of the family unit. In Arnow as in Morrison, the individual's experience of alienation is portrayed in relation to fetishisation under the commodity form. For a brief discussion of *The Dollmaker*, see Susan Willis, 'A Literary Lesson in Historical Thinking', *Social Text*, no. 3 (1980), 136ff.

4. See Georg Lukács, 'Reification and the Consciousness of the Proletariat', in *History and Class Consciousness* (London, 1971), p. 83. According to Lukács, reification occurs when the 'commodity structure penetrates society in all its aspects and remoulds it in its own image' (p. 85). This differentiates bourgeois society from previous social modes, in which the commodity form may have pertained to certain endeavours or may have been only partially developed. Reification means the transformation of all human functions and qualities into commodities 'and reveals in all its starkness the dehumanised and dehumanising function of the commodity relation' (p. 92).

5. Referred to as 'The Principal Beauty of Maine', Margaret Lenore from *Tar Baby* (New York, 1981), p. 11, comes closest to embodying bourgeois reification. Her characterisation may well be a literary allusion to another great beauty and bourgeois stereotype in contemporary fiction: 'The Most Beautiful Woman in the World', in Gabriel García Márquez's *One Hundred Years of Solitude* (New York, 1971), p. 192. Both Margaret Lenore and Márquez's 'Most Beautiful

Woman' are first beheld by their future husbands as beauty-contest winners in a parade and draped in ermine. However, neither Margaret Lenore nor Márquez's Fernanda define total reification. First of all, neither is originally of the bourgeois class: Fernanda is the sole survivor of a transplanted and bankrupt Spanish aristocracy and Margaret Lenore is the daughter of struggling Italian immigrants. Both develop forms of hysteria as a result of the discontinuity between their pasts and presents and their imperfect assimilation into bourgeois culture. Margaret Lenore abuses her infant son and Fernanda develops a relationship with imaginary doctors she hopes will cure her bodily ailments through telepathic surgery (a situation not unlike Margaret Lenore's long-distance telephone conservations with her son, which, because no one witnesses or overhears them, appear to be imaginary).

6. In Morrison's writing, candy is often associated with capitalism. In *Song of Solomon*, candy is the symbolic payoff given by the boss's wife when Guitar's father is crushed in a mill accident. In *The Bluest Eye*, candy is a penny's worth of sweetness in the life of a little girl who will never find satisfaction in human terms. And in *Tar Baby*, candy is a metaphor for all of capitalist production. The association is not gratuitous, for the connection between candy and capitalism extends far beyond the current glut of sugary breakfast cereals and junk foods. As Immanuel Wallerstein explains in *The Modern World System* (New York, 1974) sugar production in the New World was essential to the rise of capitalism. Rather than simply satisfying luxury consumption, a lot of the sugar produced under slavery in the Caribbean found its way into the daily diet of the growing European proletariat. With many peasants leaving the countryside to seek jobs in the cities, there was an increased need for food production and a shrinking rural labour force. The need for more food was met neither by increased cereal production (which would have required substantial transformations in production techniques) nor by increasing meat production (which was basically intended for the bourgeoisie). Rather, sugar became – and remains today – a substitute for real food. Capable of providing increased energy output at the expense of long-term health, sugar is the opiate of the working class under capitalism. See also Sidney Mintz, *Sweetness and Power* (New York, 1985).

7. Toni Morrison, *Tar Baby* (New York, 1981), p. 61. Hereafter cited as *TB*.
8. Toni Morrison, *Sula* (New York, 1974), p. 3. Hereafter cited as *S*.
9. William Faulkner, *Absalom! Absalom!* (1936; rpt. New York, 1972), p. 155.

6. MICHEL FOUCAULT, 'THE BODY OF THE CONDEMNED'
(From *Discipline and Punish: The Birth of the Prison*
(Harmondsworth, 1986), pp. 3–23, 30–1.)

Summary

The excerpt opens by juxtaposing an account of the ritualised spectacle of the execution of the regicide Damiens in 1757 and the rules of the House of Young Prisoners eighty years later. These are taken to define contrasting economies of punishment. Traditional accounts rely too much on a narrative of increasing humanisation and fail to acknowledge the possibility of resistance that subsists in the physical struggle between the criminal and a repressive state. In the shift from the earlier to the later regimes, the spectacular, public punishment of the body is displaced by punishment in the form of the suspension of rights. It is the certainty of punishment rather than its physical agonies that operates as a deterrent and publicity shifts from the punishment to the trial. In the period of reform the soul rather than the body is the main target or focus of the new economy: prisoners are taught to internalise the discipline imposed by society. New techniques of assessing the criminal connect with new questions of truth and a complex of scientific and juridical procedures and discourses extend a technology of power beyond the moment of judgment. The history of the prison's function within this economy must be written not as a history of the past in the terms of the present but as part of a history *of* the present.

Notes

1. The public execution of traitors described by William Blackstone, *Commentaries on the Laws of England*, vol. 4, 1766, 9, 89. Since the French translation was intended to bring out the humaneness of English legislation, in contrast with the old ordinance of 1760, the French translator adds the following note: 'In this form of execution, which is so terrifying to see, the guilty man does not suffer much pain, or for long.'
2. I shall study the birth of the prison only in the French penal system. Differences in historical developments and institutions would make a detailed comparative examination too burdensome and any attempt to describe the phenomenon as a whole too schematic.

References

Annales de la Charité (1847).
Beccaria, C. de, *Traité des délits et des peines* (1764; ed. 1856).
Faucher, L., *De la réforme des prisons* (1938).
Hibbert, C., *The Roots of Evil* (1966).
Le Peletier de Saint-Fargeau, *Arch. parl.*, XXVI, 3 June 1791.
Mably, G. de, *De la législation, Oeuvres complètes*, IX (1789).
Molène, A. de, *De l'humanité des lois criminelles* (1830).
Pièces originales et procédures du procès fait à Robert-François Damiens, III (1757).
Saint-Edme (E. Bourg), *Dictionnaire de pénalité*, IV (1825).
Teeters, N. K., *The Cradle of the Penitentiary* (1935).
——, *They were in Prison* (1937).
Zevaes, A. L., *Damiens le régicide* (1937).

7. STEPHEN GREENBLATT, 'AT THE TABLE OF THE GREAT: MORE'S SELF-FASHIONING AND SELF-CANCELLATION'
(From *Renaissance Self-Fashioning from More to Shakespeare*
(Chicago and London, 1980), pp. 11–26.)

Summary

More's fictionalised account of a dinner party with Cardinal Wolsey is read as a distillation of the author's political career, notably the interplay between his self-fashioning and involvement in the world and his self-cancellation and attempts to escape the world. More's perception of the madness of political life differentiates his views of the operations of the powerful from those of Machiavelli. If we want to understand More we must not treat his comments on human absurdity as mere rhetorical devices but as a response to existence. More's estrangement from the political life in which he was, mostly successfully, involved is compared to the mood evoked by Holbein's *The Ambassadors*. The painting's depiction of confident mastery of reality through knowledge, arts and skill is disrupted by the distorted shape which can be recognised as a skull only when the viewer moves to one side of the picture. Conversely, when the skull is clearly visible, the rest of the painting is blurred. More is likened to Holbein and his humanism and alienation are seen as changing perspectives and consistent, fused features of his career and writings. *Utopia* is read as a prose equivalent of anamorphic art, questioning its own status and that of the world it supposedly represents. More's representation of scriptural authority in *Utopia* is compared to the crucifix in *The Ambassadors* that initially seems to offer assurance of the triumph of life over death but is vulnerable to the unsettling effects of anamorphosis. The excerpt ends with a consideration of More's use of the image of the world as a stage that displays the folly of human pretension, concluding that More's perception of human absurdity leads to social criticism but also limits the practical possibilities of action.

Notes

1. *A Dialogue of Comfort against Tribulation*, ed. Louis L. Martz and Frank Manley, *The Complete Works of St. Thomas More*, 12 (New Haven, CT, 1976), p. 213. Hereafter cited as *Complete Works*.
2. *The History of King Richard III*, ed. R. S. Sylvester, *Complete Works*, 3 (1963), p. 80.
3. *The Prince*, trans. Luigi Ricci, rev. E. R. P. Vincent (New York, 1950), pp. 64–5. Machiavelli's explanation, it should be noted, has its own elusiveness: on the one hand, there is a cold observation of something akin to a law of nature – the fox always eats the hens; on the other hand, there is smouldering outrage at the stupidity, the wilfulness, of the victims.
4. In William Roper, *The Life of Sir Thomas More*, ed. Richard S. Sylvester and Davis P. Harding (New Haven, CT, 1962), p. 239. I have been deeply influenced throughout by Sylvester's seminal work; see especially, 'A Part of His Own: Thomas More's Literary Personality in His Early Works', *Moreana*, 15 (1967), 29–42. See also David Bleich's psychoanalytic attempt to correlate More's writing 'with particular infantile modalities' ('More's *Utopia*: Confessional Modes', *American Imago*, 28 [1971], 24–52).
5. The classic account of this phenomenon is Johan Huizinga, *The Waning of the Middle Ages* (London, 1924).
6. On the persistence of these hopes, see Frances A. Yates, *The French Academies of the Sixteenth Century* (London, 1947), pp. 199–235; Roy Strong, *The Cult of Elizabeth* (London, 1977), pp. 176–7.
7. Mary F. S. Hervey, *Holbein's 'Ambassadors'* (London, 1900), p. 232. On Holbein's painting, which is in the National Gallery in London, see also Michael Levey, *The German School*, National Gallery Catalogues (London, 1959), pp. 46–54; Carl Georg Heise, *Hans Holbein d. J.: Die Gesandten* (Stuttgart, 1959); Ernest B. Gilman, *The Curious Perspective: Literary and Pictorial Wit in the Seventeenth Century* (New Haven, CT, 1978), pp. 98–104.
8. Jurgis Baltrušaitis, *Anamorphoses, ou perspectives curieuses* (Paris, 1955), p. 65. The lute as a standard object in the teaching of perspective is familiar from Dürer's

'Portillon' woodcut of 1525. Albrecht Dürer, *The Painter's Manual*, trans. Walter L. Strauss (New York, 1977), p. 392.

9. Ficino, *Platonic Theology*, trans. Josephine I. Burroughs, in *Journal of the History of Ideas*, 5 (1944), 235. On perspective in Renaissance art, see especially Samuel Y. Edgerton, Jr, *The Renaissance Discovery of Linear Perspective* (New York, 1975); Claudio Guillén, 'On the Concept and Metaphor of Perspective', in *Comparatists at Work*, ed. Stephen G. Nichols, Jr, and Richard B. Vowles (Waltham, MA, 1968), pp. 28–90; and Erwin Panofsky, 'Die Perspective als symbolische Form', *Vorträge der Bibliothek Warburg* (1924–25).

10. I am, as will be clear, sceptical of Edgar R. Samuel's theory that the skull was meant to be corrected by an unidentified optical lens held by the viewer: see 'Death in the Glass – A New View of Holbein's "Ambassadors"', in *Burlington Magazine*, 105 (1963), 436–41.

11. See Baltrušaitis, *Anamorphoses* pp. 58–76; also Fred Leeman, *Hidden Images* (New York, 1976), pp. 13–14. Levey dismisses as exceedingly unlikely the suggestion sometimes made that the skull is a punning signature: *hohle Bein* for 'hollow bone'. The painting in any case is manifestly a celebration of Holbein's genius.

12. Hervey, *Holbein's 'Ambassadors'*, pp. 203–7.

13. Such mockery is a commonplace in representations of the 'Memento mori' theme; see, for example, Breughel's 'Triumph of Death'. For the heraldic use of the skull, see Dürer's 'Coat of Arms with a Skull' (1503) and Holbein's own 'The Arms of Death' (1538).

14. We might also note the strangely ominous lute case beneath the table and the emblematic significance of the sundials. On the lute as an emblem of harmony, see John Hollander, *The Untuning of the Sky: Ideas of Music in English Poetry, 1500–1700* (Princeton, NJ, 1961).

15. See Erwin Panofsky, *Tomb Sculpture*, ed. H. W. Janson (New York, 1964).

16. Hervey, *Holbein's 'Ambassadors'*, p. 205. It is typical of the pervasive irony of Holbein's work that this substantiality should be proved by a shadow. Levey observes that the times marked on three of the faces of the polyhedral sundial differ from one another: 'The variations in the cast shadows are, of course, impossible; as the times indicated are not even the same, it is difficult to suppose anything except that different parts of the instrument were painted at different hours' (*The German School*, p. 51). Possibly so; but Holbein may also be subtly furthering the unsettling of the sense of reality.

17. Professor Michael Baxandall, to whom I am indebted for several valuable suggestions, thinks that the poses are more likely to reflect the *restraint* counselled by Northern writers of behaviour manuals.

18. Roper, *Life*, p. 202. Henry VIII may have been imitating Italian princes; see, for example, Vespasiano's account of the intellectual interests of Federico, Duke of Urbino, in *Renaissance Princes, Popes, and Prelates*, trans. William George and Emily Waters (New York, 1963), pp. 99–105. Elton's characterisation occurs in 'Thomas More, Councillor (1517–1529)', in *St. Thomas More: Action and Contemplation* (New Haven, CT, 1972), pp. 87–122.

19. The definition quoted by Elizabeth McCutcheon, 'Denying the Contrary: More's Use of Litotes in the *Utopia*', in *Essential Articles for the Study of Thomas More*, ed. R. S. Sylvester and G. P. Marc'hadour (Hamden, CT, 1977), p. 263.

20. Ibid., pp. 271–2. Elsewhere in her fine article, she remarks that 'we're never quite sure where we stand in the *Utopia*.... On the smallest syntactical level ambiguity does exist of a sort which can never be altogether resolved, and probably was not meant to be' (p. 272). In *Self-Consuming Artifacts: The Experience of*

Seventeenth-Century Literature (Berkeley CA, 1972), Stanley Fish provides a powerful critical analysis of the literary equivalent to anamorphosis; see esp. ch. 3, 'The Dialectic of the Self in Herbert's Poetry', pp. 156–223.

21. Louis Marin, *Utopiques: jeux d'espaces* (Paris, 1973), p. 81. In 'Lies and the Limitable Inane: Contradiction in More's *Utopia*' (*Renaissance Quarterly*, 26 [1973], 173–80), Alan F. Nagel argues that More deliberately includes contradictions in his account of Utopia to call attention to its fictionality.
22. *Utopia* satisfies virtually all of the conditions of play described by Johan Huizinga, *Homo Ludens* (Boston, 1960).
23. For an extraordinarily subtle and complex development of the implications of meditation upon an object – here a representation of God in which the eyes appear to follow one – see Nicholas of Cusa, *The Vision of God*, trans. Emma Gurney Salter (New York, 1928).
24. As Ronald Levao is demonstrating in work in progress, this theme is developed throughout Cusa's career; the most familiar expression of it is in *De docta ignorantia*.
25. *Dialogue of Comfort*, p. 133.
26. See Natalie Zemon Davis, 'Holbein's *Pictures of Death* and the Reformation at Lyons', *Studies in the Renaissance*, 3 (1956), 97–130.
27. On the relationship between *Utopia* and More's Christianity, there has been considerable debate. The most impressive and subtle discussion, in my view, is by J. H. Hexter in his masterful introduction to the Yale *Utopia*, ed. Hexter and Edward Surtz, S. J., *Complete Works*, 4 (1965), esp. pp. lxiv–lxxxi. Hexter's argument has been endorsed by Quentin Skinner in 'More's *Utopia*', *Past and Present*, 38 (1967), 152–68, and in *The Foundations of Modern Political Thought*, 2 vols (Cambridge, 1978), 1:193ff. Skinner overstates the case, however, when he argues that More's implication is 'that it may be possible to become a perfect Christian without any knowledge of the Church or its dogmas at all' (p. 233). More is careful to have the Utopians anticipate an evolution of their religious beliefs and to depict the benign introduction of 'the name of Christ, His teaching, His character, His miracles, and the no less wonderful constancy of the many martyrs' (p. 217).
28. *Four Last Things*, in Thomas More, *The Workes... in the Englysh Tonge* (London, 1557), pp. 84, 81.

8. JÜRGEN PIETERS, 'FACING HISTORY, OR THE ANXIETY OF READING: HOLBEIN'S *THE AMBASSADORS* ACCORDING TO GREENBLATT AND LYOTARD'

Summary

The essay stages a confrontation between two exemplary readings of Holbein's painting *The Ambassadors* by Stephen Greenblatt and Jean-François Lyotard. In their analyses both authors are concerned with the possibility and the nature of full historical knowledge, a subject upon which the painting itself seems to reflect. Greenblatt's reading is taken to be a prime example of New Historicist practice which stems from a paradoxical desire to converse with the dead, a desire that, by definition, must remain forever frustrated. Lyotard's analysis of *The Ambassadors*, it is argued, shows how easily Greenblatt's practice may foster the belief that the past can be made to speak to us, directly, immediately.

Notes

1. All translations from Lyotard's *Discours, Figure* are mine.
2. My reading of the painting draws on several sources: apart from those explicitly dealt with further on in this essay, I would like to mention Baltrušaitis (1977), pp. 91–114; Butor (1968), pp. 33–41; Gilman (1978), pp. 98–104; Hallyn (1994); and Lacan (1973), pp. 92–104.
3. Some believe the exact day (April 11th) can be deduced from the sundial on the upper level of the table. There is, however, sufficient evidence (a letter from de Dinteville to his brother) that de Selve only arrived in England in May of that year (see Wilson, 1996, p. 196; Foister, Roy and Wyld, 1997, p. 14).
4. See Scarisbrick (1972), p. 403. Anne's pregnancy kept de Dinteville in England much longer than he had expected. His king, who was chosen to be the child's godfather, ordered him to stay in London for the baptism (see Foister, Roy and Wyld, 1997, p. 16).
5. The celestial and terrestrial globes next to and beneath de Dinteville's left arm are the most conspicuous examples.
6. For a comprehensive analysis of all of these see the chapter on 'The objects in the painting', in Foister, Roy and Wyld (1997), pp. 30–43.
7. In this respect, it is hardly coincidental that Holbein's globe bears the index of the line dividing the Spanish from the Portuguese possessions in the New World. Another striking (yet unrealistic) detail is the fact that de Dinteville's hometown, Polisy, is marked on the globe.
8. The lute, symbol of all cosmic harmonies, has one broken string and de Dinteville's cap is adorned with a small skull.
9. The representation of the lute in *The Ambassadors* is often taken as a reference to Dürer's famous woodcut on the art of perspective.
10. See e.g. Greenblatt (1990), pp. 166–8 and Lyotard (1991), pp. 82, 90.
11. See Lyotard (1988), p. 79 and (1991), pp. xx, xxx.
12. Derek Wilson's excellent biography of the painter furnishes ample material to answer it (Wilson, 1996).
13. In Holbein's work, he writes, 'death is affirmed not in its power to destroy the flesh, or as is familiar from late medieval literature, in its power to horrify and cause unbearable pain, but in its uncanny accessibility and absence' (Greenblatt, 1980, p. 19).
14. '[S]omething exterior, which it cannot internalise in terms of *signification*.' It will be hard to find a more appropriate definition of Holbein's anamorphotic skull.
15. Cf. *Readings* (1991), p. 13: 'The function of reference, by which language points at objects outside itself, is entirely subjugated to signification, by which language assigns meanings to things. A thing can only be pointed at insofar as language can give it a meaning.'
16. The point of transition between the two, Bennington claims, is Lyotard's fascinating reading of Mallarmé's 'Un coup de dés' (Bennington, 1988, p. 68).
17. Lyotard's criticism of Merleau-Ponty boils down to his conviction that the phenomenological space works according to the logic of difference, not opposition. It is, obviously, but a small step from Lyotard's 'disruption' of what is *heimlich* to his later writings on the sublime.
18. 'Meure' can be a *subjonctif* of both 'mourir (de)' – to die from – and '(de) meurer (à)' – to stay with.
19. Cf. Lyotard (1971), p. 217: 'To read is to hear, not to see.' This sentence receives its full meaning only in the context of the opening pages of *Discours, Figure*,

where Lyotard puts it to the reader that his study is meant as a protest against the sort of books in which the author argues 'that "the eye listens" [and] that that which is visible can be read, heard, understood'. In Lyotard's view, 'what is given is not a text [...] it has a thickness, a constitutive difference, which is there to be seen rather than read' (Lyotard, 1971, p. 9). For this reason he considers his study 'a defence of the eye' (Lyotard, 1971, p. 11), albeit a quite different one from that by Merleau-Ponty.

20. The difference between Lyotard and Greenblatt at this point is obvious. At all times, Lyotard emphasises the fact that Holbein's skull is but a representation: 'these testimonies of the inconsistency of representation are themselves representations' (Lyotard, 1971, p. 378).

References

Frank Ankersmit and Hans Kellner (eds) *A New Philosophy of History* (London, 1995).

Jurgis Baltrušaitis, *Anamorphic Art* (Cambridge, 1977).

Roland Barthes, *Oeuvres Complètes, Tôme III* (Paris, 1995).

Geoffrey Bennington, *Lyotard. Writing the Event* (Manchester, 1988).

Michel Butor, *Répertoire III* (Paris, 1968).

Peter Dews, 'The Letter and the Line: Discourse and its Other in Lyotard', in *Diacritics* (Fall 1984), 40–9.

Susan Foister, Ashak Roy and Martin Wyld, *Making and Meaning. Holbein's Ambassadors* (London, 1997).

Ernest B. Gilman, *The Curious Perspective. Literary and pictorial wit in the seventeenth century* (New Haven and London, 1978).

Stephen Greenblatt, *Renaissance Self-Fashioning. From More to Shakespeare* (Chicago and London, 1980).

Stephen Greenblatt, 'Introduction' to Stephen Greenblatt (ed.), *The Forms of Power and the Power of Forms in the Renaissance*, special issue of *Genre*, 15/1–2, (1982), 3–6.

Stephen Greenblatt, *Shakespearean Negotiations. The Circulation of Social Energy in Renaissance England* (Berkeley/Los Angeles, 1988).

Stephen Greenblatt. *Learning to Curse. Essays in Early Modern Culture* (New York, 1990).

Stephen Greenblatt, *Marvelous Possessions. The Wonder of the New World* (Oxford, 1991).

Fernand Hallyn, 'Holbein: la mort en abyme', in *Le Sens des Formes. Etudes sur la Renaissance* (Genève, 1994), pp. 111–29.

Mary Hervey, *Holbein's 'Ambassadors'* (London, 1900).

Jacques Lacan, *Les quatres concepts fondamentaux de la psychanalyse. Séminaire: Livre XI* (Paris, 1973)

Dominick LaCapra, *History and Criticism* (Ithaca and London, 1985).

Dominick LaCapra, *Soundings in Critical Theory* (Ithaca and London, 1989).

Jean-François Lyotard *Discours, Figure* (Paris, 1971).

Jean-François Lyotard, *The Differend: phrases in dispute* (trans. G. Van Den Abbeele) (Manchester, 1988).

Jean-François Lyotard, *The Inhuman: reflections on time* (trans. G. Bennington) (Cambridge, 1991).

J. Hillis Miller, *Hawthorne and History. Defacing It* (Cambridge, MA, Blackwell, 1991).

Bill Readings, *Introducing Lyotard. Art and Politics* (London, 1991).
J. J. Scarisbrick, *Henry VIII* (Harmondsworth, 1972 [1968]).
Derek Wilson, *Hans Holbein. Portrait of an unknown man* (London, 1996).

9. CATHERINE BELSEY, 'READING CULTURAL HISTORY'
(Edited extract from *Shakespeare and the Loss of Eden: The Construction of Family Values in Early Modern Culture* (London, 1999).)

Summary

The essay opens with an analysis of Belsey's experience of visiting a 'living history museum' and notes that efforts to make the seventeenth century come to life for twentieth-century visitors destabilise the present, removing the frame of interpretation. Living, or synchronic, history that attempts to isolate a single moment was conceived as an alternative to conventional narrative history, but the past cannot be recovered either as experience or as record. Belsey suggests a practice of history at the level of representation. This cultural history will be concerned with meanings and values that are connected to, but not the same as, the practices studied by social historians. Cultural history will acknowledge that history is *made* in the present and that a past is produced which is both the consequence of and motivation for the historian's analysis. The theory and practice of cultural history will, in contrast to New Historicism, foreground dissent and cognitive dissonance textually and culturally.

Notes

1. Michel de Certeau, *The Writing of History*, trans. Tom Conley (New York, 1988), p. 3.
2. Hayden White, *Tropics of Discourse: Essays in Cultural Criticism* (Baltimore, MD, 1978), pp. 84–5 and passim.
3. Cf. Certeau, *The Writing of History*, p. 287.
4. For an excellent example of the social history of the family in the period see Susan Dwyer Amussen, *An Ordered Society: Gender and Class in Early Modern England* (Oxford, 1988). Amussen analyses texts, including advice manuals, as well as the economy and demography of the Norfolk villages she discusses, and she recognises that there may be a gap between beliefs and practices. Where they differ, it is the practices she pursues.
5. Louis Althusser, *Lenin and Philosophy and Other Essays*, trans Ben Brewster (London, 1977), pp. 156–8.
6. 'Fiction' is itself a problematic term, of course. I use it here, for want of a better, in order to avoid the value judgment commonly implied by 'literature', but the category rarely exists in pure form. Mimetic fiction, not self-evidently an independent mode until the nineteenth century, depends on (the illusion of) reference to what is perceived as fact (human psychology, social convention, etc). Meanwhile, epic, chronicle drama and even romance, were not usually offered as pure invention. Current categories of 'faction' and drama-documentary also deconstruct the opposition between fact and fiction. (I owe this reservation to a conversation with Martin Kayman.)

7. Clifford Geertz, '"From the Native's Point of View": On the Nature of Anthropological Understanding', *The Interpretation of Cultures: Selected Essays* (New York, 1973), ch. 3.
8. Certeau, *The Writing of History*, p. 33. Certeau is concerned here primarily with previous historical debates, but the point also holds for the material they consider.
9. See for example Richard J. Evans, *In Defence of History* (London, 1997). For a much more thoughtful account of the limitations of constructivism, see Michel-Rolph Trouillot, *Silencing the Past: Power and the Production of History* (Boston, MA, 1995).
10. Jacques Derrida, 'Differance', *'Speech and Phenomena' and Other Essays on Husserl's Theory of Signs*, trans. David B. Allison (Evanston, IL, 1973), pp. 129–60.
11. As Patricia Parker points out, there is no shortcut to the process of learning the language(s) of the past. See her *Shakespeare from the Margins: Language, Culture, Context* (Chicago, 1996), pp. 18–19.
12. Kiernan Ryan (ed.), *New Historicism and Cultural Materialism: A Reader* (London, 1996), p. xviii.
13. These questions are not always so easily answered, of course (see Jacques Derrida, *Limited Inc* (Evanston, IL, 1988)), but that does not, in my view, legitimate ignoring them.
14. See, for example, Stephen Greenblatt, 'Fiction and Friction', *Shakespearean Negotiations: The Circulation of Social Energy in Renaissance England* (Oxford, 1988), pp. 66–93.

10. WALTER BENJAMIN, 'THESES ON THE PHILOSOPHY OF HISTORY'
(From *Illuminations: Essays and Reflections*, ed. Hannah Arendt
(London: 1970), pp. 255–66.)

Summary

The 'Theses on the Philosophy of History' resist reduction to a brief summary. Individually and collectively the theses develop a historical materialist philosophy of history which eschews the illusions and comforts of a theological or progressivist stance.

Notes

1. The Gotha Congress of 1875 united the two German Socialist parties, one led by Ferdinand Lassalle, the other by Karl Marx and Wilhelm Liebknecht. The programme, drafted by Liebknecht and Lassalle, was severely attacked by Marx in London. See his 'Critique of the Gotha Program'.
2. Leftist group, founded by Karl Liebknecht and Rosa Luxemburg at the beginning of World War I in opposition to the pro-war policies of the German Socialist party, later absorbed by the Communist party.
3. Benjamin says '*Jetztzeit*' and indicates by the quotation marks that he does not simply mean an equivalent to *Gegenwart*, that is, present. He clearly is thinking of the mystical *nunc stans*.

4. The Hegelian term *aufheben* in its threefold meaning: to preserve, to elevate, to cancel.

11. SHOSHANA FELMAN, 'CAMUS' *THE PLAGUE*, OR A MONUMENT TO WITNESSING'
(From Shoshana Felman and Dori Laub, *Testimony: Crises of Witnessing in Literature, Psychoanalysis, and History* (London and New York, 1992), pp. 93–119.)

Summary

The essay examines the impact of the Holocaust on the mutual claims of, and relationship between, history and narrative through a reading of Albert Camus' post-war novel *The Plague*, conventionally interpreted as an allegory of the Second World War. Produced as an underground testimony, an intervention in the events it narrates, the text is presented as a chronicle or objective reproduction of historical events, an act of witnessing bridging narrative and history. But why use the metaphor of the plague? As in Camus' novel the plague was seen as a historically impossible event, because it had died out, so in reality the Holocaust was unthinkable in conventional historical terms. Imaginative literary testimony reaches towards historical insight through exploring the implication and consequent transformation of the witness in and by the event. The literature of testimony is a performative engagement between consciousness and history that obliges artists to transform words into events.

Notes

1. 'Narrative Versions, Narrative Theories', in *On Narrative*, ed. N. J. T. Mitchell (Chicago and London, 1980, 1981), p. 228.
2. In the quoted passages, italics are mine unless otherwise indicated.
3. G. W. F. Hegel, *The Philosophy of History*, trans. J. Sibree (New York, 1956), p. 60.
4. Louis Mink, 'The Autonomy of Historical Understanding', in *History and Theory*, vol. V, no. 1 (Middletown, CT, 1966), p. 24.
5. Ibid., p. 33. Hereafter, page references to this article will be given in parenthesis in the text.
6. See also Chapter 1, III, 'Narrative and Testimony: Albert Camus', in Shoshana Felman and Dori Laub, M. D., *Testimony: Crises of Witnessing in Literature, Psychoanalysis, and History* (New York and London, 1992).
7. In *Confronting the Holocaust*, ed. Alvin Rosenfeld and Irving Greenberg (Bloomington and London, 1978), p. 4.
8. My re-translation from the French original: here and elsewhere, the abbreviation '*TM*' – 'translation modified' – indicates my alterations of the English version.
9. Walter Laqueur, *The Terrible Secret* (New York, 1983; first edn London, 1980), pp. 198–9.
10. Like Rambert, Albert Camus was separated from his wife Francine, because of the German military occupation, on November 11, 1942, of the Vichy-controlled Southern zone of France, where he was staying (in the town of Le Chambon-sur-Lignon) for medical treatment of his tuberculosis. Camus' plans to return to

his North African homeland and to rejoin Francine were unsettled, ironically enough, because North Africa had been liberated by the surprise invasion of the Allied troops on November 7 1942. Consequently, mainland France and Algeria were now on opposite sides of the War and totally cut off from each other. Trapped in Le Chambon-sur-Lignon, Camus could neither rejoin, nor even get in touch with, his wife.

11. In contrast to Rambert, Tarrou has no such blindness and, consequently, no illusions. That is why, however, he lives with no hope. 'There can be no peace without hope, and Tarrou *denying as he did the right to condemn* anyone whomsoever – *though he knew well that no one can help condemning and it befalls even the victim to turn executioner* – Tarrou had lived a life riddled with contradictions' (*The Plague*, p. 271).

12. The artist's role is to demolish the deceptive image of history as an *abstraction* (as an ideological and/or statistical, administrative picture in which death becomes invisible) by *bearing witness to the body*. 'In a civilisation where murder and violence are already doctrines in the process of becoming institutions', and 'where the executioners have gained the right to become administrative managers', the artist, says Camus, is by vocation 'Freedom's witness' [le Témoin de la liberté], in that he 'testifies not to the Law, but to the body' [les artistes . . . sont les témoins de la chair, non de la loi] ['Le Témoin de la liberté' (1948), in *Actuelles* I, pp. 188 and 191; *Oeuvres complétes d'Albert Camus*, Vol. 5 (Paris, 1983), my translation].
    'The work of art, by the mere fact of its existence, negates the conquests of ideology', affirms Camus (ibid., p. 189). Ideology partakes of theory: 'When one wants to unify the world in the name of theory, there are no other means than rendering this world as *disembodied, blind* and *deaf* as theory itself' (p. 188).
    As a 'witness to the body, not to the Law', the artist's role in history is, by inference (in my understanding both of what Camus *says* and of what he *does* both in *The Plague* and in this speech addressed to writers), not so much to witness *truth* (a theory) as to witness *freedom* (the body's difference; the body's otherness to theory; the body's physical *resistance to theory*). Witnessing itself becomes thus not a passive function, but an *act* (an *art*) partaking of the very physicality of Resistance. 'And, in the end, it is not combat which makes us artists, but art which makes us combatants. By this very function, the artist is freedom's witness . . . True artists testify not to the law, but to the body' (pp. 190–1).

13. 'The Holocaust as a Literary Inspiration', in *Dimensions of the Holocaust* (Evanston, IL, 1977), p. 9. See also Chapter 1, I, 'Crisis of Truth', in Felman and Laub, *Testimony*.

14. Camus, *Neither Victims nor Executioners*, trans. Dwight McDonald (San Francisco, 1972), p. 44. ('Ni Victimes ni bourreaux', *Combat* 1948, reprinted in *Actuelles, Erits politiques* [Paris, 1950].)

15. Ibid., p. 43.

16. Camus, 'Create Dangerously', lecture given at the University of Uppsala in Dec. 1957; in *Resistance, Rebellion, and Death*, trans. Justin O'Brien (New York: 1961), pp. 250–2.

17. Maurice Blanchot, *L'écriture du désastre* (Paris, 1980), p. 131. My translation. Blanchot quotes Lewental, whose testimonial notes were hidden near a crematorium: 'Truth was always more atrocious, more tragic than anything that might be said about it.' What is ungraspable, indeed, is not the content of the statement, but the survival of its testimonial utterance: the fact that it is literally *spoken* from within the ashes of a crematorium.

18. Elie Wiesel, 'Why I Write', in *Confronting the Holocaust*, ed. Alvin Rosenfeld and Irving Greenberg (Bloomington and London, 1978), pp. 202–3.
19. Ibid., p. 201.
20. Terrence Des Pres, *The Survivor – An Anatomy of Life on the Death Camps* (New York, 1977), p. 32.
21. I mean by 'existential' not 'pertaining to existentialism' (a theory), but, pragmatically, 'involving the whole of existence' (a practice).

12. KEITH JENKINS, 'WHY BOTHER WITH HISTORY?'
(From *Rethinking History*, 1.1 (1997), 56–66.)

Summary

What is the point of going to the historicised past? The main reason historians study the past is to produce historical consciousness. This is assumed to be a good thing but in the postmodern present there are many competing definitions of what 'good' and 'good history' are and we have no neutral, foundational criteria for adjudication between them. One response to this problem is to admit one's position and interests in order to be reflexive and ironic, but is this too 'historical'? Perhaps we should forget history and the past and concentrate on ethics as a way of talking about living together in the present? But ethics has also been challenged by a variety of postmodern thinkers. To performatively constitute our lives on the basis of nothing may be energising morally and historically. We cannot look to the past for ethical lessons as the past does not have an independent existence *historically*. In effect historians are treated as moral guides, legitimators of identities. Are they to be trusted? Postmodernism signals the end of history as modernists have construed it.

Notes

1. Although I don't think for a moment that F. R. Ankersmit would agree with much that I have said in this paper, his views on the aesthetic nature of historiography, his rejection of the 'historists' historical object as a reified past in favour of a 'nostalgic' historical sensation, and his qualified postmodernism as a movement beyond the 'Kantian paradigm of knowledge and meaning' into the possibilities of a new, disaggregated world that lies ahead of us, stand behind some of the ideas expressed here. See especially Ankersmit's recent collection of older papers and new essays, *History and Tropology: The Rise and Fall of Metaphor* (1994).
2. Particularly interesting in the context of postmodern ways of expressing older notions of reification is Jean Baudrillard's notion of 'the idea of reversibility' (Baudrillard, 1996). Thus, for example, Baudrillard points out that whilst much has been made of the way in which the 'subject constitutes the object' few have raised the question of the way in which the 'object constitutes the subject'. That is to say, while we post-Cartesians can now admit that we subjects constitute objects (e.g., we historians constitute history/historiography) we have not been too aware of how such an object (history/historiography) once in place, then constitutes us, tells us how to behave towards it, tells us how to treat it as if it was self-constitutive. That history would only give up its secrets if it was looked at in, say, Marxist fashion, or empirically, or if we approached it 'properly', i.e., objectively, open mindedly, in ways which were balanced, etc. In this way the reified

object really does look as if it has a life of its own as we forget that we gave this discourse all the life it has as we meekly obey 'its' strictures; in this way Baudrillard talks of the 'revenge of the object'. But a further interesting point about reversibility is not only the insight it offers into the way our demands of history are reified such that the histories we demand in turn demand us, control us, but that we can never get out of this subject–object/object–subject reversal into a higher resolution or synthesis whereby we can ever really sort out and thus know what we had made of the past/history and what the past/history (us) had made of us. . . .

References

Ankersmit, F. R., *Narrative Logic* (The Hague, 1983).
——, *History and Tropology* (Berkeley, CA, 1994).
Attridge, D., Young, R. and Bennington, G. (eds), *Post-structuralism and the Question of History* (Cambridge, 1987).
Baudrillard, J., *The Perfect Crime* (London, 1996).
Bennington, G. and Derrida, J., *Jacques Derrida* (Chicago, 1996).
Elton, G., *The Practice of History*, (London, 1969).
Laclau, E., *Emancipation(s)* (London, 1996).
Levinas, E., *Ethics and Infinity* (Pittsburgh, 1985).
Lyotard, J. F., *The Differend* (Minnesota, 1988).
McHale, B., *Constructing Postmodernism* (London, 1992).
Marwick, A., *The Nature of History* (London, 1989).
Mouffe, C. (ed.), *Deconstruction and Pragmatism* (London, 1996).
Stanford, M., *A Companion to the Study of History* (Oxford, 1994).
Tosh, J., *The Pursuit of History* (London, 1991).
White, H., *Metahistory: The Historical Consciousness in the Nineteenth Century* (Baltimore, MD, 1973).
——, *The Content of the Form* (Baltimore, MD, 1987).

13. MICHEL DE CERTEAU, 'WRITINGS AND HISTORIES'
(From *The Writing of History* (New York, 1988), pp. 1–14.)

Summary

The essay opens with quotations from Michelet that raise the issue of the dead as the other, the phantasm, of historiography, as that which it seeks, honours and buries. The historical quest for meaning could, he argues, be read as an attempt to calm the dead who haunt the present, to offer them scriptural tombs. Modern Western history is founded on a differentiation between present and past and related oppositions between labour and nature, discourse and the body. It is a heterology, a discourse of the other, that, like medicine, is built on a division between a mute body that supports a discourse and a body of knowledge that utters it. Western emphasis on the breakage of present from past is contrasted with other traditions in India and Madagascar and is connected with the West's obsession with death. The making of history has become synonymous with writing, turning the given into a construct, building a past through exclusion. Historiography was developed in relation to the exercise of political power as Machiavelli's writings attest.

Notes

1. Jules Michelet, 'L'Héroïsme de l'esprit', unpublished project from the preface to *L'Histoire de France*, 1869, in *L'Arc* (1973), no. 52, pp. 7, 5, and 8. [Unless otherwise indicated, all translations from the French are my own. – Tr.]
2. Jules Michelet, *Préface à l'Histoire de France*, ed. Morazé (Paris, 1962), p. 175.
3. Michelet, 'L'Héroïsme de l'esprit', p. 8.
4. [De Certeau refers to a passage in Freud's *Moses and Monotheism* which is crucial for the relations of historiography and psychoanalysis. – Tr.]
5. Michelet, 'L'Héroïsme de l'esprit', p. 8.
6. Michelet, quoted by Roland Barthes in 'Aujourd'hui Michelet', *L'Arc* (1973), no. 52, 26.
7. Michelet, 'L'Héroïsme de l'esprit', pp. 12–13.
8. Alphonse Dupront, 'Langage et histoire', in *XIIIe Congrès international des sciences historiques* (Moscow, 1970).
9. See especially Michel Foucault, *Naissance de la clinique* (Paris, 1963), pp. v–xv. Available in English as *The Birth of the Clinic* (New York, 1975), see pp. ix–xix.
10. Louis Dumont, 'Le Problème de l'histoire', in *La Civilization indienne et nous* (Paris, 1964), pp. 31–54.
11. See Alain Delivré, *Interprétation d'une tradition orale: Histoire des rois d'Imerina* (mimeographed thesis; Sorbonne, Paris, 1967), especially part 2, 'Structure de la pensée ancienne et sens de l'histoire', pp. 143–227.
12. On this last point, see Stanislaus Adotevi, *Négritude et négrologues* (Paris, '10/18', 1972), pp. 148–53.
13. To cite but one study, see Dieter Gembicki, 'Jacob-Nicolas Moreau et son Mémoire sur les fonctions d'un historiographe de France (*1778–1779*)', *Dixhuitième siècle* (1972), no. 4, pp. 191–215. The relation between a literature and a 'state service' will be central to the historiography of the nineteenth century and the first half of the twentieth.
14. In fact, we must go all the way back to Commynes (1447–1511), to Florentine chroniclers, and ultimately to the slow transformation of history produced toward the end of the Middle Ages by the emancipation of cities, subjects of power, and the autonomy of jurists, technicians, thinkers, and functionaries of this power.
15. [The author distinguishes between *faire de l'histoire*, what is tantamount to the task by which rhetoric is used to make an illusion of posterity, and *faire l'histoire*, the making of a limited number of material effects in a given time. – Tr.]
16. See Claude Lefort, *Le Travail de l'oeuvre de Machiavel* (Paris, 1972), pp. 447–9.
17. See ibid., p. 456.
18. In the last resort this futility acquires meaning in the relation between the historian-philosopher and *Fortuna*: the infinite number of relations and interdependencies prohibits man from hypothesising an ability to control or even influence events. See Felix Gilbert, 'Between History and Politics', in *Machiavelli and Guicciardini* (Princeton, NJ, 1973), pp. 236–70.
19. See Lefort, *Le Travail*, pp. 453–66.
20. Eugène Marbeau, *Le Charme de l'histoire* (Paris, 1902).
21. See for example Jean-Yves Guiomar's remarks in *L'Idéologie nationale* (Paris, 1974), pp. 17 and 45–65.
22. Lucien Febvre, preface to Charles Morazé, *Trois essais sur histoire et culture* (Paris, 1948), p. viii.
23. Jean T. Desanti, *Les Idéalités mathématiques* (Paris, 1968), p. 8.

24. See for instance Félix Thürlemann, *Der historische Diskurs bei Gregor von Tours. Topoi und Wirklichkeit* (Frankfurt, 1974), pp. 36–72.

25. In the fifteenth century, Agricola writes, 'Historiae, cujus prima laus est *veritas, naturalis* tantum *ordo* convenit, ne si *figmentis* istis aurium gratiam captit, fidem perdat', in *De inventione dilectica libri tres cum scholiis Ioannis Matthaei Phrissemii*, III, VII (Paris, apud Simonem Colinaeum, 1529), p. 387. The italics are mine. The foundation of this historiographical system must also be remarked: the text takes it for granted that truth is credible and consequently that showing what is true is tantamount to producing belief, of producing a *fides* among readers.

26. Desanti, *Les Idéalités mathématiques*, p. 29.

27. Gérard Mairet, *Les Discours et l'historique: Essai sur la représentation historienne du temps* (Paris, 1974), p. 168.

28. Karl Marx, *Theses on Feuerbach*, Thesis I, in Karl Marx and Friedrich Engels, *Basic Writings on Politics and Philosophy*, ed. L. S. Feuer (New York, 1959), p. 243. On the same topic, see also 'Marginal Gloss to the Program of the German Workers' Party', paragraph 1, Marx and Engels, *Critique of the Gotha Erfurt Program*, in *Basic Writings*, pp. 112–32.

29. Karl Marx and Friedrich Engels, *The German Ideology*, in *Basic Writings*, p. 249; and Karl Marx, *Die Fruhschriften*, ed. S. Landshut (Stuttgart, 1853), p. 354.

30. Karl Marx, *Introduction to a Critique of Political Economy*, in *The German Ideology*, ed. C. S. Arthur (New York, 1978), pp. 125–6.

31. Karl Marx, *Critique of Political Economy*, in *The German Ideology*, pp. 127ff.

32. Ibid.

33. See Martin Duberman, *Black Mountain: An Exploration in Community* (New York, 1973).

Glossary

Note: Words or phrases given in italics are also defined in their alphabetical place in the Glossary.

anamorphosis A deformed or distorted figure that appears in proportion or is identifiable only when viewed from a particular angle.

Bakhtin, Mikhail Literary critic who worked in the Soviet Union. His publications included *Rabelais and his World* (1965) which explored the emancipatory potential of carnival.

Coulanges, Fustel de Nineteenth-century French historian whose study *The Ancient City* stressed the impact of religion on the development of Greek and Roman institutions.

Derrida, Jacques Influential French philosopher whose work challenged Western metaphysics and contributed to the development of poststructuralist approaches to language.

Dietzgen, Josef Nineteenth-century German philosopher whose work on Hegel anticipated that of Marx and Engels.

Dietzgen, Wilhelm Nineteenth-century German socialist.

discourse Michel Foucault redefined discourse as a specific knowledge inscribed in particular language that sustains and is sustained by power relations.

Durkheim, Emile Key figure in the development of twentieth-century sociology.

empiricism The belief that knowledge is derived from experience, experiment and induction. For some historians, empiricism links their work with science rather than with the arts or humanities.

formalism In literary criticism involves the study of the formal, artificial and technical aspects of literary texts that are seen to distinguish them from other types of writing.

Fourier, François Eighteenth-century radical thinker.

idealism Is the philosophical theory that holds that the only things that exist are minds or mental states. Hegelian idealism, for example, sees all individual human minds as fragments of the sole Absolute mind or spirit.

Keller, Gottfried Nineteenth-century German Swiss realist novelist and writer whose work was concerned with the incompatibility of capitalism and artistic individualism.

Lévi-Strauss, Claude Influential structuralist anthropologist.

linguistic turn This phrase is used within the discipline of History to describe work influenced by literary or narrative theory.

Lotze, Hermann Nineteenth-century German philosopher who argued that ethics were the foundation of metaphysics and that cause and effect can only be explained in moral terms.

Lyotard, Jean-François French theorist whose extremely influential study *The Postmodern Condition* (1979) suggested that postmodernism was defined by incredulity

191

towards metanarratives, overarching explanations which legitimate accounts of the world.

metonymy   A linguistic figure or *trope* that replaces a name with the name of an adjacent or contiguous object.

Michelet, Jules   Nineteenth-century author of one of the most famous histories of the French Revolution.

nomological   Refers to the science of laws, such as laws of mind.

Other   A term derived from psychoanalytic theory describing the locus of the law and signification. Usually identified with the symbolic figure of the Father, the Other both alienates and constitutes the subject. The term is also used more generally for that which is irreducibly different or unreachable.

praxeological   Defined by practices.

Ranke, Leopold von   Nineteenth-century German historian whose dictum that the historian's task is to reconstruct the past as it actually happened is generally seen as the central tenet of empiricist history.

Saussure, Ferdinand de   Swiss linguist whose *Course in General Linguistics* (1916) set out the structuralist theory of language as a system of signs which do not label reality but allow for the production of meaning through relations of difference.

trope   Is a figure of speech, literally a 'turning' of a word or phrase to make it mean something else. Types of trope include metaphor, *metonymy*, synecdoche. Hayden White identifies tropes as the key components of historiography.

Suggestions for Further Reading

Ankersmit, F. R., 'Historiography and Postmodernism', *History and Theory*, 28.2 (1989), 137–53. One of the first and still most thought-provoking explorations of the topic.

Ankersmit, Frank and Hans Kellner (eds), *A New Philosophy of History* (London, 1995). A collection of essays on history as discourse, focusing on topics including narrative, voice, and the presence of the historian.

Appleby, Joyce, Lynn Hunt and Margaret Jacob, *Telling the Truth About History* (New York, 1994). Attempts to combine radical pluralism and the possibility of objectivity.

Attridge, Derek, Geoff Bennington and Robert Young (eds), *Poststructuralism and the Question of History* (Cambridge, 1984). Demanding but rewarding theoretical essays.

Bann, Stephen, *The Inventions of History: Essays on the Representation of the Past* (Manchester, 1990). Explores an unusually wide range of forms of historical representation.

Barthes, Roland, 'Discourse of History' (trans. Stephen Bann), *Comparative Criticism – A Yearbook*, Vol. 3 (1981), pp. 3–20. An influential essay that argued that historiography was concerned with the intelligible not the real.

Catherine Belsey, 'Towards cultural history – in theory and practice', *Textual Practice*, 3.2 (1989), 159–72. Influential manifesto for cultural history which examines the theoretical and practical issues and problems.

Brannigan, John, *New Historicism and Cultural Materialism* (London, 1998). Accessible introduction.

Callinicos, Alex, *Theories and Narratives: Reflections on the Philosophy of History* (Oxford, 1995). Marxist rebuttal of narrativist position.

Carr, David, 'Narrative and the Real World: An Argument for Continuity', *History and Theory*, 25.2 (1986), 117–31. Unlike Hayden White, Carr believes that human actions and reality have narrative forms.

Chartier, Roger, *Cultural History: Between Practices and Representations*, trans. Lydia G. Cochrane (Cambridge, 1988). Exploration of cultural history by a leading French exponent.

Davis, Natalie Zemon, *Fiction in the Archives: Pardon Tales and their Tellers in Sixteenth-Century France* (Berkeley, CA, 1988). Analysis of texts by one of the most influential social historians.

Easthope, Anthony, 'Romancing the Stone: history-writing and rhetoric', *Social History*, 18 (1993), 235–49. Succinct poststructuralist argument about the relationship between historiography and rhetoric.

G. R. Elton, *The Practice of History* (London, 1967). Classic exposition of the theory and practice of traditional empiricist history.

Ermath, Elizabeth Deeds, *Sequel to History: Postmodernism and the Crisis of Historical Time* (Princeton, NJ, 1992). Examines postmodernism's subversion of modernist ideas of linear time.

Fay, Brian, Philip Pomper and Richard T. Vann (eds), *History and Theory: Contemporary Readings* (Oxford and Malden, MA, 1998). Collection of essays exploring the nature of history after 'the linguistic turn'.

Foucault, Michel, *Language, Counter Memory, Practice: Selected Essays and Interviews*, ed. Donald F. Bouchard, trans. Donald F. Bouchard and Sherry Simon (Ithaca, NY, 1997). Includes the extremely influential essays 'Nietzsche, Genealogy, History' and 'What is a Author?'.

Friedlander, Saul (ed.), *Probing the Limits of Representation: Nazism and the 'Final Solution'* (Cambridge, MA, 1992). A collection of essays by historians and theorists on representations of the Holocaust. Many of the contributions deal primarily with problems of adequate representation and the implications of postmodern denial of traditional ideas of truth.

Fukuyama, Francis, *The End of History and the Last Man* (Harmondsworth, 1992). Polemical account of the triumph of liberalism which is also an examination of theories of history.

Geertz, Clifford, *The Interpretation of Cultures* (New York, 1983). Essays by cultural anthropologist whose work has influenced many contemporary social historians and New Historicist critics.

Ginzburg, Carlo, *The Cheese and the Worms*, trans. John and Anne Tedeschi (Baltimore, MD, 1980). First published in Italy in 1976, Ginzburg's extremely influential short social history of the 'cosmos' of a sixteenth-century miller that has been compellingly re-read in the light of poststructuralist theory.

Hall, Catherine, *White, Male and Middle Class: Explorations in Feminism and History* (Cambridge, 1992). Marxist-feminist study.

Hamilton, Paul, *Historicism* (London, 1996). Concise but wide-reaching introduction to historicism in philosophy, theory and critical practice.

'Hayden White: Twenty-Five Years On', *History and Theory*, 37.2 (1998), 143–93. Collection of essays assessing the impact of White.

Holderness, Graham, 'Shakespeare's "whole History": drama and early modern historical theory', *Rethinking History*, 3.1 (1999), 21–52. Theoretically informed exploration of Renaissance thinking about history.

Howard, Jean, 'The New Historicism in Renaissance Studies', *English Literary History*, 16 (1986), 13–43. Accessible examination of the foundations and varieties of New Historicist criticism.

Hunt, Lynn (ed.), *The New Cultural History* (Berkeley, CA, 1989). Collection of essays which explore theoretical and practical concerns.

Jameson, Fredric, *The Political Unconscious: Narrative as a Socially Symbolic Act* (Ithaca, NY, 1981). Probably the most important Marxist contribution to debates on history in the postmodern condition.

Jenkins, Keith, *On 'What is History?'* (London, 1995). Survey of debates within and about History.

—— (ed.), *The Postmodern History Reader* (London and New York, 1997). Collection of (often quite brief) excerpts from work by a wide range of historians dealing with various aspects of postmodernism and history.

Joyce, Patrick, *Democratic Subjects: the Self and the Social in Nineteenth Century England* (Cambridge, 1994). By the best-known British champion of the 'linguistic turn'.

LaCapra, Dominick, *Rethinking Intellectual History: Texts, Contexts, Language* (Ithaca, NY, 1983). A reappraisal of intellectual history that examines the work of a wide range of theoretical and philosophical writers from White, Wittgenstein and Jameson, to Heidegger and Derrida.

——, *History and Criticism* (Ithaca, NY, 1985). An exploration of connections between history and critical theory.

Le Roy Ladurie, Emmanuel, *Montaillou: Cathars and Catholics in a French Village 1294–1324*, trans. Barbara Bray (London, 1978). A history that combined a realist narrative and archive research, popularly and professionally acclaimed as ground breaking when first published, and subsequently reappraised, by Dominick LaCapra and others, as an example of storytelling that masks its own fictionality.

Levinson, Marjorie, Marilyn Butler, Jerome McGann and Paul Hamilton, *Rethinking Historicism: Critical Readings in Romantic History* (Oxford, 1989). After the early-modern period the historical moment of Romanticism has, as this volume shows, been constructed as a particularly important object of enquiry.

Marwick, Arthur, *The Nature of History* (London, 1970). Detailed and accessible account of historical practice by one of the best-known opponents of narrativist and postmodern theories.

Mink, Louis, 'History and Fiction as Modes of Comprehension', *New Literary History*, 1 (1970), 541–58. Early narrativist argument.

Momigliano, Arnaldo, 'The rhetoric of history and the history of rhetoric: on Hayden White's tropes', *Comparative Criticism*, 3 (1981), 259–68. A critique of White's constructivist approach to history.

Munslow, Alun, *Deconstructing History* (London and New York, 1997). Accessible introduction to current debates within the discipline of History.

New Literary History, 21.3 (1990). Special issue of journal, on 'New Historicisms, New Histories, and Others'.

Porter, Carolyn, 'Are We Being Historical Yet?', *South Atlantic Quarterly*, 87 (1988), 743–86. Frequently cited critical analysis of New Historicism.

Quillen, Carol E., 'Crossing the Line: Limits and Desire in Historical Interpretation', *History and Theory*, 37.1 (1998), 40–68. Exploration of relationship between interpretation and subjectivity.

Ricouer, Paul, *Time and Narrative*, trans. K. McLaughlin and D. Pellauer (Chicago, 1984). Influential study of the role of narratives in lived experience and texts.

Roth, Michael S., *The Ironist's Cage: Memory, Trauma, and the Construction of History* (New York, 1995). Explores History after the 'linguistic turn'.

Rowbotham, Sheila, *Hidden from History* (London, 1983). Pioneering feminist study.

Ryan, Kiernan, *New Historicism and Cultural Materialism: A Reader* (London and New York, 1996). Useful anthology of sources, debates and examples of two extremely influential movements in cultural criticism.

Schama, Simon, *Dead Certainties (Unwarranted Speculations)* (London, 1992). Enjoyable and thought-provoking deliberate fusion of archival fact and fiction, interpreted by some historians as epitomising the abandoning of any attempt to record reality.

——, *Landscape and Memory* (New York, 1995). Unusual exploration of the relationship between history and landscape.

Scott, Joan W. (ed.), *Feminism and History* (Oxford, 1996). Accessible collection including Scott's 'Gender: A Useful Category of Historical Analysis'.

Sinfield, Alan, *Faultlines: Cultural Materialism and the Politics of Dissident Reading* (Oxford, 1992). Exemplifies one strand of British Cultural Materialist criticism.

Southgate, Beverley, *History: What and Why? Ancient, Modern and Postmodern Perspectives* (London, 1996). Enjoyable and thoughtful with a particularly useful introduction on classical and early-modern debates.

Spivak, Gayatri Chakravorty, 'Subaltern Studies: Deconstructing Historiography', *In Other Worlds: Essays in Cultural Politics* (New York and London, 1987). Difficult but important critical exploration of historiographical work by the Subaltern Studies group.

Stanford, Michael, *A Companion to the Study of History* (Oxford, UK, and Cambridge, MA, 1994). Useful introduction to methodologies in past and contemporary History.

Toews, John E., 'Intellectual History after the Linguistic Turn: The Autonomy of Meaning and the Irreducibility of Experience', *American Historical Review*, 92.4 (1987), 879–907. Influential essay.

Veeser, H. Aram (ed.), *The New Historicism* (New York and London, 1989). Collection of essays by exponents and opponents of New Historicism dealing primarily with issues of theory, politics and methodology.

——(ed.), *The New Historicism Reader* (New York and London, 1994). Representative examples of criticism by, among others, Stephen Greenblatt, Stephen Orgel, Louis Montrose and Catherine Gallagher.

White, Hayden, *Metahistory: The Historical Imagination in Nineteenth Century Europe* (Baltimore and London, 1973). White's first text.

——, *Tropics of Discourse: Essays in Cultural Criticism* (Baltimore and London, 1978). Influential collection of essays including 'The Historical Text as a Literary Artifact' and 'Foucault Decoded'.

——, *The Content of the Form: Narrative Discourse and Historical Representation* (Baltimore and London, 1987). Collection of essays including 'The Question of Narrative in Contemporary Historical Theory'.

Williams, Raymond, *Marxism and Literature* (Oxford, 1977). Extremely influential revision of Marxist approaches to literature and culture.

——, *Keywords: A Vocabulary of Culture and Society* (London, 1983). A collection of explorations of the cultural history of words and concepts.

Wilson, Richard, 'Introduction: Historicising New Historicism', in Richard Wilson and Richard Dutton (eds), *New Historicism and Renaissance Drama* (London, 1992), pp. 1–18. Energetic, accessible and informative.

Young, Robert, *White Mythologies: Writing History and the West* (London, 1989). Examines modernist histories as white, male and Eurocentric and argues that the move from History to the Postmodern marks the dissolution of the West.

Notes on Contributors

Catherine Belsey chairs the Centre for Critical and Cultural Theory at the University of Wales, Cardiff. Her books include *Critical Practice* (1980), *The Subject of Tragedy: Identity and Difference in Renaissance Drama* (1985), *Desire: Love Stories in Western Culture* (1994) and *Shakespeare and the Loss of Eden: The Construction of Family Values in Early Modern Culture* (1999).

Walter Benjamin (1892–1940) was a relatively unknown member of the German Jewish middle-class intelligentsia in his lifetime but since his suicide his works have been among the most influential of the Marxist tradition of cultural criticism. He wrote numerous essays and his books include *The Origin of German Tragedy* (1928).

Michel de Certeau was director of studies at the Ecole des Hautes Etudes en Sciences Sociales, Paris, until his death in 1986. His books available in translation include *The Practice of Everyday Life* (1984), *Heterologies: Discourse on the Other* (1986), *The Writing of History* (1988), and *The Mystic Fable* (1992).

Robert Darnton is Shelby Cullom Davis Professor of European History at Princeton University. His books include *The Great Cat Massacre and Other Episodes in French Cultural History* (1984), *The Kiss of Lamourette: Reflections in Cultural History* (1989) and *The Forbidden Best-Sellers of Prerevolutionary France* (1995).

Shoshana Felman is Thomas E. Donnelley Professor of French and Comparative Literature at Yale University. She is the author of *The Literary Speech Act: Don Juan with Austin, or Seduction in Two Languages* (1984), *Writing and Madness: Literature/Philosophy/Psychoanalysis* (1985), *Jacques Lacan and the Adventure of Insight* (1987), and *What Does a Woman Want? Reading and Sexual Difference* (1993).

Michel Foucault (1926–84) wrote histories and theoretical explorations which made him one of the most influential of French poststructuralists. His translated texts include *Madness and Civilisation: A History of Insanity in the Age of Reason* (1967), *The Order of Things: An Archeology of the Human Sciences* (1967), *Discipline and Punish: The Birth of the Prison* (1977), *The History of Sexuality*, Vols I, II, and III (1988–90).

Stephen Greenblatt is Harry Levin Professor of Literature at Harvard University. He is the editor of the *Norton Shakespeare* and the author of several books of literary and cultural criticism, including *Renaissance Self-Fashioning: From More to Shakespeare* (1980), *Shakespearean Negotiations: The Circulation of Social Energy in Renaissance England* (1988), *Learning to Curse: Essays in Early Modern Culture* (1990), and *Marvelous Possessions: The Wonder of the New World* (1991).

Keith Jenkins is Reader in History at Chichester Institute. He is the author of *Rethinking History* (1991), *On 'What is History?' From Carr and Elton to Rorty and White* (1995), *The Postmodern History Reader* (1997) and *Why History?* (1999).

Leszek Kolakowski is a Polish-born philosopher whose most recent post, until his retirement in 1995, was as Senior Research Fellow at All Souls College, Oxford. His works available in English translations include *Main Current of Marxism* (1978), *Religion* (1982), *Metaphysical Horror* (1988), *Presence of Myth* (1989), *Modernity on Endless Trial* (1990) and *God Owes Us Nothing: A Brief Remark on Pascal's Religion and the Spirit of Jansenism* (1995).

Jürgen Pieters is completing a doctoral dissertation on the theoretical background of Stephen Greenblatt's New Historicism at the University of Ghent (Belgium). He is editor of *Critical Self-Fashioning: The New Historicism of Stephen Greenblatt* (1999) and has published articles on literary theory and drama.

Tamsin Spargo is a Reader in Cultural History at Liverpool John Moores University. She is the author of *The Writing of John Bunyan* (1997), *Foucault and Queer Theory* (1999) and essays on critical theory, gender and nonconformist culture.

Carolyn Steedman is Professor and Chair of the Social History Centre at the University of Warwick. She is the author of *The Tidy House: Policing the Victorian Community* (1982), *Landscape for a Good Woman* (1986), *The Radical Soldier's Tale* (1988), *Strange Dislocations: Childhood and the Idea of Human Interiority 1780–1930* (1995).

Susan Willis is Associate Professor of English and Literature at Duke University. Her writing is grounded in Marxist and feminist theories and her publications include *Specifying, Black Women Writing the American Experience* (1987), *A Primer for Daily Life* (1991), and *Inside the Mouse, Work and Play at Disney World* (1995).

Index